Child Sense

Child Sense

A Pediatrician's Guide
for Today's Families

by William E. Homan, M. D.

BASIC BOOKS, INC., *Publishers,* NEW YORK, LONDON

To my most dependable teachers
and flattering students,

BETTY, JANE, *and* **BILL**

ACKNOWLEDGMENTS

My sincere thanks to Dr. William McKnight, Dr. Rustin McIntosh, and Mr. Carl Dreher for their invaluable suggestions and corrections; to Dr. Herbert Hurwitz and Dr. Judah Roher for their assistance and forbearance; to my sustainer, benevolent critic, counselor, inspiration, and tutor, my wife.

My most particular gratitude to the many dedicated parents who shared their wisdom and their rewards with me.

W. E. H.

Foreword

by W. K. McKnight, M.D.

Nowadays, it must be the rare parent who is not somewhat confused, if not mystified, in the face of the vitally important task of bringing up his children. Books, magazine articles, newspaper columns, television, and other channels of communication offer the parent a steady stream of advice—some of it complicated, some of it confusing, some of it contradictory. This is one reason why I believe that the book you have in your hands may well become a major source of help for both parents and others who are intimately involved in the guidance of children.

In a straightforward, readable style, Dr. Homan deals with all of the salient issues in the personality development of the child and, most importantly, in such a way that parents can understand them clearly and can test the author's judgments in the daily events of their own children's lives. Thus, Dr. Homan, with his keen perception and kindly wit, has provided us with a handbook that has its own strong, clear voice and offers lucid guidelines for raising children in our increasingly complex society.

Dr. McKnight is Assistant Professor of Psychiatry at The Cornell University Medical College, and is Physician-in-Charge, The Mental Hygiene Clinic of the Westchester Division, Inc., New York Hospital–Cornell Medical Center.

Child Sense is both an expression of Dr. Homan's considered judgments and a unique record of his many years of experience as a practicing pediatrician. His unusual practice provides for special hours-long appointments for exploring signs of personality or behavior problems with his patients and their parents. In this way, Dr. Homan not only practices the best kind of preventive medicine but also has gained an intensive, practical knowledge of children and the needs of their developing personalities.

Dr. Homan places strong emphasis on the importance of the family as a balanced unit as well as on the necessary balance among the various other influences in the developing child's life, including those responsibilities which must be shared by schools and other agencies within the community. His concept of the "triad of basic needs for the normal development of a child's personality" is, in my opinion, a sound and practical basis for parental guidance, as it represents in a simple, fundamental way many of the truths that have emerged from observation and research.

In *Child Sense*, I believe, Dr. Homan has written an essential guide for today's families which will merit the wide readership it is certain to have.

Contents

ix

Child Sense

Introduction

This book represents thirty years of blood and sweat and worry and sleeplessness. It is an inadequate monument to agonized children I have talked to and laughed with and cried with; children who have suffered, and who have wept, and who have lost their birthright to happiness, and who have died. It distills the sacrifices and the ceaseless efforts of their twenty thousand parents—determined efforts to comprehend, to do a better job, to improve and to support their children.

If you believe that raising children is a spare-time job, if you find it incredible that guiding children is the most difficult, the most challenging, the most significant, and the least mastered and most promising frontier for man—then this book is not for you.

Or if you have been persuaded that the problems of the young can be solved by speaking "childrenese"—if you are convinced that children can reach meaningful happiness through such parental evasions as permissiveness, or can be fitted for tomorrow's problems by an egocentric preparation for responsibility and legality—if you think that the complexities of parenthood can be catalogued in an ivory tower by staring at a hundred children selected with statistical bias—if you believe that unaided parental instinct can suffice to rear an enlightened generation, or that the establishment of conditioned reflexes in the child will insure appropriate values—if you imagine that parents can successfully help their children to a productive and harmonious maturity without dedication and painstaking consideration —then this book will enrage you.

But if you can see the hope that resides in the children of this

3

generation, and can envision their progress against the burdens of the world—if you can endorse the need to prepare them as adequately as possible—if you can subscribe to the worthwhileness of making the effort to start them on their way without handicaps, I wish you would give me a little of your time to discuss and assess what we know about the stewardship of the young.

A lifetime spent with children and the problems of children yields no conclusion more haunting than this: each set of new parents approaches the formidable assignment of raising humans with meager experience and spotty knowledge; each set of parents learns by a process of trial and error, committing the same mistakes that have been committed by countless other parents; the new parents learn—some more, some less—by their missteps, and they become, in some respect, more adept at parenthood with every succeeding child; the parents wish at some point that they had known at the beginning what they have come to know by the end.

There is a striking similarity, a remarkable repetition, among the lessons learned by parents in family after family during the on-the-job training that constitutes parenthood: the same errors, the same finally acquired understanding.

It is almost as though each neophyte scientist were to be handed a flintstone and a wheel and made to rediscover for himself all the basic scientific knowledge of the ages, instead of being allowed to start from the shoulders of his predecessors, forearmed with their laboriously assembled experiences, mistakes, and facts. How many years of education in mathematics are devoted to mastering the relatively simple demands of accounting? How many weeks, or even hours, of education are allotted to preparing for the complex demands of child raising?

No other task in the world compares in consequence with that of raising children. From the point of view of the individual child, much of the balance between happiness and unhappiness that will ultimately comprise his life's experiences depends upon the orientation he receives in his childhood. From the point of view of the community, the success or lack of success with which an individual contributes to the welfare of the world depends in the main upon the environment he had as a child.

Pitifully few persons are granted the opportunity to improve this earth in any permanent manner through their own achievements. The chance, however, to have a profound and lasting effect upon the world, either for good or for bad, is thrust upon each person who is given the privilege of raising a child. In terms of personal satisfaction, the rewards of being, for instance, a good professional educator are immense, for a teacher has the daily opportunity to enrich the state of mankind through properly orienting the child. But if teaching is a notable profession, how far more exalted is the role of the parent, whose influence on the child, willy-nilly, constitutes the majority of the child's educational experiences.

At the same time, and quite aside from its importance, the job of raising children must surely be classified as the most complicated, most intricate, and most challenging of all man's tasks. To guide and shape the formative years of a human being dwarfs in complexity the problems of computer design or of international diplomacy. How strange it is, then, that for this most demanding and most vital task of parenthood one finds the least imaginable training and preparation. For the simple roles of doctor, lawyer, and Indian chief, it is taken for granted that years of preparation will be necessary to attain even mediocrity. To be a plumber, a clerk, or a soldier one undergoes months and years of training. For operating the new toaster, assembling the knocked-down carriage, controlling the three-way light bulb, precise manuals of instruction are available. But you are apparently assumed to come to the job of being a parent divinely endowed with knowledge and experience. And when you stumble along the path, and the resulting product is less than perfect, you are made to experience guilty feelings of inadequacy, and the world in its wisdom feels free to point an accusing finger at you.

If by chance you had the foresight to seek out the knowledge that would help you as a parent, you would be doomed to chaos. The fact is that the rare schoolroom course and the many in-

struction books on parenthood—unlike the plethora of material
relating to handweaving and to home carpentry—are unrealistic
and contradictory. Even in this day of specialization and unlimited wisdom, there seems not yet to be a true expert on the
subject of child raising.

Some books urge that a parent need only rely upon his instincts to guide his relationships with his child. "The normal
mother will instinctively know how to . . ." This is assuredly true
if your aim is to produce a young adult who would do well in
an aboriginal state. Unfortunately, instincts do not equip a parent
to guide his child to meet the requirements of a complex competitive society.

Furthermore, were I a perplexed parent seeking a solution
to a question, the ingenuous advice: "As a normal parent you
will instinctively see how to act" would throw me into a guilty
panic when I realized that *I* felt no surging rush of intuition
growing within *my* body. Please remember that the author or
teacher who says, "You will readily understand this without my
telling you about it," is using a shorthand for: "Quit bugging me.
I don't know the answer either."

Some books, on the other hand, insist upon the total repres-
sion of parental instincts. Great-grandma and Great-grandpa had
all the advantages over today's parents in dealing with this advice.
Uninhibited and unembarrassed by such advice from "experts,"
they often succumbed to their common sense, and sometimes
provided their children with more than enough love and approval
to counterbalance whatever other shortcomings they had as
parents.

My child has just dismembered his sister, castigated his
mother, and kindled the house, and I discover from the experts
that to communicate effectively with him I should say, presumably in a level voice, "I see something is bothering you; you are
angry at your teacher; Daddy often feels this way himself." Reading such advice, I know that, if it be true, I can never be a good
parent. Not without prolonged psychotherapy and treatment
for my colitis.

Some books maintain that heredity overwhelmingly outweighs

the effects of environment in determining the child's personality. "Stop blaming the parents for the child's transgressions. Look how often good parents produce bad children." As a matter of fact, if a normal child studies spelling, say, for sixteen years under the same teacher, and ends up a non-speller, is it not possible that the teacher shares the blame? I, for one, wherever else I looked for the cause of the failure, would at least have to wonder whether the teacher *might* be the cause. And where is the credibility in the supposition that "good" people automatically make good parents? Many "good" people are rotten plumbers, rotten bridge players, rotten parents. Sometimes entirely because of lack of knowledge of the subject. The emphasis upon heredity provides far too much sand for head burying when a child has problems, as a substitute for an honest search into the cause of the problems.

Some books overwhelm the reader with learned jargon that obscures the "whole cloth" from which the pontifical advice stems.

Some books outline in minute detail how the child will behave at age three years, two months, and ten days, based upon observations of how four other children were once recorded to behave at this age. Sometimes nothing seems to qualify one as a child expert quite so much as either being childless oneself or being secluded in a remote office in an imposing brick edifice from which one occasionally looks to "observe" a child.

Some books tell you how to prepare your child for some utopian society that does not yet exist on our planet. I commend these to you for the purpose to which they are suited—light fictional reading.

Or you will be assured that the raising of children to the attainment of normal emotional development and desirable attitudes and character traits can be reduced to the simplicity of conditioned reflexes. Know which actions to condition your child to and you will produce a man capable of feeling love, compassion, tolerance, and self-confidence! Or perhaps it will be a salivating dog.

With such scarcely intelligible guides to this complicated and important assignment, one can only marvel respectfully at the extraordinary job the average American parent, and most particularly the average mother, manages to perform. From each mistake the parents acquire skill; from each child they acquire knowledge. And from my vantage point as observer and student of thousands of typical American parents, it is clear to me that this generation of child-rearers is somehow muddling through to a better product than did their forebears.

If each parent eventually becomes self-educated in the care of children, should it not then be possible to record some of these hard-won facts to serve as a guide for future parents? As the sage mourns, "I wish I had known twenty years ago what I know now." In this book I hope to set down some of the facts or semi-facts, and some of the mistakes, concerning the raising of children which have been brought to the attention of my two associates and me through the generous teachings of thousands of dedicated parents during what amounts to a half-century of combined pediatric experience.

From well over 10,000 charts and 100,000 pages of notes recording the intimate tribulations and personal conclusions of "real, live" parents, I have tried to choose those observations which seem most often to repeat themselves in family after family, and which seem to be the most significant in helping or hindering the child. Errors in choosing and in interpretation and organization are mine. Any wisdom present is creditable to the parents of my patients.

These observations have come from "normal" parents with "normal" children and are directed to normal parents with normal children. Emotionally disturbed parents need psychiatry and sympathy, not advice. Moreover, all matters I shall discuss relate to emotional development in growing youngsters, and problems of physical health are omitted. Likewise, the subject of what values you should elect to pass on to your children I have not considered an appropriate topic.

I do not propose that I have covered the entire subject in this book, for the more you experience the difficulties and joys of being a parent the more you must realize how little you know. Nor do I claim that these pages contain immutable truth. You will clearly decide for yourself that which sounds sensible to you and that which is to be disregarded for your own use as "bunk." But if you will only be made to pause occasionally to re-examine from a fresh point of view your own beliefs concerning a topic, this book will have served its purpose. I must re-emphasize the obvious fact that there are no true experts in this field; the closest thing to an expert becomes the parent himself.

The Perfect Parent

Since it is my hopeful intention to help some of you become better parents, we should pause here to consider the attributes of the ideal parent.

Who is the perfect parent? That depends a lot upon what you mean. If you mean the parent who knows *all* there is to know about raising children, who knows *exactly* what to do, and *when* to do it, and then *unfailingly* does it, I could safely say, "Thank God, there ain't no such parent."

Furthermore, any parent who even knows *almost all* the right things to do, and who *most* of the time does them, would, I am sure, inevitably produce an unfortunate child, completely unfit and unprepared to deal with any of the meanness and inequities of the real world he would have to live in.

To me, the perfect parent is simply the one who knows a good many of the right things to do in raising a child, and who *more than half the time* does the right thing instead of the wrong. He is the parent who makes mistakes, and then forgets about them and passes cheerfully on to the next task with some thought to doing better. One of the great rewards of being this kind of a successful and bumbling parent is to have your sixth-grader come home and cheerfully announce, "Hey, Dad, I got Mr. Sweeney as a teacher. He's swell! He can yell even louder than you can."

Basic Requirements of
Normal Personality Development

One last thing, before starting upon the main topics of the book proper. I would like to introduce the single most important theme, which is indeed the unifying foundation of all that is to follow. This is the concept of what constitutes the essential ingredients that insure the normal emotional development of the child—and of how few in number these requisites are.

I am going to be using the word "personality" a good deal. It is better that we have an understanding of what this word means before we get started. I will be using the term "personality" in its broadest sense, to include the individual's sense of happiness and unhappiness, his self-confidence, his attitudes toward himself, toward his family, and toward his community, his motivation, goals, ideals, ethics, morals, physical actions, and his feelings of "security," that ubiquitous and imprecise word. "Personality," within the meaning of these pages, implies "the total mental state."

It is true that thousands of factors contribute to, and shape, the final personality of a growing human being. It is equally true that in the long run only *three* basic needs are essential to the development of a normal personality. *Essential!* This minimal need of three, and only three, factors is an important point around which to orient your thinking, both in raising a child and in searching for a cause of any aberrations of personality that may seem to be arising along the way. These three absolute requisites for the normal development of a child's personality may be stated, with some temporary oversimplification, as (1) love, (2) discipline, and (3) independence.

Each of these three factors which determine the child's personality operates in the three geographical divisions of a child's environment: (1) the home and family, (2) the school, and (3) the neighborhood and social contacts. Thus the personality development of the child may be said to depend upon love in the family, love in the school, love in the neighborhood contacts; discipline in the family, discipline in the school; and so forth. It is clear before we begin that of these nine areas some will be more important at one age than at another.

I do not want to minimize unduly the importance of hereditary or congenital factors and their influence upon the personality of the child. It is certainly true that children do come into the world with varying degrees of talents, skills, and personality attributes. I want to emphasize, however, that these inborn potentials simply make the development of a normal personality more or less easy or difficult. Most parents of more than one child quickly recognize that each child is easier or harder to deal with in one regard or another from early infancy.

Though sometimes with more, and sometimes with less, effort, the personality of *any* child, *regardless of his potentials* at birth, can be *overwhelmingly* influenced and molded by his environment. And regardless of his genetic endowments, each child requires without exception the three fundamental factors of love, discipline, and independence. Since, once he is born, we can do nothing to control the hereditary endowment of the child, little mention of this contribution to the child's personality will be made. I am concerned not with theory, but with practicality. Furthermore, I am unprofessionally disgusted with parents who "give up" on a child's problem with only half an effort, under the excuse, "Oh well, what do you expect? That's the kind of person he was born to be."

1

Love

If it can be said that one of the three legs of a tripod is the most important, then of the three requirements for the normal development of a child's personality—love, discipline, and independence —the first is the most important. It has been repeatedly shown that a child can withstand the most awesome buffetings of Fate if there is sufficient love in his life. An impressive demonstration of this fact is found in the generally good adjustment of the children who survived the bombings of London compared with the maladjustments of those English children who were sent away from their families to places of physical safety.

It is a simple matter to agree to the need for love in childhood. But it is well to spend a little time considering just what the implications of this word are.

Love is unique among the three basic requirements for the development of normal emotional health. It is unique in that of this one ingredient *there can never be too much.*

An excess or a scarcity of discipline, too much or too little independence, can be harmful. But of love, the more the merrier. This is an important point.

As a result of a popular but misguided philosophy in the 1920's of the needs of growing children, there is still an uneasy feeling among parents that to bestow too much love upon the child is to spoil him. Nothing could be further from the truth. It is imperative to understand that the withholding of discipline may spoil the child, but never a surplus of love. These two factors are not in any sense inversely related. That is, it is *not* true that the more you love, therefore the less you must discipline. Nor that the more you discipline, the less you love.

For the sake of simplicity, it might be helpful to consider that love and discipline are *entirely* unrelated and that one should in no way affect the other. In actuality, however, it is true that you bother to discipline only insofar as you love. In other words, you would scarcely bother to discipline the stranger's child down the street, because you don't love the stranger's child. This association between discipline and love, that you discipline because you love, children readily perceive and accept.

What is love? Many different things. In the interest of clear thinking, it is a handicap that we have only the one word to mean so many related but different aspects of this all-important emotion. It will be worthwhile in dealing with children (and with adults) to consider some of the implications of "love."

The type of love most important for the normal personality development of the child is the kind that says, "I love you, Joe, not for what you do or don't do, but just because you're you." We might speak of this as uncritical love. This undemanding sort of love, or acceptance if you will, is indispensable to the *development* of a normal personality. Indeed, it is strongly supportive to the *maintenance* of a normal personality, even throughout adulthood. It is the sort of love that just about says, "I love you *despite* what you do. I love you because you're alive."

Obviously, this is not the only form that love assumes. Nor is it the only type of love that affects the child. But I must make my point crystal-clear. We are exploring the three absolute needs of the child's personality. We are not considering any of the lesser factors that will have *some* significance for his self-confidence. Other influences upon the child in addition to the vital three, other categories of love, will be discussed later in this book.

In our educated, competitive society, it is far too common for the young child inadvertently to be given the impression that his parents (or his teachers or his friends) love him because of what he does. This unfortunately conveys the obvious negative corollary: "If you don't do well, I won't love you." Or: "The better you do, and the more you succeed, the more I love you; the more you err, and the oftener you fail, the less I love you." This too frequent misunderstanding is a frightening thing, a destructive influence upon the child's developing personality. It is a major cause of many problems, present and future, and is perhaps the most important of the communication confusions between generations.

Consider the analogy of the support and comfort the husband receives from knowing that his wife loves him in an amount that has no relation to whether he succeeds or fails. Not that she loves him more when he does well in the world, and loves him less when he meets failure in his work, but rather that she loves him when he succeeds and she loves him *exactly the same* when he fails. Or take the wife who must live with the knowledge that her husband loves her *in direct proportion* to how young and beautiful she is, to how well she manages the home and prepares the meals, to how successfully she conducts herself in community affairs; compare her lot with that of the wife who can luxuriate in the knowledge that her husband loves her because she *is* Jill, and will love her, not more, not less, though her charms and productivity might wax and wane.

This is the kind of love I mean when I say that love is one of the three basic ingredients that contribute to the normal personality development of children. This is the kind of love that builds self-confidence, creates a good self-image, leads to a willingness to try without fear of the consequences of failing. This is the kind of love that makes heroes and that makes well-oriented children.

This blind, accepting love from the parents is most vital during the first five to ten years of a child's life; it is not unimportant, though, throughout one's entire life. The failure to convince the growing child that this is the feeling his parents have for him is probably the single most important cause of future personality deviations in later childhood, in adolescence, and in adulthood.

There is no doubt that most parents have a good deal of this sort of affection for their children. How then do they so often manage to convince their children otherwise? There seem to me to be three common unintended errors which unwittingly suggest to the child that his parents love him for *what he does* rather than for *who he is*. To avoid them, it is helpful to keep in mind the following:

1. *Disapprove of what the child does, not of who he is.* It is imperative to keep clear in your own thinking, and to convey to the child from the beginning, the fact that, though you often disapprove of what he *does*, you do not therefore disapprove of *him*. It is the rare high-school counselor who has the uncommon good sense to say to the delinquent student, "I abhor what you are doing; I will not tolerate such actions for a moment; but I think you're a great guy, one of the most appealing students we've had around here in a long time; I would enjoy your company." Here is the essence of being a successful counselor—and also the essence of being a successful parent.

There would be absolutely nothing contradictory in correcting and criticizing a child's actions and behavior and at the same time letting him know how much you love him as a person, just because he is he. To make this point in the extreme case, there is no inconsistency in knocking a child across the room for misbehavior, and then immediately picking him up, putting your arms around him, and telling him what a fine boy he is and how much you love him. Indeed, not only are the acts not inconsistent, but in effect they convey the two notions that (a) "I bother to correct your behavior *because* I love you" and (b) "I disapprove of your actions, but I love *you* just as much, *regardless* of how you act."

There is no hint of apology in this sequence of events. A parent need not apologize for his efforts to teach or for his instinct to love his child. Nor is there any implication of parental wrongdoing or remorse. The sincere teacher may feel pride, but not doubt, in his earnest attempts to improve his student. It will not be understood, either, that the parent is trying to buy the child's affection. The bid for the child's love lies in the parent's willingness to correct the child; the subsequent cuddling is a simple affirmation of the parent's love for the child.

There is no contradiction implied to the child—simply, "I love you. I love you independently of your behavior. I love you even though your actions made me angry. I love you enough to make you behave."

2. *Praise the child more for being, more than you praise him for doing.* A second cause of misconception on the child's part stems from our eagerness to see that our children succeed in our competitive society. In this effort, we quite properly praise and reward our children when they make a good effort and when they achieve a measure of success. For instance, parents generally react favorably to a good report card or to a kind and thoughtful act on the child's part. This is all well and good, and profitable and proper. However, it is too easy to let these accomplishments become the child's major or sole source of praise, reward, acceptance, and love.

It is important that the child receive the greater measure of praise and love *unrelated to his achievements and successes.* The child should have the opportunity to see that a good report card and a thoughtful act merit a pat on the head, a slap on the shoulder, a smile, a warm word of encouragement, even perhaps a silver quarter; but he should see more often that he receives the greater reward of five minutes of cuddling, ten words of praise, a friendly tousling of the hair, and perhaps even a one-dollar bill when he is producing nothing, is merely walking through the room, is non-constructively daydreaming, or in fact has recently done something that had to be criticized.

When the wife has just, on short notice, produced a spectacular dinner for her husband's boss, has the house immaculate and the children tucked into bed, and has groomed herself impeccably, and then her husband rewards her with a dozen red roses, that's nice. When the wife has just burned the roast, the house is a shambles, her dress is slovenly, and the children are raging through the home, and then her husband brings her a dozen red roses, that's magnificent.

3. *Communicate your love.* A third thought concerning unquestioning love that parents must consciously consider, and keep in mind, involves the difficulties that people of all ages have in communicating with one another. A person can, unfortunately, love the very devil out of another person, but if that second person is totally unaware of the fact, the love is to no avail. For example, a man and wife may deeply and sincerely love each other, he sitting on one side of the room watching television and she on the other side reading her book, and the marriage may go down the drain.

In brief, it is not enough for you to feel love; you must in some manner make the recipient *aware* of the presence of this love.

You may show your love by a thousand little acts and gestures of thoughtfulness throughout every day. Some of these *indirect* expressions of love are catalogued in context later on. Among them are:

Tucking a child into bed at night while forbearing to review with him his daily misdeeds. Tucking him in long after he is too old to require such attention.

Offering a comforting arm or an unbegrudged lap even though she's not hurt badly enough to need them.

Overlooking the sermon "You're a big boy now," or "You're a big girl now," at the moment he or she least wants to be a big boy or girl.

Eliminating references to some other child, related or unknown, from all conversations with him.

Interpreting her furious "You don't love me" correctly as "Let me hear you say you love me again, even though I've just displeased you."

Understanding his outraged "I hate you!" as "Is it all right for me to get mad at you?"

Biting your lip and waiting for a better moment instead of calling him down in front of his peers.

Not asking her to perform in front of visitors or family until she has already volunteered.

Being at home when the school day ends, even if only to see the complete belief in your love demonstrated by the casualness of your child's "Hi" followed by contented indifference. Or a thoughtful note to be found on the table or a telephone call that says, "I love you though I can't be home."

Letting him off the hook with "Nice try" when an easy lob is dropped, and while your vision of a box at Yankee Stadium becomes a mirage.

Offering her your *unsolicited* help with her homework and her chores.

Protecting him from annoyance by his younger brother even though both children were culpable.

Darning his trousers without sinking in further the already self-inflicted harpoon after he has torn them in a forbidden adventure.

Being visibly proud of him when he has given you no earthly reason even to admit that he's yours.

Placing the acne medicine remindfully but tactfully in view on the pillow without shoving the blight down his self-conscious throat.

But this subtle communication is not always enough, particularly for young children. And you may wonder whether it is enough even for adolescents and grownups. It is necessary in dealing with children to take the time occasionally to be as direct in expressing your love as to say, "Gee, I love you," "You're a swell boy," "I think you're the best daughter in the whole world." And remember that the most effective time to blurt out these not-so-corny clichés is when the child is actually doing nothing. Perhaps one of the ideal times is offered by the opportunity to tuck the child into bed for his nap or at nighttime.

An elegant way to communicate your love to a child is to praise him—not so much his accomplishments as the child himself—out loud to strangers, to relatives, and to your mate, in the presence of or within earshot of the child. This method of talking *to* a child, without talking *at* him, can serve well in many areas of communication. But be conscious of the importance of its opposite number—the harm that can develop from belittling or deriding a child to a third person within voice range of the child.

How about parents who are self-conscious, and so embarrassed by such overt statements of affection as to be made uncomfortable by them? No one should pretend that it makes any sense for a parent to upset his own sense of propriety to benefit his children. But there is a simple device that can quickly become a pleasant habit in this instance, whereby you may both have your cake and eat it. If you squirm at the thought of saying, face to face, "I love you," all you need do is develop the habit of jotting down, in appropriate seclusion, one- or two-sentence notes to the child and leaving them where he alone can find them to read—or to have read to him by the other parent if he is of preschool age. Most parents have moments of warm sentimental feelings toward their children, especially when the parent is alone and the brats are long since asleep or are away from home, and the memory of their transgressions has been dulled by time. These are the fleeting moments in which to tell your children how you feel about them, in writing. Not a long, involved pageful, but just a sentence or two.

Sharing Your Love

Few, if any, parents feel exactly the same amount of love for each of their children. Nor should they. Yet most struggle valiantly to show equal affection for each child in a spirit of dedicated "fairness." This effort is utter nonsense.

I suggest to you a radical proposition: Each child has the right and the need to believe that he is his parents' *favorite* child. Not that he receives love in equal shares with his brothers and sisters, but that he receives *more* love than any of his siblings.

Does this notion offend your sense of justice? Then try telling your wife that, with utter fairness, you love her equally and every bit as much as you do your secretary, the young blond down the block, or an old flame.

Each child should, at appropriate times, be bluntly told that he is the special favorite of the parents. There is an old Hawaiian fable in which a dying father summons each of his children individually to his bedside, and distributes his greatest gift by telling each in turn, "*You* have always been secretly my best-loved child. You have brought me the greatest pride and happiness. You are the one I believe in the most."

If you do indulge in the game of "each child the favorite," how do you handle note comparing by the children? As a matter of fact, the problem arises with remarkable infrequency. Perhaps children early sense that some subjects are too intimate for public revelation. Perhaps each child feels a little personal doubt and protects himself by not putting his knowledge to the test of comparison. In any event, parents who utilize this technique tell me they seldom are confronted. On my part, I know that if you tell me I am your favorite doctor, I don't go out of my way to prove to myself that you don't really mean it.

But your children are brilliant skeptics? Or vicious gossips? Even if so, you don't have to flee in anxiety from a concerted onslaught. The truth is: "Of course I love Jill best; she is my oldest daughter. Of course I love Sally best; she has the curliest hair. Of course I love John best; he is my smallest child. Just so, I love Daddy best; he is my husband." Please take note, only, that each is best-loved for some integral part of his being, not for something he does or has done or has to do. To be "best-loved" for an accomplishment—politest, smartest, best-behaved—is to risk one's status by failing to continue to perform. To be best-loved because you exist is delightful.

Sources of Love

If we agree upon the absolute necessity for noncritical love in the development of a normal personality, we may then inquire who it is that can supply the child with this ingredient.

Ideally, of course, both parents working in harmony are best able to accomplish this.

On the other hand, if one parent is completely absent from

the family (as through death or through divorce without visiting privileges), the remaining parent can quite adequately provide the needed love.

But, when both parents are taking an active part in raising the child, and when either one of them does not supply this essential ingredient, the ultimate personality of the child becomes in doubt. It is true that by middle adolescence some children are able to obtain sufficient acceptance to fulfill their needs from persons, young and old, outside of the parent-child arena. But, in general, if both parents are present and only one of them is able to communicate some degree of uncritical acceptance to the child, trouble should be anticipated. Professional help should be sought early.

Saving Face as Part of Love

Finding ways and opportunities to communicate your love for a child is difficult. There is, however, one completely foreseeable set of circumstances which inevitably will arise more than once in every parent's experience. This situation will invite and demand a statement of your love. An ill-conceived answer will wither the child. An appropriately planned answer will enhance the parent-child relationship. I refer to the times when a third person (not the other parent) will, in the presence of the child and parent, accuse the child of misconduct.

For example, Mrs. Beauregard arrives in hot pursuit of little Johnny and berates him before his mother for having willfully shattered her picture window. Or Robert explodes into the room, blood gushing from his brow, while sister Joan hangs expectantly over the banister: "Daddy, Daddy, Joanie hit me, and I wasn't doin' nuthin'!"

The unprepared parent reacts like a human. Painfully aware of the potential of little Johnny and of Joan the Ripper, embarrassed by the apparent demonstration of his own failure as a raiser of children, the unforewarned parent jumps into the soup and alternately denigrates the accused and cringes before the accuser. In this way an opportunity to communicate love is reduced to a strong expression of rejection. Is the accused offspring guilty as charged? That's not the point. The harm is done.

Does the mother grizzly seek the wisdom of the situation before she cuffs her cub's tormentor?

The experienced parent—who has mapped his response months in advance—automatically denies the accusation and defends his child.

"Yes, Mrs. Beauregard, I am sorry someone broke your window. But I am sure that it was someone else. Or if it was my Johnny, that it was an unavoidable accident. Yes, I'll get to the bottom of it with Johnny *in private*. Yes, if *our family* was responsible *we* will restore the window." Result: demonstration of love and support; rallying of faith and family cohesiveness; avoidance of false condemnation from which there is no graceful reprieve. Much face saving on all sides.

"Let's get you patched up first, Robbie. Then I'll talk to Joan in private. I'm sure there was a mistake." No kangaroo court here. No hastily spoken parental hostility toward Joan despite the circumstantial evidence.

Regardless of who is right and who is wrong, you lose as a parent if you join an outsider (even if the outsider is another member of the family) in scolding your own child in front of the intruder.

If all accusations subsequently turn out to be true, you, by not joining in the attack, have salvaged from the debacle the great prize of having demonstrated your love to your child. If, as happens so often, some important element of the accusation turns out to have been false, you will have adroitly sidestepped the need to perform hara-kiri.

This suggested method of "face saving" will not always endear you to the neighbors or to the police. But we might just as well face this problem now. In the life of virtually every parent this moment of truth sooner or later appears. You appropriately will make up your mind in advance whether you are raising your children properly or whether you are bent first and foremost upon appeasing your neighbors. I leave this decision, as all others, to you. For myself, I see no real choice in the matter.

Subsequent correction of the erring child, and compensation of the aggrieved complainant, must be accomplished later, with no unwarranted price having been paid by yourself or your child either in terms of loss of love or in terms of loss of discipline.

Allowances

I recommend to you a method of expressing your love through a device that is erroneously approached as a way of teaching "responsibility." Indeed it cannot serve such a purpose. Rather it can symbolize a family's acceptance of one of its members for the sake of himself and without regard for his ability to contribute. This device you call his allowance.

The granting of a weekly monetary allowance to a child is a tradition based upon the concept that such a gift can have a positive effect upon the molding of the child. And so it can. Unfortunately, in many families the proper purpose of an allowance is so distorted that the whole subject becomes a major source of family discontent and wrangling.

An allowance is an important statement to the child of the willing acceptance of him into the family circle. He receives it because he is an appreciated member of a loving group, in which each member is glad to share with the others his good fortune. It represents a sharing not only of the material wealth of the family but also of the wealth of love, acceptance, trust, and faith possessed by the family.

The child earns his allowance simply by being alive and by belonging to the family. He does not earn it by performing well or by pleasing his parents through his behavior and accomplishments. This would represent wages for services rendered. Wages and an allowance are two entirely different things. The allowance is earned by the pleasure brought to the family by the child's presence, not by the child's productivity.

The allowance has no strings attached. Once the family decides how much of its financial wealth is the child's part, it becomes solely the child's. If the money must be handled in such and such a way, if part of it must be allocated to the bank, or spent for lunches, or otherwise accounted for, it is not an allowance. To foster saving, give the child money to put into the bank; to buy lunches, give the child lunch money. But don't confuse these sums with an allowance.

An allowance says, "You are ours, and we are pleased that you are ours. You share in what we have. We believe in you and have trust in you. What you do with your share is solely your decision. If your use of the money seems odd to us, we have faith enough in you to understand that from your viewpoint it is not odd."

Thus an allowance serves many useful purposes. Through demonstration it proclaims family strength in sharing, and symbolizes sacrifice for others. It emphasizes the worthwhileness to the parents of the child's being, and not of his performance. It illustrates faith and confidence, and silently invites the child to consider himself worthy of them.

Therefore, an allowance is not withheld as a method of discipline any more than love is withheld. An allowance is not increased or decreased because of deserving performance—it is already deserved just for being. And if the allowance is "foolishly" dissipated, it is not commented upon, for this is the basis of independence founded on love—initiative which sometimes results in erroneous actions which are not belittled by one's judges.

The quantity of the allowance is not important. It should be an amount that involves no serious sacrifice by the rest of the family. It should increase with age. It should conform, within reason, to community standards. It should not be so large as to represent a lie to the child concerning the family's financial status, or so small as to be demonstrative of family miserliness. It should be started at an early age, more or less coincident with the beginning of schooling.

A child who elects to perform chores for money, within or without the family, is paid for his work, and this is unrelated to his allowance. A child who chooses not to perform chores for wages is not paid, and this too has nothing to do with his allowance. Encouraging a child to work for extra money must stand or fall on its own merits, and not be confused with the good that can be accomplished by an allowance.

Perhaps it is contributory to later attitudes to insist that a child earn his extra rewards. There may be some value in establishing the connection between the willingness to sweat and the receiving of commensurate material compensation. "I am a successful individual. I learned early that I had to work hard to get what I wanted." Maybe so! Maybe so! How about the possibility, though, that what you learned early was to judge yourself in terms of material achievement? And that somewhere along the way you missed discovering that there are other reasons for working hard, such as pride in doing your best, such as the pleasure of helping those who love you? Is it conceivable that you might better have learned early to work hard for no tangible reward, and merely for the gratification of conforming to the pattern of mutual helpfulness of your family?

2

Discipline

Discipline is the second of our basic requirements, the second leg on our tripod, necessary for the normal development of the personality of the child. Unlike love, which can only be supplied in quantities that are too small, and can never be too much present, discipline is a much squirmier ingredient to measure. Unfortunately it comes in doses that are too large, in doses that are too small, and, worst of all, in doses that are mutually contradictory.

Discipline is so important in the developing personality of the child simply because we live in an organized society and in theory are preparing the child to fit into and to deal with that society—not to fit into some utopian society, but into our society, where love and acceptance will be withheld if you do not know the major rules of the game, and where, if you have not learned life's requirements at an early stage, you will be taught them later, not by those whose love tempers the lesson with tenderness but by strangers who couldn't care less about the harm they may do to your personality. No growing animal long remains normal once he discovers that he is a total misfit in his surroundings and that he is therefore ostracized and rejected by the overwhelming majority of the individuals who constitute his social environment. Discipline is the ingredient that teaches a child how best to behave in order to survive in society.

I want to emphasize here, as I did in the preceding chapter, that there is no inverse relationship between love and discipline—that is, it is not true that the more one loves the less one can discipline, or that the more one disciplines the less one can love. A parent goes to the trouble to discipline a child only if, and because, he loves that child.

I should warn the reader that what follows is the most provocative portion of this book; it confronts a myriad of ingrained fallacies that muddle the parent-child relationship.

First we must consider what we mean when we use the word "discipline." Failure to define this term is behind much of the disagreement that engulfs discussions of this subject. To start with, let's agree that "discipline" and "punishment" are not synonymous. Punishment suggests hurting someone in retribution, paying someone back for a wrong committed. It carries with it the connotation of brutalizing, of exacting an eye for an eye. You more often punish someone you dislike than someone you love.

The word "punishment," in sharp contrast to "discipline," does not imply an action directed toward a single specific goal. You punish sometimes to satisfy your anger, sometimes in the attempt to prevent a recurrence of a wrongdoing, sometimes to comply with a law, sometimes to hurt an enemy, sometimes in the hope of improving the victim. The goal is not stated in the word. This is never so with the word "discipline."

Do you ever understandably "punish" a child? Of course. Since most parents are more or less human, they punish their child vindictively to appease their anger when he embarrasses them by spitting on the minister. Neighbors punish your child when he maliciously destroys their property. They are not interested in improving the child. Oh, they may want to "improve" him so that he won't return to destroy more of their property, but they are not concerned if he goes two blocks away and attacks a stranger's possessions. In short, one punishes for one's own sake, not for the sake of the victim.

Not so with "discipline." You discipline with the intention of helping the recipient to improve himself, to learn a lesson that hopefully will make him a better person. I suggest that the word "discipline" as used here, and as it pertains to the parent-child relationship, is an exact synonym for the word "teach."

It has seemed to me that we tend to speak and to think of "disciplining" children when they are very young. Gradually, as they grow older, we begin more and more to speak and to think of "teaching" them. But I would submit that this age differential is an artificial usage, and that sometimes the answer to a problem becomes more easily seen at any age if we substitute in our thinking "teach" for "discipline."

And I would urge that when you use the word "punish," you should try to define exactly what you have in mind. Toward what goal do you mean to punish? To punish for the purpose of teaching is to discipline. To punish for the sake of hurting is a different-colored horse. If to punish is to hurt, then the more hurtful the better. It follows that the best punishment might be lighted bamboo slivers under the fingernails. To punish is to dislike.

To discipline is to love. I am not about to spend my own precious time disciplining someone I don't care about. Punishment is *not* what I mean when I say that discipline is one of the three factors essential to the normal personality development of the child. To discipline is to teach.

Why Should I Discipline My Child?

"Why should I discipline my child?" Or better: "Why do I need to discipline my child in order for him to grow up having developed a normal personality?"

The development of a normal personality requires the acquisition of a sense of one's own worth, a sense of being loved and accepted. The areas, geographically, which contribute to, or detract from, this sense of self-esteem are the family, the neighborhood, and the school. To be acceptable to any organized social structure a member must know how that society expects him to behave. He must have learned the rules of attitude and deportment that that society accepts. He does not necessarily have to agree with the rules, but he must be familiar with them.

The school and the neighborhood, each of which will affect the child's developing personality, are not likely to shower him with affection and acceptance if he has learned none of the rules of behavior before he enters the school and before he makes contact with the neighborhood. Indeed, after a few years even his own family is going to be hard-pressed to offer acceptance if he has not been disciplined to a tolerable degree.

A parent need not endorse, or even imply, conformity to society's rules. He must simply recognize that rebellion, to be meaningful, must be successful. You cannot rebel successfully if you are handicapped by an abnormal personality. Nor can one rebel successfully from outside society. Even to be a successful rebel against society it is necessary first to know enough of the rules of society to be able to operate from within it. To be an effective person, even an effective rebel, you need first to be effective. A successful rebel has acquired enough self-confidence to be able to deny and try to change some aspects of society. The unsuccessful rebel is crippled by his inadequate self-image. He must reject society to the point that he dooms his effectiveness. He is unable to struggle, with hope of success, for fear of anticipated failure.

You say, "All right, I'll concede that discipline may be a necessary requirement for the child's personality. But that's not why *I* discipline *my* child. Sometimes I discipline him because he annoys me and I get mad at him; sometimes I discipline him because he acts like a brat and it embarrasses me because it makes me look foolish." Of course you do. You treat him thus because you too are human, with feelings and with needs of your own. But you *punish* him at these times, for your own sake. The valuable *discipline* the child may derive from such an encounter is the lesson that people *are* human and *do* react in a primitive way when their privileges are threatened. And this too is a profitable lesson to be learned, if it is not the only relationship you have with your child.

The "What" of Discipline

There are so many things a child needs to learn between the cradle and adulthood. In our complicated world there are too many things he has to learn. How many years of teaching do you have at your disposal—ten years, twelve years, sixteen years? Your child can't possibly learn all there is to know, not even in his entire lifetime. We must establish priorities in deciding what to teach.

Given such time restrictions, we might readily agree to teach the child only that which is important. Have you ever thought about what you would wish your child to be like when he is a teenager? Catalogued, so to speak, the attributes you would consider it important for him to have acquired? This is one way of beginning to get at the problem of what you must concentrate on in disciplining the younger child.

There is one—just one—basic lesson that *all* children must learn, and must learn first. This is the *sine qua non* of teaching, the first lesson upon which all the others must rest. No matter what else you want your child to learn, he must learn this lesson first. It can be taught at virtually any age, but if it is not learned there can be no successful future teaching. If at any age your child has not yet learned it, it is necessary to stop all other teaching to concentrate upon it.

How can I best describe this "first discipline"? It is so important that I will try to explain it in two different ways. Expressing it differently, but signifying the same thing, I might say either: "A child must first learn regard for authority," or: "A child must first learn that he can rely upon his teacher."

Authority. I haven't the slightest doubt that all children, in order to survive normally, must learn early in life that there is a mysterious force called "authority." They must deal effectively with this force in all of their future social experiences.

This force permeates our society and therefore one must be prepared to deal with it. Indeed, authority in some form has been the backbone of all civilizations, and without its cohesive influence, anarchy and chaos would of necessity prevail.

Whether authority more often serves the interest of good or of bad is not a question we need be concerned with here. Nor is it a question that should be raised in the mind of the young child. The truth is that authority can and does exist, and a most important fact in disciplining a child for the purpose of helping him to develop a normal personality is that he must learn early to deal appropriately with authority.

Thus, the first, and kindest act in disciplining any child is to teach him that there is an unquestionable, sometimes blind, sometimes unintelligible, and even sometimes erroneous, force in this world which may be called authority. This blind force will someday say, "Jump!" and there is no recourse but to jump. One gets, and one learns to expect, no explanation from authority.

Do you shrink a little at the statement: "A child should first learn to obey authority blindly?" Do you wonder whether there may not be too much authority in the world already? And too much blind acceptance of it? And do you half suspect that this, in fact, may be one of the roots of much of the trouble in the world today? Well, so might I. I am not saying that the teenager should be taught to accept dogma uncritically. I am simply saying that the acceptance of authority is the first lesson to be taught the *young* child so that his subsequent lessons will be easier for him.

Look at this first lesson from a different point of view. Even discard the word "authority" as being too charged with emotion for some people. To help our children to develop normal personalities we want to assist them in learning whatever is necessary for them to fit comfortably into their later lives. We need a good teacher to help them learn. A good teacher is one whose information can be trusted to be true without the need for constant checking and doubting by the pupil. Therefore, *the first lesson the young child needs to learn is that he can trust the reliability of the teachings of his parents.* He is thereafter spared the confusion of testing and doubting their every lesson. This rephrasing of the matter expresses to me exactly the same idea that I mean to convey by "obeying authority." Perhaps it could be said in this manner: *Establish early in the child's life the dependability of the parent's word, so that he may have the faith to be supported and directed by it.*

Can the foregoing statements be interpreted as an argument for conformity, for blind acceptance of the world, or for mediocrity of thought? No, not in any sense! They are simply a recognition of the fact that the mind of the young child is not capable of grasping abstractions or of interpreting complicated instructions. When the child grows older he may be allowed or encouraged to question the wisdom of various authorities, and may be instructed in how to combat effectively those he considers wrong. But the first step in discipline, as the first step in teaching, must be the lesson that the teacher is correct and is to be trusted and obeyed.

I want to repeat, at this point, that we are considering "what to teach a child" or "what is important in disciplining a child." We should not waste our time in teaching unimportant things, and certainly it is unimportant to teach a child things that he could as well learn by himself, things that, indeed, we would have to go out of our way to *prevent* him from learning.

How can you tell whether a child will learn something regardless of whether or not you teach it to him? One easy way to decide is to look around at all the sixteen-year-olds you know. If they all seem to know something equally well, you can bet that their knowledge on this subject doesn't depend upon who taught them or how well.

For example, how much valuable time is squandered on teaching a child to be toilet-trained? Certainly enough in some families to have taught the child six *important* things that somehow or other he never does get around to learning. Now, I defy any parents to succeed in preventing their children from ultimately becoming toilet-trained. How many normal sixteen-year-olds do you know who haven't learned this lesson well? To prevent them from learning, you would have had to bolt the bathroom doors at home, at school, and at Howard Johnson's. Indeed, institutions that house groups of young children without parents have long known that this is one subject upon which they need not squander their limited teaching time. No matter how little time you spend upon toilet training (and the less the better), your child will one day walk up to you and lead you to the bathroom.

Another example: How many hours are wasted on, and how much agonized bickering and worrying goes into, teaching a child to give up his bottle? What foolish nonsense! Provided you do not hide all the cups and all the glasses in the house, I challenge any parent to *make* a child continue to drink his milk from a bottle forever. I don't know a single neglected teenager who does. Sooner or later the child would insist, "The heck with you. I refuse to take this bottle any longer."

So in partial answer to the question, "What shall I teach?" please think about this aspect of disciplining, and don't waste valuable teaching time, which you are going to need so badly, on the lessons that you can't keep your child from learning without you.

A third measure for separating the important from the unimportant in discipline derives from a consideration of what attributes society will judge your child by after he has matured. What is the likelihood that a college admissions board or a personnel manager or a prospective mate will inquire whether or when a given lesson was mastered? The application of this criterion would lead us to agree to waste little valuable time upon such transitory disciplines as toilet training, weaning, thumb sucking, age of walking, self-dressing, and so on.

With those broad but simple guidelines we can begin to plan what it is we need to teach our children: Is it inevitable that he will learn it, whether I teach it or not? Is it really an important lesson that will contribute substantially toward my image of my grown child? Will it matter to his future happiness?

How to Discipline

This section might equally well be entitled "How to Teach." The simple rules of how to discipline apply to any teaching situation, whether it involves parent and child or teacher and student, and whether the subject is elementary behavior or advanced calculus.

The basic requirements are: (1) be an authority, (2) be consistent, (3) criticize the act, (4) avoid premature explanations.

Be an Authority. If you were to choose a teacher for yourself, would it be someone who half the time put out information that you could see for yourself was wrong? Or would you prefer the teacher whose statements were consistently accurate? It soon becomes hard to learn from a person once you have discovered that she is not an authority and that you must mull over her every statement to decide for yourself when she is speaking wisdom and when she is speaking nonsense. It is comforting, on the other hand, to realize that the teacher knows her subject and is an authority upon whom you can rely with comfort.

Don't panic, Mom and Dad. Though you and I may know very well that you are not absolute authorities, you can and must assume the *disguise* of an authority if you are to be helpful to your children in the area of discipline. Here is the key: An authority is nothing more than a fellow who knows more about a subject than the person he is addressing and who has sense enough to stay away from other subjects.

In the beginning a good teacher takes pains to establish her reliability in the eyes of her students by sticking to facts that she can easily substantiate. Later she ventures to present subjects harder to prove, but only after she has planted in her pupils a belief in herself. A successful parent takes pains to establish his position as an authority in discipline *before* he risks exposing his fallibility by plunging into areas that he cannot easily dominate. First things first. Allow your child to develop confidence in you as a teacher first. Don't demonstrate your ineptness needlessly by disciplining in matters that are difficult or impossible for you to prove until after you have first convinced him to trust you.

There are two areas, for example, in which even the most unself-confident parent can establish his reliability as a believable disciplinarian in the eyes of the unsuspecting child.

The first example involves learning to sit in the high chair for meals. "You will stay in the high chair" is a fact readily proved to the child who tries to climb out, proved by pinning a folded diaper around the doubting infant's middle and the chair back.

A second circumstance in which the odds guarantee that the parent will emerge as an authority involves dressing and diapering the crawler. "Please hold still while I dress you" is an incontestable request if the parent firmly and calmly holds the wriggling infant still until he relaxes from his struggles, proceeds with the dressing until the struggles start anew, then counters by more immobilizing.

See how easy it is to be an unquestionable authority if you choose the right subject? Let me generalize a bit from these examples. Until the pupil's confidence in the discipliner is established, the subject matter is always chosen so that the teacher can prove his point if it is challenged. The lesson is conducted with no more display of emotion than befits any classroom; the child is not scolded, not reasoned with, not nagged, not punished. He is simply made to comply!

Notice particularly that the lesson, though accompanied by words, is communicated by action. The physical enforcement coincides with the spoken command. A fact can be demonstrated to be true by physical action *before* the pupil has gained confidence in the teacher, and therefore physically provable facts can be used to establish the reliability of the discipliner. Words unaccompanied by action can be relied upon by the child only after the reliability of the discipliner has already been established.

The creeper headed for the lamp cord is called back only as he is being bodily carried back. The toddler in the backyard is summoned to lunch only as his mother grasps his hand and leads him indoors. The biter is told to quit it only as he is being physically removed from proximity to the victim.

Thus, by concentrating his early discipline on lessons which can be promptly backed up by physical means, which accomplish the performance of the task, the parent begins to establish his infallibility as an authority. The experienced parent does not think of appealing to a child by verbal commands alone until he is certain he is well along toward persuading the child to trust his reliability as a teacher. Confine your early discipline to areas where you are certain of success.

The converse must be observed. Avoid disciplining in matters which you cannot enforce until the child's actions show that you have established a reputation as a convincing teacher. Each time the young child witnesses your attempting a lesson which you are unable to prove, you deprive him of the comfort of having a reliable teacher.

To illustrate: It is unwise to instruct a young child to "eat your food," "do it on the potty, not in your pants," "go to sleep," "stop that crying," because in each instance if the child says, "I don't believe you," you cannot possibly enforce the lesson, and you detract from your image as a teacher upon whom the child can depend.

Many mothers lack the confidence in themselves to believe that they can properly instruct their children. But no amount of self-assurance is required if you choose the first lessons carefully. Pick subjects that you are master of, if only by virtue of being bigger, and avoid subjects which may reveal your weaknesses until the child accepts your lessons as incontestable.

Do you imagine that "perfect parents" ever make the mistake of asking the child to do something they cannot enforce before they have succeeded in establishing credibility? Continually! Then what to do? A knowledgeable parent, having inadvertently trapped himself by commanding of his young son, "Stop that crying this instant" (an unenforceable demand on a yet-unconvinced child), bites his lip and changes the subject. He does not pursue a lost cause.

If confidence in the parent's competence as a teacher has not been established early, it must be attempted later, by the same technique, but with more difficulty.

If you have sired your progeny too soon, or come by this book too late, so that you already have a five- or ten-year-old who has come this far without having learned to believe in your discipline, start from the beginning. Stick to only a few commands that you can enforce and avoid for a while, like the plague, giving orders that are doomed to challenge and to failure. Improve your batting average by choosing winning games and avoiding losing ones, and your stature as a dependable teacher will grow.

Are you afraid your child may come to believe in your infallibility too much, and that you may exercise too much unquestioned influence on him? Believe me, it is not likely that you will be so successful over the years in hiding your human weaknesses as a teacher from even the most retarded youngster.

Be Consistent. Convey to the child the *same* fact as many times as necessary for him to accept it. Inconsistent or contradictory discipline is far more confusing and, therefore, harmful to the child than are the extremes of too much or too little discipline.

No one would quarrel with the observation that a mother who spent Mondays and Wednesdays instructing her seven-year-old that six times six equals thirty-six, and Tuesdays and Thursdays that six times six is thirty-four, would end up with a bewildered mathematician. Nor is it unclear that a father's proclaiming The Hague to be the capital of Belgium, over the mother's claim of Antwerp as the capital, would result in confusion rather than learning on the part of the child.

So too does inconsistency of discipline on the part of a single parent, or inconsistency between parents, produce a sense of confusion and panic within the child, so that he ultimately says, "The heck with it," and gives up trying to follow *any* teaching. It is better to be consistently wrong in discipline than to be right and inconsistent. Parents who constantly disagree about the teaching of their children had best compromise their differences between themselves—if need be with the help of outside counseling, if they are mature enough to do so—or had better match their child's college fund with a child psychiatrist fund.

"Well-meaning" persons outside the mother-father-child sphere—grandparents, older siblings, servants—can equally well contribute contradiction to the discipline of a child. Such outside "help" often constitutes one of the many "put up or shut up" situations that confront parents. They must early decide for themselves whether their first allegiance is to the child or to the outsider, however closely related.

How often must you repeat the same fact to a child before he should be expected to learn it? This depends upon many variables—upon the child's age, the complexity of the fact, previous learning in the same area, how lucidly the fact is presented, the child's innate skill in that area, how many other facts are being introduced at the same time, and so forth.

Among the most complicated lessons are those that concern learning regard for authority and confidence in the teacher. These lessons take a long time, often years, and should be unencumbered by the simultaneous introduction of too many other less important facts. Other lessons, of less immediate value, which seem to be going slowly are often better postponed till a later year when the child can learn more rapidly.

In being persistent in teaching and in disciplining, try to see the distinction between nagging and patient repetition. If you say, "Johnny, stop hitting your sister with that hatchet," and there is no response, and you say for the second and third and tenth time, "Johnny, stop—" until your voice rises to such a crescendo that Johnny stops from amazement, then you are nagging.

If, on the other hand, you say *once*, "Johnny, stop—" and, there being no compliance, you move in and disarm Johnny; then when Johnny rearms himself and returns to the attack you again say *once*, "Johnny, stop—" before again physically enforcing your command, you are being patiently persistent.

Children—and adults—all too rapidly learn how often a teacher will repeat a command before enforcing it, and will inevitably come to wait for the umpteenth repetition of the request before believing it. On the other hand, they learn with equal alacrity to obey the first command if it is known to be followed by proof without being repeated. Repetition comes each time *only after* effective action.

To generalize this advice, please learn to tell a child something only once before following up with enforcement. If the request is unenforceable, it is better not to repeat the request; instead drop the subject until some later date, by which time the child hopefully will have learned to respond to the first utterance through the experience provided by requests which *have* been enforceable.

If your darling has already adjusted himself to years of chronic nagging, try surprising him by limiting your requests to the "spoken only once" kind. Then either drop the subject or enforce it, whichever course is possible. You may be pleasantly startled by the ultimate results. At worst, your child will be pleasantly surprised.

Criticize the Act. When the child gives the wrong answer, let him know that it is wrong; but be certain that he understands that you are criticizing his answer or action, and not belittling him as a person.

It is obvious that the role of a teacher includes signifying to the student that his answer is correct or incorrect. It follows that in disciplining a child of any age he must be told when his behavior is improper.

But it is of crucial importance to the personality of the child that it be clear in the teacher's mind and in the child's mind that what is being criticized is his action and not himself as a person. A child's self-image depends upon what he considers his parents' opinion of him to be. The image must not inadvertently be attacked by your disciplining.

For example, there is a mountainous difference between "You are a bad boy for kicking me in the shins" and "Kicking me in the shins is bad and I won't tolerate it." If at first this sounds like hair-splitting, let me spend a little time convincing you that this is one of the major mistakes parents make in raising children.

It is relatively harmless to attack another person's actions, which, after all, he can learn to change. It is disastrous to attack his self-esteem, for he cannot change from being himself. The ability to see the difference between declaring an action or an answer unacceptable and declaring the individual unacceptable is *important* in any teacher-student relationship. It is *vital* for the parent playing the role of teacher, since the parent cannot give up the position of parent in the child's eyes—and a seeming rejection of the child by the parent is a deep and permanent hurt.

Many of the pathetically unself-confident personalities of children stem in large part from the parents' failure to distinguish between denying the action and denying the person.

Such methods of signifying to a child that his behavior is wrong as "How can you be so stupid!" "Why aren't you as good as Sally?" "You're a mean, naughty, thoughtless child," are all attacks upon the child's self-image and do not properly imply that his action was at fault. They demean the person and not the act.

The successful counselor of delinquent children, as I have mentioned earlier, is he who says, in one way or another, to the child, "Your actions are intolerable, deplorable, and I have no intention of putting up with them; but I've watched you around school and you yourself are a fine, appealing person and I like you and would enjoy being your friend." The person is accepted, the action is rejected; and the two things are kept quite separate.

Are you convinced of the importance of this approach? Do you solemnly resolve that you will use it at all times? Please, don't be so gullible. Of course the mature parent knows and thinks about this principle—when he is in solitude. But, since most parents are human, how does he react in the natural anger that his child's misbehavior incites? Much of the time he rants at the child himself. Part of the time, after his rage has subsided, he forces himself to go back to the child, not to apologize, but to put his arm around him and let him know he is still loved. Occasionally he succeeds in confining his outburst to the non-destructive "Damn it, quit that!" And once in a millennium he may actually catch himself in time to tell the child simultaneously that he loves him and that his behavior is wrong. Accept the reality of being a fallible human as well as a well-intentioned parent. Try to come close to doing the right thing as often as you can, especially by preparing yourself in advance. But don't expect the impossible of yourself. And don't berate yourself for spontaneous behavior. Perfection is not necessary in order to qualify as a "perfect parent."

I should mention the opposite situation, overpraising the act, though it is of less destructive import. When a child's actions are praiseworthy he should of course be told so. But not out of proportion to how much he is praised when there has been no action at all, neither good nor bad. In other words, as I have stressed in the preceding chapter, if a child gets most or all of his praise and acceptance from "good" actions and "good" behavior, he may easily decide that he is loved for his actions and not for himself. If the only words of praise a child hears are when he brings home an "A" report card or remembers to wash his hands before dinner, he may conclude that he is loved in proportion to what he produces; it follows in his mind that if he should fail to produce he will be loved the less. This equating of acceptable behavior and success with love makes the stakes too high for many children, and they refuse to play the game for fear of losing their most valued possession—parental love. Do you too know the little boy who won't play baseball if his father and mother are watching?

We are still at this point considering the subject of how to tell a child his behavior is wrong—in other words, what method to use in disciplining him. Actually all that is required is some way of conveying to the child that his answer is wrong. Does someone imagine that a spelling teacher or a math teacher is a more effective or a less effective teacher if she indicates a wrong answer by a red check or by a black star or by a raised eyebrow or by a ruler across the knuckles or by turning a somersault? One method of saying "right" or "wrong" is no more meaningful to the student than another.

You may effectively discipline an erring child by confining him to his room, by stretching him on the rack, by smacking him across the rump, by raising an eyebrow, or by saying, "That's wrong." One form of "nay" is neither more educating nor less than the other. Keep in mind that, until the student has learned to trust and to depend upon the teacher's reliability, *no* method will work, and *any* method must at first be accomplished by physical demonstration. When any method of saying "no" is continually unsuccessful, it is not the fault of the method, but rather in the application of the method.

Methods of correcting a child which fill him with instant terror are, however, doomed to failure. Reduced to a state of anxiety, not even the most eager student is capable of learning. And the one thing best designed to bring instant terror to a child is the threat of losing a parent or the parent's love. Therefore, methods of disciplining which include such comments as "If you ever do that again I'll leave home," "You make me wish I were dead," or "You make me so ashamed of you," are not recommended.

Since we are anxious, for the child's sake, to preserve as long as possible the myth of the omniscience of the parent, it follows that methods of disciplining a child which involve tit for tat are also not suggested. If a parent attempts to show a child that biting or shin kicking is not permitted by biting or kicking the child back, if a parent signifies that deliberate destruction of a book or shrieking with rage is not acceptable by himself tearing up other books or screaming louder, he puts himself on the same age level as the child, and thus too readily abdicates his position of alleged intellectual superiority.

Avoid Premature Explanations. Don't force the child to make decisions before he has the facts upon which to decide—and the self-confidence to do so.

Remember that we are considering how to discipline a child—that is, how to teach him, how to help him through learning. You are not helping a child to learn if you ask him how much the square root of nine is before you have first taught him square roots. It is unfair to ask the child to help you to discipline him before you have taught him the facts from which he can derive an answer.

For this reason, it is not fair to offer the young child an explanation in order to show him that what you tell him is right. So much nonsensical illogic has gone into perpetuating the myth that one should *explain* to a child as one disciplines, that it behooves us to consider the facts concerning explanations.

On behalf of children everywhere, I beg of you, "Don't terrify them with explanations. Just support them with the facts." Would you have preferred an explanation of our number system before or after you had learned that two plus two is four? Would you have chosen to have an explanation of Newton's Laws of Motion before or after you had learned that the earth rotates around the sun?

Explanations of discipline properly come *after* the facts are thoroughly mastered, not *as* the facts are being presented.

"Anita, come in for dinner" ("Why?" "Because I say to") is a hard enough fact to master. "Anita, come in for dinner because I am your mother and ask you to do this both for your own sake and because I have had a hard day and I want to get dinner over with to go to a show," is terrifying. Instead of teaching a proper behavior it thrusts upon Anita the frightening burden of deciding for herself whether it is more important for her to continue to play or more important for her to consider her own nutritional health and the happiness of her mother. As far as being helpful to the child, you might as well, to "help" me, hand me a set of surveying instruments when I ask you the shortest route to the corner drugstore.

By giving an explanation before the facts are learned the teacher is burdening the student with the necessity to figure out right from wrong for himself. And at a time when the child does not have the knowledge to make a valid decision.

Explanations of discipline should come only after Anita has long since mastered the fact that when mother calls her for dinner it is correct behavior for her to go.

Explanations can be a method by which a teacher evades the responsibility of herself deciding what is true and what is false, and by which she shares with the student the burden of perhaps being wrong. To be a teacher you must be right or wrong; but be it. It doesn't hurt the child if you are wrong. It does hurt him to force him to help you decide whether you are right or wrong.

In this connection we should consider rewards and bribery. "Bob, you behaved well in front of Great-aunt Agatha today." You have just rewarded Bob. "Bob, if you behave well in front of Great-aunt Agatha this afternoon you will make me proud of you." You have just offered Bob a bribe. The first is legitimate, the latter destructive.

A reward is a prize presented *after* an accomplishment, with no certain commitment made before the act. A bribe is a prize offered *before* the accomplishment, and implies a choice of behavior on the part of the recipient. In other words, a bribe, like an explanation, thrusts upon the student the necessity of choosing between right and wrong, supposedly after carefully weighing the facts and the consequences.

"If you pass French this semester I will let you watch television," is a bribe. It says that I demand that you decide whether it is better for you to do something other than studying French and pay the price of forgoing television or better for you to devote your time to French and be compensated by television." Such disciplinary efforts harm the child by burdening him with a decision he knows he is ill-equipped to make and at the same time relieve the parent of seeking out and helping to remedy the cause of the French problem.

Of course, there are "negative bribes" too. "If you don't pick up your room, I'll thrash you" is as much of a bribe as "If you pick up your room, I'll buy you a pony."

How about "Please behave when Aunt Agatha comes to visit this afternoon?" Bribe? No. No value is placed in advance upon the good behavior. No weighing of the pros and cons is required of the child. Only instructions or advice has been issued in advance, no payment promised.

But doesn't the knowledge gained by repeated experiences of being *rewarded* allow a child to anticipate in advance what the prize will be for good behavior, so that in effect this anticipated prize becomes analogous to a bribe? Of course. This is the way all mature life decisions are made. At this point it is no longer a bribe. The decision is now made on the basis of facts and experience, and there is no stated commitment, only anticipation.

Another aspect of discipline is shown in the following consideration. When before a party your slip is showing or your tie has tomato soup on it, it's nice to have someone who loves you point out to you that something is wrong. It's not so nice to have that same someone remind you hour after hour thereafter of what a slob you have been. When you have disciplined Barbara for something she's done wrong, forget it. There's nothing to be gained by bringing it up later in the day or during the following week. That's nagging and belittling, not teaching.

Can anyone look back over his own childhood and recall with fondness and respect a teacher whose method of teaching was based upon reminding and rereminding the student, as the days and weeks went by, of an error he had committed in the past? This process of repetitively correcting a past mistake rather easily evolves into a system of nagging belittlement, which is a far cry from successful teaching. You cannot expect successfully to train a puppy by slapping him with a newspaper day after day for weeks following his transgression.

It is for this reason that I would consider the popular method of withholding from a child a prized possession or privilege as a means of disciplining him a somewhat dubious procedure, rather more apt to boomerang than to teach. I have in mind the discipline that goes: "Because you were rude to Aunt Sadie today, there'll be no television for a week," "Since there are two D's on your report card, you may not ride your bicycle for a month," or "Because you were fresh to your mother today, you'll get no allowance for the next three weeks."

While such methods occasionally *seem* to have the desired effect, one may suspect that any beneficial results will be only temporary and that in the long run the teaching value may be nil. These are merely elaborate ways of nagging a child over the days and weeks that he has done something wrong in the past. Surely you can find something in the present to criticize and let the past be gone.

Let's face it, if you have judged your child old enough to

spend a certain amount of time before the TV set, or to have a bicycle, or to profit from an allowance, and you honestly come to feel that *your* judgment was in error and that your child is *not* old enough for these privileges, then rectify your error and take away the privileges. But not as a form of discipline. Properly teaching a child that what he has done is wrong consists of letting him know *now* that it is wrong and then dropping the subject until he makes the mistake again.

A magnificent rule in disciplining a child is never to compare him with someone else. I wish all parents would train themselves from the birth of a child never to mention one child to another. Would you enjoy learning to speak Spanish if every time you erred the teacher pointed out to you that Helen would never have made such a mistake, and especially if Helen happened to be your own sister? It is really not fair fighting to tell your husband how much better a provider Mr. Jones is as a method of teaching your husband that he should try harder. So it is not very appropriate to wish out loud in front of Sandy that he could be as well behaved or as smart as his brother (or sister, or cousin, or friend, or imaginary playmate). The best way to avoid such errors is to cultivate the habit of not mentioning one child in any context while addressing another child.

I have tried to put proper stress on the fact that, in dealing as parents or teachers with children, the method used to discipline is of minor and, indeed, of almost insignificant importance. This subject, though, is often a source of considerable concern to parents and a basis of many of their doubts and questions.

"How can I get Johnny to mind me?" "How can I get him to behave better?" "Which is the best method to make him understand that he has to do as I say?" "What punishment is best to teach him not to lie?" "I've tried spanking him, and he only laughs at me; I've confined him to his room, and he defies me the minute he's allowed out; I've tried reasoning with him, I've threatened him, I've taken away his privileges; no matter how I try to correct him, he seems to delight in displeasing me."

Generally the honest answer is that Johnny's misbehavior has nothing whatsoever to do with the *method* being used to discipline him. The fact probably is that *no* change in method is going to make much impression on Johnny.

If Johnny is not performing up to your expectations and if your expectations are realistic, then agonizing over what method of discipline you are using is of little use. Better inquire into the likely reasons behind Johnny's confused behavior. From his point of view, is he seriously doubting your love and acceptance of him? Are you squashing his evolving need for independence, or are you trying to push him toward independence? Are you disciplining him too often? Are you disciplining him too seldom? Are you consistent when you try to discipline him? Are there several people in his life who are teaching him different standards of behavior at the same time? Is he confused and frightened at never having learned that there is a comforting and protective authority who is willing and able to guide him in his learning?

In understanding the cause of Johnny's confused and confusing behavior, the method of meting out discipline is small potatoes compared with these important aspects influencing his developing personality. Johnny just will not, because he cannot, learn if his personality needs are not being met.

When Shall I Discipline My Child?

No one ever knows the precise answer to this question, but there are certain valuable guidelines. Only a few of them will be meaningful to any set of parents.

However painful it may be to the ego of the parent-teacher, it is well to recognize in advance that most of what we teach our children is done with no deliberate effort on our part. The great bulk of the disciplining of children is accomplished through their natural instinct to copy and to imitate the actions and the attitudes of the older persons who are close to them. This, plus their tendency to be influenced more by conversation they overhear than by conversation directed at them.

This willy-nilly influence parents have in teaching their children is of course a double-edged sword. They equally well learn the good and the bad. But in any event, many families would be happier groups if the parents would depend upon emulation to teach the children rather than make issues over lessons that they could hardly prevent the children from learning.

Assuming a moderately normal parent-child relationship and assuming a normal personality development in the child, how many teenage girls and boys with slovenly rooms are influenced to become neat adult housekeepers by their parents' tirades, and how many on the other hand become neat adults because their parents kept a neat home? How many normal young people are influenced away from promiscuity by parental admonitions as compared with the number who are influenced by fifteen years of observation of their parents' deportment?

One guideline concerning when to teach a child is to teach him what he needs to know by the time he needs to know it. For instance, teach an infant to conform to a schedule that fits into the family routine by the time he is six months of age and before the family ostracizes him. Teach a child to have some respect for authority (to have confidence in the teacher) by the time he is two or three, starting perhaps at six to nine months, and before he tastes the scorn of his society. Teach a child the impropriety of biting and kicking by the time he is two or three and before he loses his companions, starting the lessons when he starts the activity. Teach a child to tolerate his peer group before he enters kindergarten, and to appreciate authority to a large degree by the same age. Teach him to respect the value of education before he is far along in school. Teach him the appropriate attitudes of a teenager long before he is a teenager.

Another guideline is to remember that at any age, even up to high school or college level, only a few new subjects can be mastered at one time by even the most brilliant student. Too much discipline, too much to learn at one time, results only in confusion and predictable failure, which then leads to withdrawal from a willingness to learn. Teach only four or five things at a time, continue to teach them till they are mastered, *let the child pause to enjoy the fruits of his success,* and then move on to other lessons in discipline, a few at a time. It is clearly too much to expect a child who is occupied with learning to get along with the kids in the neighborhood and learning to dress himself and learning not to pull the cat's tail, to take on the further load of learning table manners and not to leave his bike down the block and not to run across the street.

Still another guideline is to list mentally and realistically the important attributes you would like your child to have at sixteen years of age and to space out the time available, teaching a few things at a time until those are mastered before passing on to the next. Sixteen years is a long time from this point of view. Don't sprint at the beginning of a long race.

A most sophisticated guide is to watch the child himself. If he is being offered too many new lessons at one time he will learn none of them well; if too much is being expected of him, he will act unhappy, confused, rebellious, ornery, sleepless, stubborn, lazy, overly sensitive, aggressive. Unfortunately, he will also act this way if too little is being expected of him, or if his disciplining is contradictory or threatens his self-image. One art that some parents (usually those with several children) develop is to offer a lesson in discipline to a child and then, if he is slow to accept it, to conclude that the time is not propitious and the lesson should be postponed to a later date.

One natural guideline which is an outright trap is to expect your child to be able to do things at about the same age as you did, or, worse, at the age at which your mother remembers that you did them. *Never* expect your children to be as capable as you, the parent, were at a given age. The only safe way to use this rule is to employ the factor of two—that is, multiply the age at which you became proficient by two in order to estimate the age at which your offspring may be expected to master the same skill. Blame the factor on your wife's side.

Each child enters life with certain hereditary gifts, talents, skills, and perhaps personality tendencies. It follows, then, that a particular child will be able to accept discipline more quickly along the lines in which he is natively talented. And, conversely, will only be able to learn more slowly in areas in which he is less gifted than another child. This does not mean that he *cannot* learn. It simply suggests that one child may need to be taught a given fact thirty times before he can learn it, whereas his colleague may grasp the same fact after five tellings. Yet at the end of the thirty tellings and of the five tellings each child will have accepted the same lesson equally well.

The majority of the succeeding pages of this book concern themselves with details of disciplining children. No book, however, could hold enough words to cover all the particulars of this subject. Nevertheless, parents can be helped by broad suggestions and by a few examples to understand meaningful discipline, and then they should judge what teaching they prefer to choose for their own children.

Parental discipline strives to teach, not to punish. The basic lesson for the child, upon which all the others stand, is to believe the teacher, to regard the authority as dependable.

It is wasteful to discipline in matters that will be learned automatically or that will have no later importance.

Effective disciplining requires the establishment of the reliability of the teacher through action-proved words and through avoidance of unenforceable lessons; consistent presentation of the facts without nagging, bribing, or explanation; avoidance of declaring the child to be at fault instead of indicating that it is the behavior which is wrong.

Teach a child of any age a few things at a time and teach until they are learned before adding new problems. Judge from the student's reactions whether you are going too fast or too slow.

Periodic Review of Plans for Disciplining

No matter what plan for raising and disciplining a child may in the beginning be adopted by parents, it should be subject to frequent review and revision. It is an excellent idea for a mother and a father to sit down together in the quiet of the evening to ask themselves, "How are we doing?" Perhaps once a month, perhaps twice a year will serve the purpose.

Three questions should always be raised: "Have we been disciplining too much?" "Have we been disciplining too little?"

"Have we been too inconsistent in our discipline?" Often the answers will be all too obvious. When the correct answer seems seriously in doubt, it is certainly to be suggested that the question be discussed with the family physician or the pediatrician who has had the opportunity to become familiar with the child.

It is generally true, however, that a given set of parents will repeatedly tend, year after year, either to be too strict or to be too permissive. It is often apparent to the trained observer, long before a child is a year old, whether the parents are going to have to guard against being too demanding or against being too lax in their teaching of the child. With this in mind, it is generally only necessary for the too strict parents to ask themselves occasionally, "Have we been pushing too hard recently?" and for the too permissive parents to ask themselves, "Have we been trying to teach too little in the past few months?"

Milestones of Learning

Admitting that children differ markedly from one another in their ability to learn at a given age, and recognizing that within any one child there will be variations from month to month in his willingness to learn, are there still rough guidelines to learning that one might tentatively lay out? Probably. But they must be susceptible of alteration as one evaluates the child's response to them.

Most of us believe that for the first three or four months a child is sort of a non-malicious vegetable with a poor memory who needs mostly to be duped into believing that the world is not such an awful place after all. For this reason we believe in demand feeding, and we feel that the parents should feel free to love and to cuddle the baby whenever he is not asleep and whenever they themselves feel inclined to do so, and that they should comfort him freely when he cries.

By three to four months the baby apparently has some vague memories, and can begin to learn, on the one hand, that food and comfort will come in a short time after he needs them whether he screams or not and that, on the other hand, when he does cry out the world does not necessarily immediately rush to his assistance. He is ready to learn a bit of patience. It is reasonable to quit demand feeding and to put the baby on a rough schedule if he has not already put himself on one by this time.

By five to seven months the baby can learn that his mother does not always appear at his whim, and can start to learn that she sometimes immediately comes to him when he cries and sometimes does not.

By seven to nine months the baby can and should learn that when placed in his high chair for short intervals it is forbidden to climb out, and that while he is being dressed and undressed struggling and protesting is of little avail and he might just as well lie back and enjoy it. His first lessons concerning authority.

By the time he can toddle around, the child is able to begin to learn that there are a few things that he is not permitted to touch—for example, electric light cords. He is *not* able to learn that there are 720 valuable and reachable objects in the room which he is not permitted to explore. These should at first simply be placed out of his reach so that the issue does not present itself. Later, when he has learned some control, they should be replaced for further teaching.

By one or one-and-a-half he can learn to accustom himself to being handled and cared for by persons other than his parents, preferably at first for short intervals.

By two or two-and-a-half he should be learning to obey the command "No," unaccompanied by physical restraint. At least he should occasionally and momentarily obey the command, still reinforced often by physical enforcement.

By three or four he should have learned to leave alone most of the valuable breakables in the room most of the time. By this time he should be able to be separated from his parents for part of a day, though you could hardly expect him to wave a joyous good-bye to them as they leave.

By five he should have learned to obey simple orders, without explanation, and to stay, however unwillingly, more or less in one spot for a reasonable number of minutes. He should by this time also have learned that the world sometimes goes its merry way despite his protests. How delighted all kindergarten teachers would be if all children had been brought to this level of learning by the time they entered school!

By two or three he can begin to learn to share his possessions, if he is clever enough to have observed that when he gives away a small toy he is promptly presented with a larger one in return. By five or six he can learn to share his possessions with a scowl and with a bitten lip, as long as he sees that there is an adult observer nearby. By ten or twelve he can learn the deception of cheerfully giving away his possessions because he recognizes the value of the greater gift he receives in return, admiration and approbation by adults. By sixteen he may even have learned to give away things anonymously, in return for the greater value of being able to pat himself on the shoulder.

Keep in mind that most children are in large measure emotionally and intellectually babies until they are about five years of age. If this were not so, and if children under five were capable of prolonged concentration or of unfailing obedience, our school systems would undertake their formal education at an earlier age. Let us suppose that your own child is brilliant—say, one and a half times as smart as the average child. This would qualify him as a genius. Nevertheless, by age five he would be capable of learning readily only that which, say, the average seven-year-old could learn. If you are saddled with a genius, let him and expect him to learn faster, but not twice as fast as the average child.

By five or six a child can learn to tolerate his peers most of the time. He can sit reasonably still and out of the way for perhaps a half-hour at a stretch—but not if the temptation of a butterfly goes by. By seven or eight or nine he can begin to catch and throw a ball for periods of ten or fifteen minutes with enough interest and accuracy so that a strong-willed father with gritted teeth can put up with it. By ten or eleven or twelve he can begin to demonstrate sportsmanship. That is, he can begin to lie when he loses instead of crying, and can see the advantage of mumbling the absurdity, "I'm glad you won."

Beyond these few milestones I know of no expertise to predict safely the rate at which a given child may be capable and willing to learn.

If your child is not learning as fast as you think he should be, consider at your periodic review sessions with your mate, "Are we expecting too much? Are we expecting too little?" If you are in serious doubt, ask your family doctor or pediatrician.

3

Independence

The third leg of the tripod of factors indispensable to the development of a normal personality is the emergence and fulfillment of independence. One can err in the "love" aspect on the side of too little; in the "discipline" department by too much or too little or by being inconsistent. How does one go wrong with independence?

There are two important attributes of independence. The first is that the development of independence can be inhibited or prevented, but it cannot be forced. The second is that independence is best permitted to grow at its own rate, but not so fast that it results in serious harm to the child or to his environment. Let us look at these characteristics in more detail.

The normal maturing animal instinctively seeks independence as it acquires the ability to become independent. This inborn behavior is as certain as the instinct to suck, to breathe, and to reproduce. It is present in all but the very lowest forms of animals, and is part of the complex impulse that eventually results in procreation. Without the hereditary characteristic of independence our species would soon have become extinct. So feel no need to instigate your child's independence, nor any doubts that he will know the urge. As with other instincts, you may guide it or pervert it; you cannot prematurely kindle it to good avail.

The animal cannot successfully be pushed into independence before it is ready. Indeed, trying to push the child prematurely toward independence has generally the opposite effect of making him cling to the nest. It is akin to pushing the reluctant non-swimmer into the water. This reaction of withdrawal, learned early in life by animals that are to survive infancy, is based first upon the necessity of avoiding physical harm and destruction. Later, in the case of the human, protection of one's self-image becomes of dominant importance, often overriding even the need for physical preservation.

When any creature, humans included, feels sufficient content-ment and satisfaction in the warmth of the nest, and feels, further-more, that it can always retreat back to this protection, it then becomes willing to venture tentatively out into the world. In other words, when a child has had his bellyfull of being loved and protected, and if he feels reasonably certain that he can always return to this safety, he will then naturally begin to strike out on his own.

The only thing that will then prevent the normal develop-ment of his independence is to have the opportunity to do things for himself denied him by those about him. For example, the infant will start to convey food to his own mouth and to feed himself when he is capable of doing so, provided only that he is given the opportunity; not urged or forced to—simply given the opportunity. The baby will learn to balance himself and to walk when he is ready to if he is not prevented from doing so. He will automatically try, and eventually learn, to dress him-self if his parents are not constantly too impatient to allow him to make the effort.

So too will he learn independence of thought and of decision making on his own, provided simply that the opportunity to do so is not kept from him. But it is not possible to push him into acting independently before he feels himself ready without making him fearful of the consequences, and therefore making him pull back from independence.

Independence and a normal personality, you will note, are reciprocally related. The early development of independence requires a satisfactory self-image, and the completion of an acceptable self-image in the pre-teens and teens requires the adequate attainment of independence.

Allowing a child to make decisions of thought or action before he is capable of understanding the consequences, if the consequences could be dangerous or serious, is not realistic or appropriate. The consequences may be too harmful either to himself or to those around him who must suffer from his decisions. In other words, the need for the development of independence should not permit the toddler to fall down the cellar stairs or the ten-year-old to decide to stay home from school for a week. Minor hurts, physical and mental, however, are pretty much essential to the development of independence. The toddler must stumble and fall a score of times before he masters walking. The first-grader must suffer the scorn of his colleagues when he chooses to dress inappropriately for school. The fifth-grader must endure the displeasure of the principal when he dawdles too long on the way to school. Perhaps the way to put it is that the child throughout his life should be permitted to make minor errors of judgment but not be allowed to exterminate himself.

And then it must be added that, the child having misjudged the situation, and having been hurt thereby, the incident should be forgotten by all concerned. It will not serve to encourage independence to keep reminding the child of his mistakes.

It is also fair to point out that, in the enthusiasm for promoting the development of independence, it is not realistic or necessary to permit damage to valuable property. Harm to the feelings of the parents may properly be considered "serious damage" of "valuable property" and not tolerated in the quest for independence. A child can develop tons of independence without being allowed to make decisions or to act in such a manner that his parents experience the bitterness of embarrassment.

To allow the child to develop his independence at the expense of property or of the feelings of others is to do him the great disservice of teaching him an unreal way of life that will only cause him hurt when he finds himself out in the demanding world. Or, as has been said before, it is better to teach him the undesirability of trespassing upon the rights of others while his teachers are still those who love him, rather than to force him to learn the lesson from strangers who will not be so thoughtful in their method of teaching.

Though the ground rules of independence are rather more easily set down than those of love or discipline, they are not always so easy to follow. It is not a simple matter for "normal" parents to forgo doing things for their children and to watch them heading toward certain hurt, in the interest of cultivating their independence, without making a protective but stunting gesture to help them.

It is even harder for parents, with their own faulty personalities, to give up the relative security of the parent-infant relationship in favor of the more difficult relationship of parent to young adult. Nor is it possible sometimes for these mothers and fathers, because of the threat to their own self-confidence, to endure the criticism of the community, real or imagined, invited by the ineptness and stumbling of their child's tentative efforts at independent thought and action.

In this current generation, in contrast to those of the recent past, it is not fashionable to stunt a child's independence via momism. It is more in the mode to err in the requirements of discipline and love. I have little urgency therefore to bend your ear at length to strengthen this leg of the tripod. On the other hand, by the time you read this book perhaps you will have once again shifted the emphasis of your uncertainties. So I would like to try to give you a few examples of an acceptable rate for the growth of independence.

Fortunately, children are remarkably resilient and resourceful and readily survive great errors in any parental or pediatric timetable. They also vary delightfully in the ages at which they can master different physical and intellectual skills, thus effectively disproving any prediction of "stages."

But the really important limiting factor in any plan based on age is not the child but the readiness of the parent. Can your state of emotional maturity permit you to do these things at the ages I suggest? If not, don't worry too much; you will grow with parenthood under the tutelage of your child. Just don't turn the timetable completely around.

One other thing. As in several areas of parent-child interplay —loving your child, teaching him values, guiding his attitudes, censoring his emulatory exposures—in this arena of independence it is not always possible to reconcile your social conscience with your parenthood. Make up your mind in advance that if "everyone else in the neighborhood" is doing it in a way that contradicts yours, you will still do it your way—supported by your spouse, reinforced by your pediatrician, and criticized by your in-laws.

Below are a few examples. Each of them is predicated upon the following vows:

1. "I will wait for my child to show a willingness and not regard my own subtle coercions as originating in the child. If I buy a bike or an evening gown before she is interested, I will put it silently aside and patiently wait."

2. "I will coordinate my judgment with my spouse's, and I will compromise serious differences outside of the child's hearing. Unresolvable conflicts I will mediate with my physician, instead of sulking."

3. "In view of the great investment of time, money, and emotions that my child represents, I will not tolerate his destruction in the quest for independence. An independent dead youngster is of less value than a live dependent one."

4. "I will not visibly flinch from minor physical and emotional hurts that I recognize will be necessary to his welfare. Since I

have brought him into this sort of world, I will prepare him for this sort of world until I can change the world."

5. "I will not permit him to hurt others in more than a trivial way, either physically or verbally. I will not see my cherished possessions threatened—only my expendable ones. I will not subject myself to repeated embarrassment in the delusion that this is the role of a parent. Nor will I confuse myself with the belief that it profits the child to learn it is his right to disregard the feelings of others, including myself."

Independence in the Infant

The first primitive stirrings of independence in an infant are his lifting and turning his head, his refusal of the proffered nipple when he is full, his waving of his arms and kicking of his legs, his batting at nearby toys, and his first successful turning from his back to his stomach. These first six months' activities create little panic in Mom and Dad because they are too busy worrying about other things. They require little cooperation from the parent except leaving the child unswaddled with free arms and legs, and on his stomach so that he can raise his head; removing the nipple without argument when he says he's had enough; providing a cradle gym for him to swat. The most threatening adventure is turning over, usually between four and six months. This perversely occurs when mother's back is turned for an instant, and is announced by a chilling crash which culminates the trip from the diapering surface to the floor. It needs to be foreseen. It also needs to be forgiven by Father.

Between six and twelve months, excursions into independence become a little more provocative. At this age some, but not all, normal babies start to crawl, to hold their own bottle, to feed themselves a bit, to resist dressing and undressing, and to depart from the high chair. None of these activities need be taught the child. And many infants skip one or several of them entirely, to no disadvantage.

Crawling brings the first real threat of self-destruction, which is intensified in the toddler and will be considered next. For both safety and mother's sanity the infant should be accustomed to the confines of the playpen or a safe room before he masters crawling. Ignore his protests, or your psychiatrist will accuse you of death wishes toward your beloved.

If a baby elects to hold his own bottle, there's no harm done. But it had better be a plastic one, because some excel at pitching. If he is smart enough to see the advantage of being waited on, and chooses not to hold the bottle, that's O.K. too, because eventually he'll be off it anyway.

The mastery of shoving finger foods into his mouth, such as Zwieback and bits of table foods, is accomplished simply by putting them within his reach. Be sure the child cannot choke on them, however. They should not be round and slippery, or too hard, or of a size to cork the trachea—such as peas, nuts, corn kernels, hard cubes of meat, buttons, or tablets.

Solo handling of spillables via spoon or glass is permitted only by mothers who like sloppy kitchen floors. Despite widespread printed advices to the contrary, they are not necessary achievements at this age. *You* hold the spoon and glass, and let Junior "help" you if he wants to.

Falling out of the high chair and acrobatics during dressing are also better curbed than encouraged. Not by shouting however; by unemotional physical restraint.

Independence in the Toddler

Locomotion starts at about one year of age (earlier if you have a crawler) and reaches a diabolical peak at about two. This is the era of the toddler—and of gray hairs. Walking, climbing, falls, poisonings and burns, disrobing, self-feeding, invasion of sibling privileges, all characterize this age of independence. If you need proof that independence comes of its own accord without any encouragement, this year will make you a believer.

The child needs to be allowed to climb onto objects, to walk and run, to negotiate stairs. This means he needs to be allowed to hurt himself, be comforted, and allowed to go back to hurt himself again. But he doesn't need the opportunity to exterminate himself. Low objects to be climbed are great. Ladders, second-story windows, and bathroom sinks are physically prohibited. So too are articles of furniture worth keeping.

Stairs are fine, if the flight is short and the tread padded. Cellar steps and brick or slate surfaces are forbidden, by means of gates if necessary.

Indoor walking is admirable—but not in the presence of reachable poisons, peanuts on the cocktail table (for choking), marble-topped tables that can lacerate heads like razors, or hot liquids.

Unchaperoned outdoor play is fine, *if* the fence is unscalable or the tether unslippable, and the neighbor's dogs not loose.

Self-feeding is often accomplished by the second birthday, but accidents have to be managed by parents smart enough to have been looking the other way. And requests for assistance should be granted, without grumbling or sermons about being "a big girl now."

Efforts at undressing are laudable, but only at times that help Mom perform the task. At other times they are thwarted by double knots, safety-pinned zippers, and unmanageable buttons or pins.

Invasions of the activities and possessions of older siblings are physically prevented by removal, restraint, gates, bars, handcuffs, or straitjackets.

But if he gets into your lipstick or the chocolate pudding for tomorrow's party while your guard is down, be sure you have a loaded camera ready before you go up in smoke.

Independence from Two to Five

This is the age of the cleverness of Jimmy Valentine and the judgment of the town drunk. It is also the age of climbing out of bed, revolting against bedtime, dashing into the street, riding tricycles, wandering away, helping to dress and undress, deciding that dinner should receive two hours' attention, and drowning.

I suppose it is the prerogative of each pair of parents of this age to determine for themselves what value they place on a ten-thousand-dollar investment. This might take into account how many similar investments they have and how easy it would be to acquire a replacement.

Representing the cheap-skate parent, and not being all that dedicated to independence, I would forbid my investment, my preschool child, *ever* to cross the magic barrier of the curb without adult accompaniment. No playing in the street, no dashing across for *any* reason. And having set this rule I wouldn't depend upon his memory but would occasionally make a visual check. And I would land on transgressions like a threatened hen.

You say your street is a quiet one, or a dead end? I say it only takes one-car-a-month to squash an exuberant kid. And *I* withstand bereavement poorly.

If I were a country parent, I would want to know that there were no uncapped wells, no available bulls, no abandoned iceboxes within a mile before I'd allow my preschooler to leave the immediate environs unescorted.

The independence to stay up beyond bedtime to enjoy the company of the parents is flattering, but not necessary. I would simply honor the privilege of age—that is, the youngest goes to bed before the next older, and so on.

Helping to dress and undress is attractive, but allow plenty of time, and feel free to rescind the privilege temporarily when you have five minutes to make the doctor's appointment.

Dinner in a democracy ends for all when the majority is finished. It is undemocratic to berate the minority or to seek to influence its opinion by threat, bribe, cajolery, or badgering. But when congress is adjourned the dishes are cleared without passion or sermon.

Independence in the Early School Years

The elementary-school years bring a new status with new factors which directly affect the growing personality and which also enlarge the neighborhood sphere of influence. These are the years of independent travel, bicycle riding, responsibilities and chores, tree climbing, allowances, and selecting one's own dress. They are also the years of attitude formation and of diversity of human contacts.

By school time the child's personality is already badly distorted or solidly flourishing. His broadened horizons now reinforce or neutralize the favorable and the unfavorable persuasions of the family.

When Susie starts kindergarten or first grade, you have to bite your lip and let her walk to school, crossing streets other than highways on her own. From then on, quiet streets are crossed without escort. Street play cannot be far behind.

Bicycle riding can try the mettle of even the most unimaginative parent. Considering only the dangers of spills while riding on a level area with no cars, I would permit six- and seven-year-olds to start two-wheelers if they show the interest. At worst you might have to suffer the concern of a cracked wrist or a mild concussion. But add the elements of fast or heavy traffic and steep hills which hinder controlling the speed and the steering of the bike, and I would raise the ante to fourteen or fifteen years. The dangers of cycling can range from those of playing tennis to those of motorcycling, depending upon the conditions.

Tree climbing and fence climbing are also lethal or powder-puffy depending upon the circumstances. Low branches and low fences that promise only cracked heads are allowed for first-graders. Thirty-foot trees and barbed-wire exclusion fences are for teenagers, if they are for anyone.

The responsibility of getting ready for, and to, school on time is appropriate for the first-grader. Mom needs to supervise the waking up, and to have at hand an appropriate choice of clothes, and to have ready a suitable breakfast if Sam has saved enough time to eat it. She does *not* have to nag or scold if Sam dawdles. If the choice of clothes is bizarre, or the arrival at school late, Sam will learn his mistakes from his peers and his teacher, and not at the expense of his mother's love.

If Mom and Dad need help from their children to maintain the home, chores are relevant at this age, but these have to do with dependence rather than independence, and I refer you to the section on "Responsibility" (page 250).

The elementary-school years are not yet the age for being alone in the house or alone in the car without supervision. No matter how justified your confidence in the maturity of your child's judgment, death by fire is most unpleasant and very permanent. By the same evaluation, indoor baby-sitting is not a privilege accorded the pre-adolescent.

If you would care to escape anxious hours in the future guessing the whereabouts of your overdue teenager, this is the age to administer the antidote. Give your school child the dignity and the independence of knowing where you will be and how he can reach you in an emergency when you are away from home. Keep him informed of when you may be expected home and of unexpected delays in your plans. If this becomes a family habit, you can depend upon its absorption as a way of life by the time your child is a teenager. If you demur that it is beneath your dignity, think of the physician on call whose whereabouts must be continually transmitted to a stationary base. It's not really so demeaning, but rather flattering that your services might be valuable. Of course, you encourage reciprocation by the youngster if he drops into a neighbor's for a snack or is detained by the teacher after school.

The choice of one's own friends is a function of independence. Given a wide enough choice, the child should have the right to pick those companions whose interests and values attract him. But I say this with generous reservations and qualifications. What kind of reservations? Well, I'm just not sure at what age a given child is firm enough in his own orientation to choose with any accuracy companions who won't be harmful to him.

Some conditions *are* clear. I know that a child will seek playmates. And he will seek them among the children with whom he can make contact. If all those he can reach are totally different from him in interests, attitudes, ethics, morality, character traits, and personality, he will nonetheless select some as companions.

And I know that few children of less than high-school age can forever maintain their vocabulary, social values, educational standards, sexual viewpoint, vocational goals, and value scale against a concerted assault by a solid phalanx of their peers.

Therefore I conclude that it is the parents' responsibility at least to see that their child has the opportunity to select his friends from among a group which contains individuals with whose views his family expectations will not clash.

A disturbing number of parents are oblivious to the fact that while they are championing certain values at home, their children are constantly being exposed to contradictory values by their colleagues. Whose viewpoint will prevail? The parents' in time, I suppose. But it sure makes the trip a longer and harder one before it's completed.

Of course, if the attitudes of the peer group are superior to those of yourself, the parent, your child may be in luck, and I congratulate you.

And I am well aware that there is an age at which your child benefits by contact—though not continuous—with children of different standards. This obviously provides an opportunity for you and your child to compare, to question, and eventually to strengthen his own beliefs. But in furthering his independence, just what is the age that you can permit your child, unsupervised, to choose with some safety his own friends?

You see, there is no absolute answer. A child is old enough to be relatively immune to the teachings of his peers when his own personality is not adrift and after you have taught him to have a firm confidence in the integrity of his own values. Until this point is reached—and God grant that it will be reached—you cannot, under the excuse of "independence," allow your child to select at random his constant companions.

This is the age to be formulating the attitudes of your child in preparation for exposing them to the rebuttals that will necessarily come as the independence of adolescence demands that he have a freer choice of companions.

The Teenager

All of the foregoing excursions into independence are but preliminary gestures. They are training experiences for the surge of independence that characterizes the teens. It is true that satisfactory negotiation of preadolescent samplings of self-determination serves also to build the maturing personality. But basically they are tentative ventures in preparation for the emergence of the rebellion that is a prerequisite for severing the ties between childhood and adulthood.

Sometime between entering junior high and leaving high school, the metamorphosis of adolescence takes place. This is the age when decisions concern themselves with choosing and buying one's own clothes, hair styles and makeup, cleanliness, bedtime disagreements, dating, driving, unchaperoned parties, drinking, smoking, petting, educational goals, sexual intercourse, drugs, civic activities, and jural disobedience.

The same rules of behavior for the parents apply here as at an earlier age, but the threatening aspects and complex qualities of the decisions make it more difficult for the mother and father to interpret their roles with confidence.

To repeat, the nature of independence is such that:

1. It cannot be forced. In the case of the teenager, social and sexual maturity cannot successfully be coerced.

2. It should not be smothered. The willingness to think and to act as an independent individual is so crucial to normal adulthood that its emergence should be tolerated in all permissible forms.

3. Independence in an area that would result in permanent serious harm to the child must be prohibited. The improvement in the product cannot sanely lead to its destruction. The equivalent, in the teenager, to permitting the toddler to explore his way under the wheels of a truck, is to sanction immorality or illegality.

Since attainment of independence is the hallmark and the quintessence of adolescence, I would like to examine with you the characteristics of the teenager.

First we had better agree upon what a teenager is. It's not simply and exclusively a child in his teens, for as soon as children enter puberty they become, in any sense of the word, "teenagers." A few, particularly girls, may start to be teenagers when they are only nine or ten. Occasionally, especially among boys, the teenager doesn't start to emerge until fourteen or fifteen. In any event, the species I am talking about includes all boys and girls from the time their mature hormones begin to stir until they leave home permanently and hopefully for a better life.

If I could pass along only one single bit of advice to the parents of teenagers to enable them to enjoy their lot better, it would be this: Learn to treat your own teenager as though he or she were the son or daughter of your good friends down the street, rather than as someone you have lived with all his life.

Teenagers are clearly the most enjoyable group in our population. But one has to get close enough to know them and far enough away to see them.

As everyone knows, an adolescent child is experiencing all sorts of new surges and conflicts, which make him a hard person even for himself to understand at all times. He has a certain similarity to the unpredictable two- and three-year-old, who is outgrowing his cocoon but who frequently wants to crawl back into it, to be sure its warmth and protection are still there, and yet who feels the exhilaration of being at last able to have some control over his environment. The awful fact is that the teenager, if you have raised him successfully, *needs* to rebel, to flex his muscles, to demonstrate to himself and to the world that he is able to stand on his own feet and to be an adult. At the same time, and often without being able to admit it even to himself, he wishes *not* to have to assume responsibilities, which seem from his point of view (and indeed often are), almost insurmountable.

Undoubtedly the hardest temptation for the parents of a teenager to resist is the urge of the painter to continue to retouch his finished work. When your child becomes a teenager, recognize the fact that the mold is set, the job is done, and step back with confidence (which of course you won't feel at first) to admire and enjoy your product.

There is a need, and a responsibility, on the part of the parent not to let go of the reins which pertain to any issue of morality. The teenager needs and wants to have the whip cracked on matters of *moral* behavior. When he asks for the keys to the car to double-date in a parked car til 1 A.M., he may at the same time be saying, "Gee, Dad, I gotta do this or the guys will think I'm square. But if you really still love me, say 'No,' so I can save face by telling the guys that my jerky father wouldn't let me." How often anyone who deals with teenagers in trouble has heard this lament!

But with anything that doesn't involve moral issues, let your teenager go. You may well be surprised at what a good job you have done.

No more "reminding" about rubbers, about overcoats, about elbows on the table, clean ears, time to go to bed. No more trying to influence his attitudes toward education, his goals in life, his religious leanings, his use of his spare time, his choice of clothes, his manners, his hair. At least not as a parent to a child. The family rules of morality stand firm. The efforts to shape the *child*, who no longer is a child, must cease.

Hold tight the reins against the permission to promiscuity, drugs, and illegality.

To repeat, treat your teenager as though he were the son of a friend. You would not criticize my teenager visiting in your home for his manners, his dress, his academic achievement. You would, I hope, protect his morality.

They say that Americans fear most the inevitability of growing old. Your teenager is your last opportunity to have the flattery of the companionship of a young adult. Mom and Dad both can know the occasional pleasure of having again a young escort, of sharing vicariously in the exciting dreams of youth. Remember, though, that dreams and plans and hopes are exciting only because they are impractical, visionary, wrong, unattainable, and in conflict with existing codes and regulations—those disillusioned compromises of middle age.

Mom knows how to nurture the friendship of a young adult, or else she was a wallflower in her youth. Dad knows how to encourage the confidence and trust of young people, or else he cannot succeed in his vocation. But it takes a deliberate effort to apply these social skills to your own young adult.

You certainly wouldn't keep *my* young adults as friends of

yours for long if you laughed at their manners, pointed out their faults, argued about the practicability of their goals, belittled their dress, hair, or companions, scoffed at their heroes, denied them courtesy and respect, overlooked their efforts to control their problems, or took their minor achievements, graces, and compassions as a matter of course.

Nor would I expect you to try to usurp all of my teenagers' free time with your attentions or your tasks. Nor to have a seductive or possessive friendship with them. Nor to court their favor by trying to emulate their own activities and dress.

The time to change the opinions, attitudes, and values of your teenager is five years ago. No properly raised teenager, worthy of your efforts to prepare him to face adulthood, is going to learn much more from a lecture by his parents at this late stage concerning why this or that is wrong. On the other hand, the things he grew up with between birth and puberty are things he believes in without stopping to question. How did you teach him what his religion is? By refusing to mention the subject until he was fourteen and then delivering a two-hour lecture on why he is a Catholic, a Jew, or a Protestant? Of course not. A dozen times a week he overheard in part, or glimpsed, casual conversation and convictions directed not at him, but flowing around him.

If you want your teenager to have certain attitudes and values, you need to discuss them and to comment on them within his earshot, starting from before he enters elementary school. Do you care whether he plays football or not, joins a fraternity, has liberal or conservative political or economic views, values education, admires or rejects nationalism?

If any of these things, or others, are important to you, then they must be a part of the casual adult conversation during his early childhood. But when he is already a teenager and feels that education is for eggheads, don't bother to estrange your son and perforate your ulcers with lectures and ravings. Better at that point to slap him on the shoulder and say, "I don't agree with you, but I believe in you, son. Do what you think is best."

Indeed, this is one of your last remaining ways to influence your teenager. Bite your tongue before you criticize him. Tell him you trust him, you believe in him, you are proud of him. You don't have to agree with him—you don't have to like or understand his friends, or his haircut, or his chosen vocation. But you do have to let him know that you trust his opinions and his decisions. And when he stubs his toe you cannot gloat over him, or you will close for him whatever avenues he has left open to err and for himself to correct his error, without loss of prestige.

If you have not thoroughly estranged him, he can still absorb some of the values he hears discussed within his earshot. But forgo the lectures.

Learning to grow up means developing the willingness to make decisions for yourself. If you have properly raised your sons or daughters, during adolescence they *must* prove that they *can* make decisions. Not that they can always make right decisions, but that they can make decisions.

To make decisions means to become an authority. To become an authority means to question the authority of others. To question authority means to rebel against the authority of others. Be grateful if, in assuming his normal role in society, your teenager proves himself by rebelling in relatively harmless areas—haircuts, coiffures, clothing styles, homework, vocation or avocation—instead of permanently harmful areas—drugs, burglary, parenthood.

What becomes of those who traverse their adolescence without ever convincing themselves that they are capable of independence and self-sufficiency? For one thing, they continue to be children, who eventually become child-parents, who plague pediatricians by being able neither to prepare their own children for independence nor to prevent their own children from wandering into destructive experimentation. They become self-doubting young adults who parlay the urgency of their need to prove their competence into ordeals that defy legal and moral bounds. Or more often they emerge to escape the restraint of their parents and, in a neutral environment, in a few years they mature into functional and happy adults.

There is a delightful surprise in store for many parents of teenagers who can deliberately force themselves to give up their long accustomed relationship of mother and father to little boy and girl. And who can bring themselves to say, "I trust you, I believe in you. I will not allow you to transgress on moral issues. I will not necessarily pretend that my likes and dislikes will coincide with yours. But I will respect and trust your decisions. And I will stand ready to help you if ever you request help, as I hope you will be ready to help me when I need help."

It may help a bit to remember the cigarette smoking, the gin drinking, the petting, the goldfish swallowing, the zoot suits, the Mairzy Doats music, the dirty saddle shoes of your generation— by your friends, of course, not by you—and to recall how many of the peers of your youth are staid citizens of today. Winston Churchill flunked how many exams and was denied admission by how many schools? Today's teenagers are tomorrow's Democrats and Republicans—who knows, maybe even Conservatives.

Sure, we didn't fool with marijuana, or wear our hair as long as a girl's, or neck in parked cars, or get unmarried girls pregnant, or unwed boys fathered—we didn't know about marijuana; it was two generations before us who wore their hair long, not us; we didn't own a car; and I take back the last denials: I just remembered Kinsey.

To this point in our dialogue concerning the personality of the child, we have been considering a framework for organizing our thoughts on the needs of the developing emotions of the maturing individual. We have arrived at a triad of needs which constitutes *the* essential elements and which includes *all* the elements necessary for a normal personality structure.

By understanding this outline we may arrive at some practical solutions to the art of helping the child and some insight into recognizing the cause of the warning signs of personality deviations, as well as some inkling of how to back away from impending trouble.

Now we may turn to a more detailed examination of some of the aspects of family life which contribute to and which threaten the child-parent relationship. Each of these specific situations may be interpreted and understood in terms of the love-discipline-independence tripod.

4

Common Problems
with the
Younger Child

This chapter deals with everyday living experiences common to most families. These activities, and the problems that frequently arise in connection with them, provide a major arena for the interactions which influence the personality of the child. But before dealing with specific areas, I would like to spend a moment with you considering some of the simpler motives that lie behind human behavior.

What Determines How Parents Act?

Since this book concerns itself with how parents *should* act toward their children, we ought to think a bit about what factors influence parents to behave as they do in the first place.

Why does Mrs. Zinzindorff insist that Barney wash his hands

and face before each meal, while Mrs. Kirschwasser seems completely oblivious to Bobby's state of cleanliness, and Mrs. Jones-Jones makes a fetish of son Larry's cleanliness but is unconscious of daughter Carol's? Why does Mr. Snodgrass become enraged when four-year-old Janet roams the house at night, whereas Mr. O'Levine considers Susan's nightly meanderings to be cute?

Roughly speaking, we may say that a parent's behavior is governed by two different kinds of impulses. The first type of impulse is controllable, *conscious*, and based upon knowledge. Perhaps Mrs. Zinzindorff has read or heard that dirt carries germs and that germs are a serious threat to her child. Perhaps Mrs. Kirschwasser has heard or read that an overawareness of cleanliness is harmful to the child. Or Mr. Snodgrass remembers his own mother's admonition that a child must have adequate sleep, while Mr. O'Levine has recently attended a lecture which persuaded him that children should not be frustrated. Behavior dictated by this type of intellectual impulse is rather easily changed by the acquisition of new knowledge which demonstrates a better way of acting.

On the other hand, there is a second group of impulses, which are not controllable, are not generally changeable, and are *not* based upon any *conscious* knowledge. These impulses are really, in fact, part of the personality of the parent himself. They are based upon past experiences and past relationships, long since forgotten, but which determine the "intuitive" attitude of the parent. For instance, Mrs. Zinzindorff, when she was a child, may have blamed herself for her younger sister's serious illness because she had pushed her sister into a mud puddle; and she may now *unconsciously* live in dread of dirt. Or Mrs. Kirschwasser, when she was a teenager, may have, for good reason, hated her own mother, who, incidentally, always criticized her dirtiness; and Mrs. K. may therefore *unconsciously* be completely unable to bring herself to tell her children to wash. Behavior on the part of the parent which is dictated by his or her own personality is not easily changed by the acquisition of new knowledge. It is appropriate to point out, though, that, if necessary, attitudes that are based upon the parent's personality can be changed to a considerable degree by psychiatric and quasi-psychiatric experiences.

It is also possible, but to a much lesser degree, for such deeply motivated behavior to be altered by deliberate forethought on the part of the parent. For instance, if you know from experience that you will fly willy-nilly into a rage at Margie's minor transgressions, you can *sometimes* plan on Monday night to ignore something that you can foresee happening on Tuesday. You can sometimes decide on Monday night that when Margie drops her coat carelessly on the living-room floor Tuesday afternoon, you will ignore the matter. And then by reminding yourself Tuesday at noon of what you had planned Monday night, you may successfully ignore Tuesday afternoon's coat dropping despite your instinctive urge to scream. In other words, planning your reaction as a parent in advance can sometimes help to avoid the pitfalls that intuitive reactions may lead to. Thus, the acquisition of new facts and information can be expected to alter the motivation and the behavior of parents toward their children—to alter that behavior which stems from conscious motivation to a large degree, that which arises from unconscious motivation to a lesser degree.

What Determines How Children Act?

It seems only fair turnabout to inquire briefly into what determines the actions of children. This subject, of course, can be approached from a hundred different points of view. Indeed, it would be reasonable to conclude that this entire book concerns itself with a partial answer to this question.

In trying to understand any rational or semi-rational animal, it helps to stop occasionally to ask, "Now why the devil does he act that way?" In my own attempts to understand and therefore presumably to help children, I accept, and ask you to join me in accepting, two basic premises. These two assumptions may or may not be true, but they do help me to see through to the cause of the child's problem. The first assumption is that the child always wants to do what is right. The second is that, from the child's own unique point of view, what he is doing is for him the best possible behavior.

The child always desires to do what is right. What exactly does this mean? Well, to me it means that the overwhelming force driving a child is the desire to be able to look upon himself as a decent, acceptable, lovable, worthwhile person. The main motivation behind the behavior of children, and of adults, can be seen as a desire to live comfortably with themselves in the certainty that they have proved to the world and hence to themselves that they are valuable, meaningful persons. Thus, if the child comes to understand that he receives the greatest approbation from doing what is considered by his own immediate society to be right, he will always strive to do exactly that. This statement, of course, specifically and completely denies the presumption popularized by the behaviorists of several decades ago— that a child is born malicious and that his activities will naturally be mean and destructive unless they are curbed. Behaviorism leads to understanding essentially nothing about a child's behavior.

The second assumption is that a child's actions, however annoying and reprehensible, stem from his own conclusion that his behavior is the best possible for him under the circumstances, the best possible to help him achieve his goal of wanting to be approved and to be thought worthwhile. His conclusion is based upon the sketchy knowledge and understanding available to him at that time.

Implied in this, of course, is the basic assumption that all human action does arise from some cause or reason—that is, that no person performs any act without having some reason, conscious or unconscious, logical or illogical, for that act.

From these assumptions it follows that all of a child's behavior stems from his interpretation of the facts (as he understands them), that his behavior is the best possible action he could take in order (1) to gain the approval of those near him and (2) to gain self-approval.

When his actions seem to *us* destined to bring him, on the contrary, only disapproval, rejection, scorn, and hate, it is to be understood that our conclusions as to the outcome of the acts are based upon a different set of facts from those which limit the child's reasoning. The facts available to the child upon which he bases his deductions must, therefore, be erroneous, incomplete, or perhaps totally lacking.

If you bother to inquire, "Why does he arrive at this illogical conclusion? What is missing from his understanding that leads him to this bad decision? What does he fear more than I realize? What does he value more than I sense? What accounts for his failure to have learned the true facts? What am I taking for granted in my reasoning which he is oblivious to? If I saw things from his point of view, would I arrive at the same bad decisions?" —you can then sometimes begin to understand the child's illogical logic.

In sum, the child always has a reason for his actions; the child strives *above all else* to gain love and acceptance; the child proceeds from the facts and fallacies available to him and adopts a course most likely in his mind to carry him to his goal. If his course toward this goal is improper, it can be assumed that his knowledge and view of the world about him are false and improper.

Now, with this simplistic review of behavioral psychology in mind, consider with me some of the earliest relationships between the parent and the child. These first interactions—which concern the primitive functions of eating, sleeping, sucking, and excreting —are doubly important in the formation of the child's personality because (1) they are his earliest learning experiences and (2) their successful or unsuccessful resolution will serve to determine the parents' attitude toward the child, which, once established, tends to perpetuate itself.

Breast Feeding versus Bottle Feeding

Mealtimes in a family are important factors in molding the personality structures of the children, if for no other reason than that so much of a family's time together is spent in eating. Moreover, pleasant first impressions and getting off to a good start are so much more helpful than later frantic efforts to correct bad habits. On these grounds, the parent's decision whether to breast- or to bottle-feed becomes meaningful.

Some fortunate mothers and fathers come to their first parenthood with calm convictions on this point, free from unresolved doubts. But there are many who, during the mother's pregnancy, have not yet made the decision, have not previously concluded on the basis of experience or background whether to breast-feed or not. These uncommitted parents may be imagined to approach the problem the same way they handle other important decisions —first they seek out whatever facts and information are available on the subject in order to make a more intelligent judgment.

Here, in one respect at least, the young parents-to-be are in luck. They will find a superabundant amount of information and advice on breast feeding. The pediatrician-author, the psychologist-author, the psychiatrist-author, living, dead, and neither, writing for the private publisher and for the government, have provided the American public with a mountain of "facts" concerning the pros and cons of bottle and breast feeding.

But alas, the voice of the zealot, the missionary, and the reformer resounds through the land. In the twenty-seven "authoritative" volumes before me, I do not find a single factual presentation of the controversy. Prejudice, emotionalism, evasions, innuendo, myth, and superstition bias each presentation according to the preconceptions of the author. Let us review some of the preposterous "facts" of the sermonizers.

"Of course, breast feeding saves money. Breast milk is free." In our "affluent society," where poverty is defined in terms of denying oneself color television, you might doubt the persuasive impact of such a statement of economic advantage. But it typifies the specious propaganda of the "experts." In truth, breast milk is among the most expensive of foods. The human factory, as any factory, does not produce goods from nothingness, but rather converts raw material into a finished product. Even proponents of motherhood must forgo their belief in alchemy, and nursing enthusiasts who seek converts are not free to anticipate in their sophistry the repeal of the laws of thermodynamics. If a mother yields thirty ounces of milk each day, representing six hundred calories of energy, she must have eaten six hundred calories' worth of food over and above what her own body required. Six hundred calories of steak in the mother's diet cost fifty to seventy-five cents. Six hundred calories of cow's milk for an infant cost about twenty-five cents; of evaporated milk, still less.

Suppose the mother ingested all her extra calories as inexpensive milk rather than as a balanced diet. Since she is not the imaginary one hundred percent efficient machine, she would need, perhaps, eight hundred calories of milk to render six hundred calories of breast milk—not a free product by any means. Are the authors who say otherwise mentally retarded? Yes, like biased foxes.

"Breast milk is for babies; cows' milk is for calves. It's safer to do things the natural way. Breast feeding is natural, therefore best." If the reasoning of experts cannot be factual, it might at least be expected to be consistent. A consistent application of this equating of "natural" to "best" would then logically commit the author to recommending that the mother eat the placenta after the birth of her child and to the withholding of antibiotics from the infant dying of pneumonia—in the interest of the pursuit of naturalness. Shades of Rousseau!

"Mothers' milk contains antibodies which protect the infant from disease." A typical misleading half-truth. Mothers' milk *does* contain a trace of gamma globulin, which includes protective antibodies. And the baby digests and thus destroys part of this trace, while absorbing the rest of it. But his body already is saturated with a hundred times as much gamma globulin derived from the mother via the placenta. If additional antibodies were highly profitable to the baby, doctors could administer in five minutes the quantity of gamma globulin that would be supplied in an entire year's worth of maternal milk. Such routine administration of gamma globulin has been often thought of, considered, and universally discarded as being of no practical value to the baby.

"Breast milk is the best nutrient known for babies; a near-perfect infant food." This may be true—or it may not. The average healthy full-term infant does well on breast milk and does well on formula. Sometimes a critical choice must be made, when the most digestible food is needed for a baby whose digestive processes are poor—most commonly the small premature baby. When the chips are down and choosing the best nutrient may be a matter of life or death, do the centers for premature babies search frantically for breast milk? They do not. Three decades ago banks of mothers' milk went out of existence because hospitals were getting better results with their premature and their sick babies on artificial formulas, whose proportion of protein, fat, sugar, and calories can be varied to suit the baby's needs.

"Breast milk is safe, fresh, and clean. A big advantage of breast feeding is that the milk is always pure." This type of statement is so false that the promulgator has to be either deliberately lying or unpardonably ignorant. Breast milk often contains a hormone which interferes with the liver's function of ridding the baby's food of bilirubin, and an accumulation of bilirubin can be directly poisonous to the baby. Mothers' milk sometimes carries staphylococci or yeast germs which harm the baby. If the mother is taking certain medications, such as anticoagulants, these will appear in the milk in sufficient quantity to injure the infant. A large number of foods eaten by the mother appear in the milk and are capable of inducing allergic symptoms in the baby. Too much alcohol in the mother's diet will give the baby gastrointestinal upsets.

"The shape of the mother's breast and nipple is better suited to conform to the baby's mouth, to make the baby happier, to stimulate the normal development of his jaw and palate." The sad truth is that human breasts come in an infinite variety of shapes, and babies' mouths come in a similar variety. Some fit well, some not at all well.

"There is less thumb-sucking among breast-fed babies." "Not only does the breast-fed baby have fewer colds and fewer face and diaper rashes, but also he is very rarely constipated." "Breast-fed babies are less likely to have emotional upsets than bottle-fed babies." Such propaganda, when it is based upon anything more than wishful thinking, is based upon studies done in clinics. When such statistics prove anything, they prove that clinic patients get poor instruction in proper breast feeding and in proper bottle feeding from doctors, nurses, and books, and that with improper directions it is easier to commit a major goof with the bottle than with the breast. Breast feeding without knowledge provides at least mediocre protection for the baby. Bottle feeding without directions can sometimes be catastrophic. Careless breast feeding is less likely to result in contaminated, unsterile, or nutritionally inadequate milk than is careless bottle feeding. It is harder for the uninstructed breast-feeding mother to deprive her infant of emotional fulfillment than it is for the uninstructed bottle-feeding mother. But no studies done with educated and informed parents suggest any superiority of breast over bottle or of bottle over breast in the emotional or the physical health areas.

The compendium of Dr. Spock suggests that breast feeding is simpler for the mother. He then devotes thirty-eight pages to instructions on breast feeding and twenty-two pages to instructions on bottle feeding.

"Breast feeding is a form of birth control." So, too, is a diaphragm with a hole in it. But don't bet money.

"Any healthy mother can, with the proper encouragement, successfully breast-feed her infant." So she can, if she is prepared to pay the price. As any prosperous milk farmer can certify, adequate lactation depends upon two things: sufficient physical rest, and maintenance of a placid, unstressful, contented emotional state. Many mothers have too great a commitment to the unending needs and wants of their families to pay the price of withdrawing for the sake of personal rest and tranquillity. It is more the emotional and physical demands upon the modern woman that make her less successful as a milk producer than it is a lessened femininity or physiological incompetence. Speaking of a mother with plans to breast-feed, one authority says, "By arranging ahead for congenial part-time help, tactfully postponing visits from relations and friends, canceling social engagements, and ignoring a growing stack of TV dinner trays and dust curls [not to mention her husband and other children], she created a home environment that almost guaranteed enjoyable, successful breast feeding." Yes, and the waters parted, and lo the land was dry.

"Breast feeding has official sanction in Russia." Good!

"Nursing an infant spoils a mother's figure." This is not true. Breast feeding may actually improve a woman's physical contours.

"Women with small breasts cannot produce as much milk as more generously endowed girls." False. The size of a breast is virtually entirely a measure of the amount of fatty and connective tissue in it. All breasts contain approximately the same amount of glandular tissue, which is the only part of the breast concerned with milk production.

"Small or retracted nipples make it impossible for a mother to breast-feed her infant successfully." Actually a little pre-delivery attention can prepare even the most retracted nipples for nursing, and the baby himself in short order will generally manage to improve the nipple's configuration for better accessibility.

This, then, is a sampling of the more commonly propagated myths regarding breast feeding. What are the established facts?

First, from the point of view of the baby. With a few instructions, virtually any woman can, if she wishes, provide her baby with adequate, good-quality milk from her breasts. Equally so, she can supply him with adequate, good-quality formula from a bottle. He will thrive nutritionally on either.

A baby can receive excellent emotional satisfaction if he is breast-fed and if he is formula-fed. But neither form of alimentation assures, in itself, the fulfillment of the emotional needs.

An infant can become ill *while* being breast-fed and ill *from* being breast-fed—allergies, rashes, respiratory infections, contagious diseases, gastrointestinal disturbances, colic, and so on. And he can become ill with the same range of problems *while* being bottle-fed and *from* being bottle-fed. All of these unpleasant eventualities can be guarded against whether breast or bottle is the container.

In brief, neither method of feeding prevents or mandates the physical and emotional health of the child. Therefore I would conclude, whichever course you elect, do it properly with necessary forethought, but don't decide on the basis of imagined advantages or disadvantages to the baby.

Second, from the mother's point of view. Hopefully your baby is welcome because of the pleasure and satisfaction that you and your mate will derive from helping him to grow. And the more pleasant are your contacts with him, the better you automatically will be as a mother. Then choose the method of feeding that will give *you* the greater pleasure. If it appeals to you to breast-feed, let no one discourage you. If it appalls you to breast-feed, don't give it a second thought. You will be neither more nor less feminine, neither a better nor a worse mother, neither more successful nor less successful for having breast-fed or for having bottle-fed, unless you do either against your own desires.

If your husband or mother or mother-in-law is misinformed or immature or confused enough to urge you on a course that would distress you, or tries to coerce you with sincerely held myths, and if you understandably do not want to provoke hard feelings, mention the fact to your doctor. He will promptly forbid you to breast-feed or to bottle-feed on medical grounds, as the situation requires, and gladly accept his accustomed status as a protective ogre. You can then, in good conscience, insist, "I desperately wish I could do as you want, but that old doctor won't let me." You can thus have the best of all possible worlds.

If you are terribly undecided about whether you want to breast-feed or not, try it for a week or a month, and then chuck it if you are displeased. (Obviously you cannot try the two alternatives in the opposite order!) And if you find you *are* displeased, don't listen to a soul who tries to dissuade you. Just switch to the bottle and again be ingeniously ingenuous enough to blame it on the doctor.

"A mother who has tried without success to breast-feed one infant is ill-advised to attempt to nurse subsequent children." Stuff and nonsense! With the exception of rare medical contraindications, which your doctor can identify for you, any woman can breast-feed any of her offspring, regardless of past experiences, if she decides that the price of the effort is worthwhile to her in terms of whatever satisfaction or happiness she might derive from the relationship.

To insure success, you might well seek out the counsel of a knowledgeable person, professional or lay. But beware of biased fanatics. If the adviser holds the opinion that a nursing mother is either a better mother or an inferior mother, the adviser is a kook. Seek elsewhere.

Among the constructive hints you may expect to receive will be these—which will add up to part of the price tag of the commodity you are anticipating purchasing, and whose relative value to yourself you must rightfully decide:

A month or two before the predicted delivery date, start to toughen the delicate nipple area by daily gentle stroking with a clean object such as a terrycloth towel. If the nipples are extraordinarily retracted, and do not become erect upon stroking, begin to mold them with the fingers to more prominence, but gently enough to avoid pain.

After delivery, within forty-eight hours of birth, depending upon the advice of the doctor, begin to acquaint the baby with the wondrous adventure of sucking. You should know in advance that your milk will not "come in" till the third to fourteenth day. The evolutionary wisdom in this phenomenon lies in the fact that babies are born waterlogged and need time to urinate away their excess body fluid. Premature babies are often allowed nothing to drink for several days, whether bottle-fed or breast-fed, in order to improve their health. Your newborn baby may properly and profitably lose over a pound of excess water. Let the baby's doctor decide whether or not the infant needs sugar water from a bottle during this period; he has successfully decided this matter for countless other newborns.

Your baby's first several introductions to the breast will generally be like all other first introductions—confused and nonproductive. He may well be sound asleep and totally uninterested. Or he may treat you like a strange wretch. These are the days of getting acquainted, before any meaningful quantity of milk appears anyway. Touch his lips or cheek with your nipple. If he is interested, he will turn by instinct toward the nipple, and might even by accident grab on with his mouth. Support his head with your hand at the back of his skull; if you touch his face with your hand, he will turn toward your fingers instead of toward your nipple. His school days are long in the offing. Press the flesh of your breast back from the nipple with your free hand to make the nipple more readily available to his mouth. If he shows no signs of interest, hold him and love him until the nurse picks him up. But don't worry about his lack of a meal. His stomach is wiser than you.

Often the day or so before your milk flow establishes itself, your breasts will be swollen and sore and sometimes unbearable. Don't despair. Take something for the pain. Soon they will soften and your distress will pass.

On the first or the umpteenth trip to the breast, the baby will latch on and suck, to your amazement and his. The first day he sucks, two or three minutes at the nipple is all you should permit per feeding. He can make your nipple raw and unusable. Remove his grip by breaking the suction with your finger, introducing it between his lips and your skin. If he howls at you reproachfully, smile back. Many doctors recommend feeding at both breasts for the allotted time at each meal, alternating the starting breast. If your nipples are not made sore by the short nursings of the first day, increase the time allowed on each breast by a minute or two on each succeeding day. If your nipples begin to be sore, slow down, and report the soreness to the baby's doctor. Usually it is not well ever to exceed feedings of about twelve minutes per side, no matter what the baby's age.

When you get home, feed the baby *something* whenever he screams blue murder. When he is pleased to sleep, be pleased to let him. If he calls for food two or three or more hours after a breast feeding, give him another breast feeding. If he cries as though he might be hungry two minutes or two hours after a breast feeding, feed him again. But since you can't manufacture milk this fast, feed him a bottle of formula—as much of it as he willingly takes. Next time he cries, back to the breast.

If he persists in wanting to be fed every hour or so for more

than a day or two, consult his doctor. He will help you to decide
what is bothering the baby.

Get plenty of rest—lie down on the couch, nap, go to bed early,
let the housework slide temporarily. You need more rest than you
did before you became pregnant, and you will be getting up at
night in the bargain.

Preserve whatever emotional tranquillity you can. Get a
mother's helper to ride herd on the older urchins. Send disturbing
visitors on their way with the threat that your doctor is a horned
devil who prohibits visiting. Smile when your husband protests
the baked beans for dinners.

Eat whatever you want—provided it is food which you have
been accustomed to eating and which has not previously dis-
agreed with you. "The book" says you should avoid lobster and
cabbage? So you should, if they have not been part of your
routine menus. But the Chinese mother subsists on cabbage, and
the Maine lobsterman's wife eats shellfish daily—and their nursing
babies thrive. Shall you eat highly seasoned foods? Well, if you're
a "first generation" gal who has been raised on garlic and pepper,
you should. If you've been a bland "American style" eater, you
shouldn't.

You need an adequate source of calcium—milk, cheese, tablets. You may need vitamins. If you ingest drugs and alcohol,
they will appear in your milk; your doctor knows how much the
baby can tolerate.

Once in a while the breast-fed baby deserves a bottle of formula, even if you have a ton of milk. He deserves it so that he can
learn that such a thing exists. Then, if you are struck by lightning,
he can make the switch without too much anguish. He deserves
it so that he can have a mother who goes out and has a good time
once in a while. He deserves it so that his father can feed him
occasionally.

Bottles of sugar water are confusing during breast feeding at
home. Confusing to the baby, the mother, and the pediatrician.
They might have a legitimate place in "stalling off" a hungry
baby for an hour or so on occasion, to give the mother time to
produce some milk. But often they fill up a hungry baby, who

then goes to sleep for three or four hours in confused contentment. He may then wake, cry, nurse at an empty breast for twenty minutes, cry immediately, take another bottle of sugar water, and again fall asleep. Thus the mother and pediatrician are confused by the picture of a contented baby, who in actuality is being starved. I prefer the bottle of formula for a breast-fed infant who needs to eat before sufficient time has elapsed since the prior feeding to permit the mother to accumulate some milk of her own.

How long should you continue to breast-feed before weaning? Exactly as long as you are enjoying it and having fun. One day; four months; two years. Isn't family pleasure the reason you went through those nine months?

Should you wean suddenly or gradually, to the cup or to the bottle? Just as you please, and with your doctor's agreement.

Should you have intercourse while you are a nursing mother? I should hope so. Are you temporarily sterile? Not for certain. Can you use contraceptives? It is not yet agreed that "the pill" itself is safe for a nursing mother to take. All other forms of contraception are known to be harmless, except intrauterine devices.

These are some of the helpful suggestions that you can get from a counselor experienced in breast feeding. Listen to his or her advice and you can successfully breast-feed, if you elect to, whether you have failed in the past or not. But avoid "salesmen" who are "pro" or "con" nursing because their grandmothers were frightened by a polar bear. It's your baby and your breasts.

Eating Patterns

One of the most fascinating, and truly astounding, aspects of modern American culture is the tremendous impact upon parent-child relationships that the simple act of eating so often produces. In many families, feeding the child is fraught with so many misunderstandings and superstitions that it becomes a major factor in molding his personality. The simple matter of nutrition becomes a significant cause of conflict and misunderstanding between the parent and the child, and it is so utterly unnecessary.

In this respect it is perhaps rivaled only by the inane over-attention that is similarly paid to toilet training.

Eating occupies perhaps five to ten percent of the total lifetime of an individual. The minutes spent at the dining table constitute an even greater proportion of the brief time that a family spends together. They afford, therefore, a remarkable opportunity for influencing the personality of the child, either for good or for bad.

You can hardly help but wonder why so many misconceptions concerning eating are still prevalent among the sophisticated mothers and fathers of today. One obvious reason is that our modern knowledge of nutrition, established during the past three decades, has been thoroughly beclouded and obscured by pseudo-scientific literature, charlatanism, and flamboyant advertising. A second source of confusion is the ingrained idea that the amount of food you bestow upon your child is a direct measure of the love you have for that child. This notion must linger from the days when parents, with insufficient food for the family's needs, sacrificed their own portions in order to nourish their offspring.

Feeding Requirements and Problems of Infancy. During his first two to four months of life, an infant's eating habits are natural, instinctive, and generally unencumbered by emotional distractions. Doctors commonly recommend that these young infants be fed "on demand." Every modern mother understands that this means to feed the baby *when* he cries to be fed, *whenever* he cries to be fed, and *only when* he cries to be fed, and that he should be allowed to sleep or play as long as he wishes between feedings.

It is not so commonly understood that "demand feeding" equally strongly implies two other things. The infant is to be allowed to drink his formula as *rapidly* as he is comfortably able, so that he may obtain as much nourishment as his appetite dictates and is not influenced in his food consumption by the element of exhaustion, caused by too slow a nipple. That is to say, an infant is not being demand-fed who, at the end of forty minutes of struggling with a slow nipple, falls asleep from exhaustion, with his stomach still partially empty. A formula-fed baby should be able to obtain enough milk to fill his stomach in ten to twenty minutes. A breast-fed baby whose mother's milk supply is ample will be able to get his milk in about the same period of time.

Another requirement of demand feeding is that the infant should be allowed to take *as much* milk at each feeding as he desires. This condition obtains naturally in breast feeding, partly because the mother is fortunate in never knowing how much the child has taken and partly because the emptied breast produces more milk at the next feeding. In bottle feeding there should always be more formula present in the bottle than the baby is able to take willingly. The word "willingly" should be emphasized here, for demand feeding does not include urging or coercing the baby into taking three more swallows beyond what he actually wants. The extremes seen in the demand feeding of healthy babies are sometimes remarkable. Normal babies may consume anywhere from two to fourteen ounces at a feeding, and may take from fifteen feedings a day down to as few as two feedings in twenty-four hours. It is not unusual to see babies imbibe as much as sixty ounces of formula in an occasional twenty-four-hour span.

The advantages of demand feeding are many, both to the baby and to the mother. It enables the mother to feel free to comfort her child with a feeding whenever he cries, without being concerned with the clock, rather than having to subject herself to the unpleasantness of hearing him scream for an hour, awaiting a scheduled feeding. It provides a warm, comfortable early life-experience for the infant, which introduces him to the fact that he is in the hands of someone who loves him and who will support and comfort him when he is in distress. With demand feeding, the number of feedings per day is usually more quickly reduced and the infant begins sooner to sleep through the night.

When the demand-fed infant awakens to be fed too frequently, or continues to cry despite having been fed, it is not that the method of feeding has failed, but rather that something else is amiss. Either the child is not getting his formula easily enough, or he is not being allowed to have as much as he wants, or the formula is disagreeing with him, or he is suffering from the ubiquitous "colic," or he has a minor illness. None of these situations suggests that demand feeding is at fault, but rather indicates that the physician should be called to discover what is wrong.

The mother should be aware that demand feeding was devised partly with her well-being in mind, and she need not feel that she must rush to the baby the instant he cries, if she is at that moment occupied with something more important—namely, enjoying a rest period herself, dining, playing with an older son or daughter, or being loved by her husband.

An alternative method of feeding young infants, which is still used by some mothers and by some doctors, is "schedule feeding." This usually means feeding the infant every 240 minutes as though one were running a railroad system. As a matter of fact, it is a rare mother who is able to listen to her child's screams for two hours until the clock says it is time for him to be fed, or who can shake a sleeping baby into sufficient wakefulness to interest him in his mealtime if he has chosen to sleep beyond it.

The principal purpose of demand feeding is to give the mother confidence in, and firsthand experience with, the unalterable fact that a normal growing animal will take, without urging, enough food to satisfy all his nutritional requirements. This concept is so basically a part of proper feeding attitudes that its development in the mother is worth considerable time and familiarization.

The Introduction of Solid Foods. It has become a dubious custom to introduce solid foods, such as cereals, vegetables, and fruits, into an infant's diet at an early age. There is a popular and thoroughly erroneous belief that solid foods "fill a baby up" and encourage him to sleep longer between feedings. A moment's deliberation on the fact that, in the stomach, milk itself is quickly converted into a cheeselike solid substance (to which any mother whose baby has vomited thirty minutes after feeding can attest) will expose the fallacy of this belief.

Nor is there any basis for the notion that solid foods are necessary to the proper nutrition of an infant. One need only bear in mind that, until twenty or thirty years ago, generation upon generation of thoroughly healthy infants were raised without ever seeing solids until they were eight to twelve months of age.

Indeed, each new food introduced into the diet of an infant is an experiment and a risk. There is no known food which has not, in one baby or another, produced cramps, vomiting, rashes, or diarrhea. Herein lies one disadvantage of the early starting of solid foods. And for this reason it is not proper to offer more than one new food at a time or a new food oftener than every three or four days, so that offending substances can be identified. Nor should a previously untried food be offered to a baby who already has cramps, diarrhea, vomiting, or rash, because the effect of the new nutrient will be scarcely discernible.

In choosing appropriate solids for your young baby, can you rely upon the integrity of the food packagers to offer only those foods known to be relatively safe for infants? You can depend upon them to make available whatever they can entice the uninformed mother to purchase. Statistically speaking, among the foods proven to be most likely to disagree with babies are chocolate, citrus fruits and juices, tomatoes, onions, spinach, berries, cherries, fish, pumpkin, corn, thickening agents such as acacia, and excessive quantities of starch. It is appalling how many of the proffered infant foods contain these identifiable trouble-makers.

The single valid reason for offering any solid foods to a young infant lies in the hope that while he is still young and ignorant he will accept these strange tastes without having the brains to protest. Whereas, occasionally, if one waits until a child is eight months of age before introducing him to solids, he will intelligently spit out these strange substances.

If, then, it is the purpose of early feeding to teach a baby to like solids, how ridiculous it is to persist in shoving cereal or vegetables down the protesting throat of the young infant who happens to be keen enough to perceive that he prefers the breast or the bottle. Far from teaching him to like solids, this can only accomplish teaching him to hate solids, hate the spoon, hate his mother, and hate the whole darn business of mealtime. If your infant, after a few attempts, makes it clear that he detests any solid, or all solids, please put the offending substance back on the shelf. And don't offer it again until a few weeks or months have elapsed, during which time he may have changed his mind. A child can easily and properly be raised in good health, well-nourished and happy, to a year of age or beyond, with adequate milk, plus perhaps a few drops of vitamins and a few drops of iron.

Feeding from Three to Twelve Months and Its Problems. I have just suggested that during this period an infant who detests solids may be fed satisfactorily with nothing but milk and supplements. On the other hand, if your chow hound does like solids, he may be fed the variety your doctor suggests, always in quantities suited to his desires. That is, he may have as much or as little cereal, as much or as little fruit and vegetable, as much or as little meat and egg as he *enjoys* eating. Always the important question is, "Is he enjoying his food?" and not "How much or how little of it did he eat?" The only minor nutritional requirement is that if he likes solids so thoroughly that he cuts down to much less than a pint of milk per day for long periods of time, your doctor may see fit to prescribe temporarily a calcium supplement or to limit his intake of solids somewhat.

During this period you should have occasion to observe and to learn several things. There will be mealtimes, and even whole days, when your baby will mysteriously refuse to eat any or all of his foods. Sometimes it may be because he doesn't feel quite well, sometimes because he is teething, sometimes just because he is being human. It is *not* your job to coerce him into eating when he doesn't feel up to it. Rather, learn to respect his judgment and to remove the food promptly. The next day, or the day after, his appetite will return and he will make up for lost time.

Develop the attitude: "I love you enough to bother to prepare your food; but I also love you enough to remove it when I see that you don't want it, rather than foolishly try to force or to bribe you into eating it." Unless you are unwilling to credit your child with having as much intelligence as a pet dog, you may safely and properly follow this course. You don't really try to make your cat or your dog eat its food when it doesn't seem to want it, do you? And your child has at least as much intelligence as your dog—certainly enough intelligence to know better than to starve himself to death in the presence of food.

It is a good safety measure, during the latter part of this period, to allow Junior to begin to feed himself whatever he can without destroying the kitchen, not only to allow his independence to develop but also to remove from yourself the temptation, when you are wielding the spoon, to shove one last bite down him that he really doesn't want. This is the period during which good eating habits are established. Fall into the habit of allowing him to climb out of the high chair during mealtime, or of forcing food down his protesting throat, or of playing "The Star-Spangled Banner" so that he will "finish just this last bit of applesauce," and you are off to a rousingly poor start.

And when he has finished what he eats willingly, take him out of the chair without comment, not again to see food until his next mealtime.

Feeding from One to Three Years of Age and Its Problems. Be amply forewarned that, toward the end of his first year or during his second year of life, your child's appetite will fall off dramatically. If he continued to eat and to grow at the same rate as during his first year, he would weigh over two hundred pounds by the time he was ten. Remember that children during their second year of life eat far, far less than they do when they are infants. Failure to anticipate this all too commonly results in the mother's striving to force or to urge the unhungry toddler to eat the way he previously did.

Offer him more to eat than his body requires and he will quickly turn away from all foods, or he will eat the one or two things he prefers and leave the rest. "But, Doctor, he only wants a spoonful!" That's right, and that's all he needs at this age.

To keep some perspective on how much food the toddler requires, divide his weight, say 25 pounds, into your weight, say 125 pounds. You are thus five times his size. Multiply what he eats by five. He drinks ten ounces of milk a day? That's equivalent to a quart and a half for you. He eats one quarter of a sandwich? That equals one and a quarter sandwiches for you. And so on.

How about what kind of food he eats? Is his diet balanced? Well, in this day and age, it would be a real challenge to a mother to unbalance her child's diet deliberately. In this era of enriched foods, for a balanced diet he requires daily (1) the amount of calcium contained in about a pint of milk. And remember that all the milk on his cereal and in his custard counts, and that one to two ounces of cheese are approximately equivalent to one pint of milk. Moreover, if he takes no milk for a while, his body has ample stores of calcium, and if he continues to take no milk for long periods, your doctor can prescribe a few spoonfuls of calcium solution per day. He requires (2) the amount of iron contained in one egg or in a small portion of meat. The daily requirement of milk, and of egg or meat, supplies more than enough (3) animal protein. He requires (4) the amount of plant protein contined in two small portions of either vegetables or fruits. He needs (5) the vitamins that are contained in, or added by the processor to, his cereal, milk, bread, egg or meat, fruit or vegetable or fruit juice. And that's *all* he needs nutritionally.

Does the diet have to be balanced each day? Not at all. All nutritional requirements would be perfectly met by consuming a week's worth of eggs and meat one day, a week's worth of milk the next, of vegetables and fruits the third day, and then enough calories in the form of bread each remaining day for the rest of the week.

How about the need for green vegetables? They're pretty. Nutritionally that's all there is to it.

What about three proper meals each day? Nothing but custom. There is neither Biblical nor biological endorsement of three meals a day. So far as I know, man is the only animal who commits himself to dining this way. One meal a day, or six—neither is better or worse than our customary three. No need for a "nourishing" breakfast to get you off to a good start? None except custom and Madison Avenue.

The normal body is perfectly capable of storing up and of releasing when needed the food elements required for the moment. In fact, it is quite likely that the food you lived on today was that which you ate the day before yesterday—not what you had at today's breakfast and lunch.

Here are a few miscellaneous hints. Most children prefer soft meats such as hamburger, frankfurters, or delicatessen meats to steaks, roast beef, or chops. Why? Even after his full set of twenty baby teeth have erupted, by the age of two and a half or three, a child still does not have equipment that compares to your molars. Next time you have a steak, count back two teeth on each side from your own canines (eye teeth and stomach teeth) and try eating your meal with just these front twenty teeth. You'll soon understand why your three-year-old does not share your enthusiasm for steak.

Junior doesn't like vegetables? Well, if you haven't already suspected it, I'll tell you a secret. Neither do ninety-five percent of the rest of the Juniors in the world. And neither do you, in all probability. Limit yourself to eating a vegetable dinner several nights in a row and you'll know better what I mean. The fact is, if Junior eats his fruit, he doesn't need vegetables. But if you're lucky, he might drink a vegetable juice, or nibble on raw vegetables, or eat vegetable soup or vegetables in a jelled salad.

"But I want him to eat all foods and to enjoy tasting new foods." Very well, try a little simple psychology. Dollars to doughnuts he enjoys ripe olives, or potato chips, or a sip of a cocktail. How did you manage this? First you sat around consuming them in front of him. Second, either you didn't go out of your way to offer him any or you may even have told him, "No, those are not for little boys." Human nature being the perverse thing it is, this same approach will work on any food. Just make it plain that he is not allowed to have such and such a food, while you eat it in front of him. Sooner rather than later he will become a fan.

How about desserts? Same approach. As the redoubtable Dr. Spock says, if you want him to love desserts and hate carrots, tell him that he cannot have his dessert until he eats his carrots; if you want him to love carrots and hate desserts, tell him that he cannot have his carrots until he eats his dessert.

Of course, any child intelligent enough to be worth raising will be smart enough to fill up on his favorite foods, and leave behind the others, if he is able to get enough of those things he prefers to satisfy his appetite. If a child is hungry enough to eat four tablespoonfuls of food and you put before him four table-spoonfuls of hamburger, four of stringbeans, and four of ice cream, unless he is retarded he will eat the ice cream and pass up the rest. But if he *is* hungry enough to eat four tablespoonfuls and you place before him one-tablespoonful portions, he will eat the one tablespoonful of ice cream, the one of stringbeans, the one of hamburger, and then will ask for a second one-tablespoonful portion of something.

And keep in mind, when you are figuring his capacity, that liquids (milk, juice, water, Coke) fill his appetite requirements just as surely as do the solids.

There are a few cardinal rules to establish early. (1) He who eats or drinks enough at mealtime may be permitted to eat or drink between meals. He who doesn't eat or drink enough at meal-times may not eat or drink between meals. A small word of warning here. If your child is bright and is not eating well at mealtimes, it is a sad mistake to explain to him that he cannot nibble between meals *because* he did not eat well at mealtime. He will auto-matically accept your challenge, and continue not to eat at meals, in order to play the ever enchanting game of "Who's going to win?" Safer to tell him, when he wants to nibble, either simply "No," without any explanation, or "Gee, I'm sorry, there's nothing here to eat right now," or "I wish I could give you some, but I'm saving that for supper (for tomorrow's bridge party, for your Aunt Emma)."

Other good rules to establish early while you are still the con-trolling teacher: (2) No eating allowed, either at mealtimes or between, except when seated at the table. (3) No eating per-mitted while walking about the house. (4) When you're finished eating you may leave the table, but once you have left the table, the table is cleared and there is no more food until the next meal.

If you dawdle over your food and are only half finished when everyone else is through, the table is cleared, not because you dawdled, and not because I want to punish you, but simply because I've got to get on with my work of washing the dishes. (Here again, don't throw down the challenge; the bright child will be only too glad to pick it up.)

Feeding from Three to Eighteen Years of Age and Its Problems. Here's the time to enjoy the results of your earlier teaching. If you missed somewhere along the line, back up and start again. Don't forget that, especially at this age, to introduce a new food you mustn't be so unsophisticated as simply to put it on the child's plate and avoid urging him to eat it. Instead, deliberately refrain from including it in his diet, but see that you and your husband or your older children enjoy eating it in front of him. If he asks, unsolicited, for a bite, fine, but give him just a bite. Maybe next time you'll remember to buy enough so that he can have some of his own.

Now use mealtimes to their best advantage. Those attitudes and values which you and your husband remember to discuss, and which the children "accidentally" overhear, are those things which they learn the best.

Also, learn from the United States Government. Aboard many ships in the Navy, anyone who brings up a topic of business or an unpleasant subject during mealtimes forfeits twenty-five cents into a kitty. Mealtime is not the appropriate occasion for reminding the children of their transgressions of the day.

No matter how you look at it, both eating and toilet training fall into the category of things that, regardless of how big and how strong and wise you are, you cannot force your child to obey. Really now, are you prepared to pass a stomach tube and to push down that pile of carrots you told him he *had* to eat? Therefore, as with all other teaching experiences with the young child which the teacher cannot directly enforce, eating must be approached by the indirect method as described above rather than the direct method.

Sleeping Patterns

Sleeping patterns, after the first few months of age, are learned responses. Just as there is nothing instinctive in the learned response of eating three times a day, so there is nothing instinctive in one long stretch of sleep at night. The newborn infant sleeps virtually all of the time, except when he is awake to eat. By three or four months of age most babies have learned to sleep in an apparently uninterrupted stretch of eight or even twelve hours, generally at night, and their wakeful hours are mostly confined to the daytime. Certainly all babies from seven to nine months of age should have become accustomed to taking their long sleep period at the family's convenience at night.

Close observation of babies of this age, however, reveals that they all awaken periodically several times during the night, raise their heads, move about, and even remain awake for some minutes at a time. This suggests that the long period of silence occurs not so much *by instinct* at *night*, but rather because the darkness and the quiet are not conducive to prolonged activity. The "light sleep" of this age is frequently noted by the parents, whose stealthiest footstep may bring a wide-eyed head popping over the crib bumpers.

For these reasons it is strongly recommended that the baby's crib should be out of the parents' room not much later than six months of age. Indeed, when feasible, it is usually best for the baby to *begin* his domicile in the home in a room other than the parents' bedroom.

The notorious bad sleeping habits of babies who occupy the parents' bedroom during the second half of the first year are partly explained by the child's awareness of the mother and father's presence through sound and sight. Where continued three-in-a-room occupancy is unavoidable, it is preferable at least to screen off the baby's crib.

There is no longer any doubt that a child between six and twenty-four months of age who does not sleep through the night, or at least remain silent, should be allowed to "cry it out" until he acquires the notion that this is "quiet time" for the family.

This is a simple learning experience for the child, and a highly profitable one both for him and for the household. After briefly checking his first outcry to be certain he is neither ill nor hurt, the parent should not thereafter return to the cribside. The commonest pattern of learning under these circumstances, varying some with the intelligence of the child, is for the baby to scream for three or four hours the first night, two or three hours the second night, and then for increasingly shorter periods over the next several nights until he no longer rouses.

A note of caution here. If you, the teacher, are not going to be able to hold out the first couple of nights, *don't start the lesson.* A child who is allowed to cry out for an hour, and who then has his parents relent, learns this lesson all too well. He quickly learns that by screaming long enough he can make his immediate world succumb to his demands, and he is apt to carry this lesson to other fields of encounter.

What if he screams and carries on to the extent of causing himself to vomit? The lesson is most quickly learned if he is left unchanged until the morning. If your delicate sensibilities forbid this, change him and clean him up without taking him out of the crib, and leave him without comment in the shortest possible time. If the delicacy of your nature or the loudness of the neighbor's pounding makes this course untenable, ask your physician whether he is willing to sedate the baby for two or three weeks for the sake of the lesson to be learned. Incidentally, you can pretty well soundproof a small room by hanging several blankets from lines strung across the room. If the baby does not relent in his waking in a few days, have his pediatrician check him for sources of discomfort, including perhaps a review of his food intake for excessive starch or indiscreet tidbits.

If a child much past two years of age is in the habit of waking regularly at night, a cause, physical or emotional, should always be sought. Perhaps he has pinworms. Perhaps his two-year molars are giving him unusual trouble. Ask his doctor to check him. If he is physically tip-top, give some thought to his daytime activities and try to identify anything that might be causing sleeplessness or bad dreams. Is he playing too wildly with children older than himself? Is he being too frequently disciplined during the day? Is television playing a part in his disturbed sleep? Any of the many factors that may disturb his personality structure in the areas of love, discipline, and independence can cause distressing dreams. Aside from seeking and rectifying the causes of his poor sleep, it is often considered permissible and desirable to encourage his rest, and to alter an established habit, by sedating him periodically for a few weeks at a time.

Nightmares, or night terrors, are nothing more than unusually severe, frightening dreams which children of all ages may experience, particularly during periods of febrile illness. They are characterized by the child's waking in a screaming and anxious state. Though ostensibly awake, and with eyes open, for several minutes or more the child is incoherent, panicked, and unaware of his surroundings. He should be gently held, cuddled, and talked to in a reassuring voice until he regains his composure and orientation. Frequent nightmares and frequent sleepwalking are both taken as signs that undesirable factors are influencing the child's personality. They deserve to be recognized as warning signals, and a search should be undertaken to discover their cause in the child's daily experience, if need be with the aid of his pediatrician.

A young child should grow up with the firm conviction that he is not permitted to leave his crib or bed without permission until morning. This, too, is an easy lesson for children to learn, provided they do not first learn the equally easily learned lesson that it is great fun to hop out of bed the moment Mother's footsteps trail off down the hall. If the child is still in a crib, his first successful attempt to exit without permission should be promptly countered by putting extensions on the sides of the crib which he cannot scale. In an occasional instance a length of tennis net placed over the top of the crib is necessary to frustrate the budding gymnast.

The average child is able to give up his crib in favor of a standard bed by the time he is two years of age, and even sometimes by eighteen months. At the opposite extreme, he probably should be out of his crib before he is four years of age, if only to prevent his pediatrician from suspecting that his mother is refusing to allow him to grow up.

Youth beds with side rails are a wasteful excursion down a blind side-street. A standard-height single bed is suitable for a child old enough to be out of his crib. A few pillows or folded blankets on the floor will adequately cushion his first one or two falls, and thereafter he will fall out no more often than you do.

An essential accompaniment to the occupancy of a grown-up bed is an on-the-toes attitude of the parents for the first few weeks to see that Junior is promptly and authoritatively popped back into bed at the first patter of little feet. Incidentally, a double bed is probably not easy for a young child to adjust to.

For the youngster with orchestra-leader instincts, who discovers the pleasure to be derived from rocking in his crib (a pleasure that we oldsters still know in the form of the swaying hammock), the standard treatment is a sturdy two-by-four bolted to the crib to prevent its squeaking, or angle irons on the legs fixing the crib to the floor, or transference to a regular twin bed, which will permit rocking without noise.

On the subject of going to bed at night: If you have succeeded in creating a reasonably happy family, very few intelligent children of any age will gladly and cheerfully sever their relationship at bedtime and march whistling off to bed. Isn't it a little insulting to your attractiveness as a hostess if they do? Don't look hopefully forward to the time when they will outgrow this "childishness," unless you have full intentions of living to be one hundred. How easily do *you* tear yourself away from an exciting party? And a few last-minute appeals for "just a little drink of water" are indeed flattering to those at whom they are directed. But the emphasis is on a *few*. The guest who lingers forever at the door to say good-bye may be flattering, but he's also a pest. None of this is to suggest that, at Junior's bedtime, be he two or twelve, he should not be escorted briskly to his pillow. Just don't expect him to volunteer.

Insomnia—that is, the inability to fall asleep within an hour or so of going to bed—in a child from two to twenty, can signify one of only three possible things.

1. Especially in the older child, it may mean that his bedtime is a bit too early. If you can't stand him in the living room another instant, send him outside or to his room, but try letting him stay up a bit longer.

2. Or it may mean, at any age, that he is deliberately, though not necessarily maliciously, keeping himself awake. Remember that you can successfully tell a child to go to bed, and expect him to obey, because you have the power to enforce the order by physically making him. But don't be foolish enough to order him to go to sleep. Try enforcing *that* order—unless you keep a hypodermic syringe handy. But for the child who is avoiding sleep by whistling, humming, sitting up, tossing from side to side, or otherwise doing what you or I do when we want to keep ourselves awake, at least close his door so that the rest of the family is undisturbed by his transgressions.

3. But sometimes a child's insomnia has the same cause as that of an adult—worry. Consider whether you need to help him by finding and eradicating the cause of his anxiety and concern.

Just how many hours of sleep does a healthy child of any given age really require for health's sake? I am sure that this is such an individually varying need that no average figure makes any sense. If a child is physically and emotionally sound, however, I am quite certain that, with perhaps rare exceptions at the high-school age, he cannot in any way harm himself by lack of sleep. Make himself unbearable the following afternoon, yes; harm himself, no. Indeed, one of the most meaningful gifts you can give your child as he progresses into adolescence is the expression of trust that goes with saying, "You're quite grown-up now, and I have faith in your judgment and in your sense of responsibility. So from now on you may go to bed when *you* think it is appropriate."

An urgent suggestion: All children, once they discover the delight of it, enjoy the warm, cuddly pleasure of sharing a bed with the mother or father or both. This is equivalent to offering heroin to a five-year-old; an addiction can be acquired in short order. Even leaving aside all Freudian connotations, it is a hard-to-break habit which, if you are a sexually normal parent, you will quickly live to regret. Take my word for it, don't let it start. Send Junior packing the very first time he tries to crawl in. If, for some extraordinary reason, you feel it urgent that he be comforted until asleep, lie down beside him on *his* bed, you dressed and on top of the covers.

If your two- to five-year-old child roams the house at night, look to see whether there is an emotional cause, but meanwhile protect him and yourself by a securely fashioned screen door or unscalable gate on his bedroom door. (A locked solid door is panic-provoking.) If he regularly roams at night much after five years of age, you can be sure that there is an emotional or physical cause and should look until you find it.

Finger Sucking

A normal, healthy infant is born with a few well-developed instincts. Foremost among these is the sucking instinct. An infant has an inborn urge to suck whenever he feels uncomfortable. If this instinct were lacking, the infant could scarcely survive, for it is his sucking in response to the discomfort of hunger which enables him to be fed.

Since his hunger pains are alleviated by sucking, the infant very early learns to associate the act of sucking with a feeling of comfort. Thus, enlarging upon his discovery that sucking brings him pleasure, a young baby will suck upon any object that comes within reach of his mouth. Then comes the marvelous day when he discovers that he can, at will, maneuver those soft, pink, ten little somethings into his mouth and suck away content-edly, no longer dependent upon an outside giant to offer him a sucking utensil. This is the day when all the generations of myth, misconceptions, and fears on both sides of his family tree spring into action. What actually are the known facts concerning both the harmful effects and the benefits of finger sucking?

There are many who still believe that breast-fed babies show less tendency to suck their fingers than do bottle-fed babies. This conclusion is based upon observations of parents with inadequate instructions in child rearing. Among a group of parents with little or no knowledge of how to deal with a baby, it is far more difficult to make mistakes with breast feeding than it is to make a shambles of bottle feeding. Thus *these* breast-fed babies tend to be more comfortable than their bottle-fed colleagues, and it is this factor of comfort-discomfort which accounts for the difference in finger sucking.

In recent years it has been shown that babies can even be raised on the cup from birth without ever receiving either a bottle or a breast, with no resulting increased incidence of finger sucking.

There is no reason to believe that finger sucking will have any effect upon the position of the permanent teeth, provided that the habit is discontinued before the second teeth have erupted. It is true that certain techniques of finger sucking may cause the front baby teeth to protrude or to be recessed, but the position of these teeth has no effect whatsoever upon the ultimate position of the second teeth. In fact, to use an extreme example, even if all eight of the front baby teeth are literally knocked out of the mouth in an accident, no malpositioning of the permanent teeth results.

Most parental reaction to finger sucking is determined by the parents' own confused emotional response. Daddy thinks it looks "sissyish." Mommy finds it "distressing." Great-aunt Sally thinks it is "disgusting." Evil he who evil thinks.

I myself feel a bit sorry for the poor little guy who is already beginning to understand that life is not all honey and roses, and wish that I could give him some other way of comforting himself in addition to—not in place of—the solace of finger sucking that he has discovered for himself. But I would be the first to insist that the parents who don't approve of finger sucking, whatever their reasons might be, have the right to put an end to it —but only if they know an effective way to do so. It seems to me the height of futility to engage in an ineffective nagging battle with the baby if no assuredly successful method is worked out in advance. This falls right smack into the middle of those things which a parent is ill-advised to attempt to teach a child, unless he, the parent, is fully certain of the success of the outcome. Mittens don't work. Yanking the hands out of the mouth whenever you pass by doesn't work. Bitter solutions applied to the fingers only end up with a screaming baby with a chemical burn of the eyes. The only effective method I can think of is to put plaster casts or tubular cardboard on both arms. This works. Do you really want to go to this extreme?

How about pacifiers as a substitute for finger sucking? Sure, why not? You say, "They're disgusting"? Only because someone taught you to think they're disgusting. There's really nothing inherently disgusting or attractive about a pacifier. But if you don't like them, don't fight your psyche—don't let your baby use them. Are they better than finger sucking? Not really. They are softer, in general, so they don't have as much tendency to move the baby teeth. But we've already noted that, except for the immediate cosmetic effect, the position of the front baby teeth does not matter and has no effect upon the permanent teeth. Aren't pacifiers dirty objects? Investigations by bacterial culture have shown repeatedly that pacifiers carry fewer germs than do a baby's fingers. While this is not in any way an argument in favor of using the pacifier, it certainly demonstrates that they are not sources of disease.

The majority of children give up the habit of finger sucking, except in moments of severe duress, by the time they reach school age. This comes about either because of outside social pressures, mainly the taunts of their playmates, or because they discover a better way to comfort themselves, such as torturing baby brother. After that, they may suck cigarettes. One suspects that at least some of the children who persist in finger sucking beyond the age of five years have been encouraged to do so by the artificially increased value of the act, demonstrated to them by their parents' futile efforts in urging them to desist.

Since the second teeth begin to appear during the early school years, and since orthodontistry is expensive, an effective method of dissuading the continuing thumb-sucker must be found. As in breaking any habit, there are two essentials: (1) The possessor of the habit must desire to give it up and (2) he must have some opportunity to remind himself that he does want to change the habit. An excellent motivating force, which lies safely outside the family, can be the kindergarten teacher. After the first few months, during which she has presumably gained the admiration and respect of her young charges, the teacher is in a superior position to present the proposition, not to any one individual but to the class, that school children generally will want to give up their baby habits such as finger sucking. If this is not in the curriculum of your child's school, most kindergarten teachers will gladly respond to a suggestion. Now the parent is in the catbird seat. He is no longer the nagger, but is now the buddy. Through the kindness of his heart, he is going to help his child to attain what the child already wants. As a result of great generosity, the parent is willing to supply the means by which the child can remind himself of his own desire. He will be willing, as a friend, to buy a bottle of "reminder medicine" so that the child can be helped to remember. As a co-conspirator he will see that the bitter potion is readily at hand for the child himself to apply to his fingers, so that when he thoughtlessly pops them into his mouth he will be immediately reminded of his own desire to give up his childish habit, as the teacher has suggested, but which the parents couldn't care less about.

A somewhat less ideal solution for the school-age child is for the parents to provide the motivation through a strong bribe. But the bribing object must be carefully conceived; it must not be an object that the child may decide he would eventually get anyway. It must be a foolish expense that no child could remotely look forward to for his birthday. But it need not, and indeed should not, upset the family budget. If you have carefully avoided bribery in the past as a method of disciplining your child, play the ace here and it may work.

Nail biting and nail picking, both of the fingers and of the toes, seems to be an analogue of finger sucking. It is usually developed as an outlet for distress at a later age than finger sucking, but we have seen many babies, scarcely a year of age, who regularly nibbled their nails.

Those who worry about finger sucking as a cause of tooth malpositioning are quite content with nail biting as a substitute, because this comforter cannot in any imaginable way harm the teeth. It is, however, a more meaningful sign of pressures being applied to the child.

Nail biting is at least a yellow caution flag, warning of the possibility that the child is under pressure. Under too much pressure? Probably not, if it is the only sign of tension in the child. It is not (perhaps unfortunately) possible to prepare a child to fit into the society we live in without putting him under *some* pressure. A child who is never frustrated, never taught to act contrary to his instincts, never disciplined, might be in the long run inordinately happy. But only in some utopian social milieu, not in ours.

On the other hand, if nail biting is one of several signs of unhappiness or confusion in a child, one might well begin to run down the several possible causes of his distress in the areas of love, discipline, and independence.

Otherwise, the stopping of nail biting is approached in the same manner as that of finger sucking; just motivation to stop, coming preferably from outside the family; and help to stop, coming from the family.

If nail biting is indeed a sign of the pressures of civilization upon the child, it should be quite clear that adding to the pressures by nagging and badgering him to stop can only result in adding to the pressures upon him. Of course, if one or both parents bite their own nails, it will be next to impossible for the child to desist.

Toilet Training

If you have read almost any other part of this book before turning to this topic, you already suspect much of what I believe about toilet training. From my observation, this subject is one of the major, and also one of the most ignominious, causes of destructive intrafamily relationships.

As a pediatrician, I have many earnest apprehensions about the possible outcome of efforts to toilet-train a child. My major fear is that parents will undertake bowel training or urine training before they have instilled obedience into the child—that is, before they have taught the child to believe the spoken word of the teacher or before they have taught the child regard for authority. Under these circumstances, efforts to teach bowel or bladder control are extraordinarily disadvantageous choices of early teaching experiences for both the student and the parent.

If your child does not yet have reason to believe in you, to have confidence in you, to obey you as a parent, how quickly he may learn to distrust you, to disobey you, if you elect to help him learn toilet training. With no intelligence at all, he may perceive quite by accident that you are unreliable as a teacher if you tell him he is supposed to deposit his excreta here and he manages to put it there.

Worse, if he is bright, he will promptly see that you are quite serious about this lesson, but that he can at will prove you are wrong and that as a teacher you are ineffectual and utterly unable to back up your lesson or to enforce it. It is a great blow to his developing personality to discover so early that the teachers upon whom he is so dependent have such unsupportive feet of clay.

A second fear of mine is that the parents, upon whom the child depends for love and acceptance, will feel normal human anger and resentment if their efforts to toilet-train are unsuccessful—unsuccessful either because the child is too young to cooperate or because the child is clever enough to relish the rewards of uncooperativeness.

Another concern is that parents will waste so much precious teaching time on toilet training. So much unnecessary time, since *all* children *always* learn to be trained without and even despite help from Mother or Father. Show me the untrained teenager.

Further, I know that success engenders success, and defeat

begets defeat. I fear that a child will sense that he is expected to be able to control his bowel movements and his urine, will find himself unable to do so, and consequently will feel that he has failed to live up to his parents' expectations. You see, in any well-chosen and safe learning experience at this age, the parent can support the child. For instance, in "Don't climb on the sofa with your muddy shoes," the child can be guaranteed the satisfaction of success because if at first he fails to learn he can be bodily removed and so achieve success. How do you manage to help a child to control his bodily functions?

With all these reservations about the wisdom of attempting toilet training, is there any wonder an elderly pediatrician would prefer to have parents ignore the subject until the child presented himself to say, "Please take me to the bathroom"?

However, since it is unlikely that in a short time I can improve the orientation of all the country's parents—and grandparents and neighbors—I want to discuss with you how to toilet-train with a minimum of undesirable repercussions.

Bowel training is far simpler for the child to master than urine training. It involves much less complicated muscle coordination; furthermore, defecation occurs far fewer times in a day than does urination. A child, then, is intellectually and physically capable of being bowel-trained before being bladder-trained. If you know a child who is urine-dry before he is feces-clean, you can be certain he was first taught to be bowel-untrained! So we shall speak first of bowel training.

At anything less than the second or third birthday, bowel training must depend upon learning by association. That is, the child learns that he is expected to deposit his bowel movement in a certain place because *by coincidence* he happens several times to excrete in that certain place. Thus he begins to associate such and such a place—the toilet, we hope—with the act of defecating. How do we manage this coincidence?

You can legitimately start bowel training whenever you can reasonably predict when the child is going to have his next bowel movement—in other words, when the child's movements occur at a fairly regular time of the day. The bowels do tend to assume a certain regularity because of the gastrocolic reflex, whereby the colon is automatically stimulated to empty itself whenever the stomach is distended. So at any age bowel movements tend to occur during or soon after feedings.

When, by astute observation, you can predict that Junior will probably have a bowel movement after breakfast and after supper, or at 9:30 in the morning, then you can tote him to the john at those times in hopes of accidentally catching the feces in the assigned receptacle. With a few children there is another way to predict the coming of a bowel movement; they will give some sign of being about to defecate, such as grunting or squatting or holding their bottoms. If you are gifted with such an expert in communication, you can accept this forewarning as the signal to whisk him to the toilet.

If your timing is good, and your feet fleet, you will sometimes, with luck, manage to have Junior's rear over the toilet when he parts with his stool. By this process he soon (?) begins to associate in his mind the trip to the bathroom with the act of moving his bowels. And after a while he begins to hold back his stool until he is on the toilet and then to push it out after he is enthroned.

There are several pitfalls of which the training parent should be aware. If you make ten or twenty fruitless excursions to the bathroom with no success, Junior may very well start to associate sitting on the toilet with the act of *not* having a bowel movement. Since this is the very opposite of what you intend, it is best to stop for several weeks to let him forget his wrong learning before trying again.

Next, it is wise not to show provocation if the child manages over and over to have his bowel movement immediately before or immediately after his visit to the bathroom. It is best to postpone the training for a time if this happens, for it suggests that he is realizing that he can thwart the learning process and thus prove you an undependable teacher.

It is also *not* advisable to (1) leave him on the toilet so long that he begins to hate the lesson, (2) play with him while on the toilet, lest he associate play rather than defecation with the bathroom, (3) praise him excessively if he manages to have a bowel movement on the john, (4) frighten him by flushing the toilet while he is on it or near it, (5) exhibit disgust or distress at the sight or odor of the bowel movement, (6) continue to put him on the toilet if he cries at the experience or is physically pained by the passage of a hard stool, or (7) if he usually has loose movements, which would be virtually impossible for him to control, or (8) if he is sick or out of sorts for some reason, or (9) if he is involved already with learning several other lessons in behavior, or (10) if he has recently had a frightening change in his environment, such as a change in homes, a new bed, the advent of a sibling, or the sickness or absence of a parent; finally (11) he should not be left alone on the toilet at first, lest he associate the bathroom with lonely imprisonment.

Some authorities stress that one or another type of toilet seat or potty is to be preferred. Certainly the seat should be safe and comfortable and not frightening. One expert, who has parlayed the subject into an appointment of prominence for himself, emphasizes that the exact position of the body is important and that the feet should be set against a solid support with the thighs forming a proper angle with the body. I am inclined to doubt the meaningfulness of such details, since the baby has been accustomed to having bowel movements while lying on his back, lying on his stomach, walking around, and so forth.

At what age might you start bowel training? Before six or eight months you could conceivably, with great alacrity, catch a few stools, but the baby could not physically sit upright on the toilet.

Until the child walks alone, between ten and eighteen months, he does not have the muscle coordination deliberately to hold back or push out a bowel movement. Neither is he exactly a highly intellectual student. Nevertheless, he might be "caught" on the toilet occasionally, if not actually "taught." Keep in mind, though, that if you frequently succeed in catching a bowel movement at this age thanks to the regularity and predictability of the child, he may not actually be "trained" for the toilet. If then in later months his movements become irregular in their timing, so that you no longer are able to catch them, get angry at yourself if you wish, but not at the child.

For my part, I have never seen a child who was bowel-trained at less than two years. Oh, I've heard of many, particularly from a generation or two back, and I've had second- and third-hand reports of some dozens in the present generation. It's just that I myself have never seen one. It is usually at about two and a half or three that the children of my ken are able to be trained. And at about this same age they begin to train themselves anyway.

Now we may turn to the urine training of children. As I have noted, control of the bladder involves far more complicated musculature than that of the rectum; so a child cannot be expected to be bladder-trained before being bowel-trained. Furthermore, a young child voids as often as every fifteen to sixty minutes, so that training too early would involve an unceasing parade.

If you are enamored with making work for yourself, sometime around the third birthday is a reasonable time to start urine training. If you are really asking for it, you might start anytime earlier than this, if the child is holding his urine for about two hours or more at a stretch in the daytime. A common signal to start urine training is when the child begins to awaken dry from naps.

In any event, when the child has been dry for a relatively long period of time, you lead him to the toilet hopefully. If your timing is good, as with bowel training, you are on your way. But all the warnings of impending trouble that apply to bowel training apply here too.

There are those who favor training little boys sitting down, and there are advocates of starting with the standing position. I doubt that it matters one iota to the child's personality.

There is some logical preference for warm weather as the season to bladder-train, for the child is wearing less clothing and he does not urinate as often as in colder weather.

Please remember that it is not intended that a child should wear training pants until *after* he is trained. To use them before and during training is unsportsmanlike. Moreover, it places constant pressure on the child to measure up.

Must you get yourself into trouble trying to toilet-train? Of course not. But if you do you will have joined a mammoth and not very exclusive club.

Am I against early training, which would spare Mother the burden of washing diapers? No, I am against Mother getting herself into trouble which is more burdensome to get out of than is the laundering of diapers.

You should realize that there is no earthly way for you to keep your children from becoming toilet-trained. But, unfortunately, you can do all sorts of things to make it worth their while to train later than they would if you left them on your own. On the other hand, you can speed up their training safely by giving them the opportunity to imitate older children or adults.

One of the pleasant unanticipated bonuses of allowing a child to train himself is that often within a week or so of becoming bowel-trained he will gratuitously also become urine-trained, and clean and dry at night.

So-called "training" for nighttime is no part of the subject of toilet training. I refer you to the subject of bedwetting for this topic. Teaching an unconscious student is no job of my liking.

Are you pressured by the older generation to start training early? Does your mother-in-law gall you with how she trained her son at three months? The appropriate answer to such comments is: "So that's what caused the trouble!" An acceptable answer for the more chicken-hearted is: "Yes, Mother, I agree with you, but my doctor won't let me."

Masturbation

Masturbation is a subject so charged with emotional overtones in the minds of many parents that it evokes in them reactions which may have a significant influence upon the personality of the child. Masturbation itself, however, has no direct influence upon the child's personality, although it may eventually be adopted by the child as a predominant way of demonstrating his disorientation toward life.

During his first year, as his muscle coordination improves to match his curiosity, the infant discovers the various parts of his body. His hands chance upon his ears, his nose, his toes, and his genitalia. Though a normal male infant has erections of the penis, there is no observable difference in the sensations experienced by the baby as he explores the various parts of his body; he or she does not at first appear to differentiate between the pleasure of fondling the ear and of fondling the genitalia. But at this time, in one way or another, society, in the form of the parents, intervenes.

Some parents (though their number is, happily, decreasing) still react to their young child's masturbatory gestures with shock, disgust, anxiety, and embarrassed guilt—despite the fact that at this stage most children have not even attained the sophistication of enjoying masturbation. Among those whose background decrees the response of horror at their child's self-manipulation, there are fortunately not too many who still believe, and who will therefore ultimately convey to the child, the myth that masturbation leads to physical deterioration, or impotence, or lunacy.

Another group of parents will hasten to chastise the offending hand, while delivering a learned and impassioned lecture to the effect that good boys and girls don't indulge in such animal activities.

A third group will feel no chagrin at their child's behavior, or will successfully conceal their embarrassment, while casually moving to distract the infant.

The parents of fortunate children will see, but not notice.

In all events, the message more often than not gets through that this particular type of activity has at least a special meaning to society, and it thereafter unfortunately assumes a special place, to a larger or smaller degree, in a child's evaluation.

To the extent that the child perceives that masturbation has some special influence on the behavior of the parents, or that it

is a forbidden fruit, he will be more and more attracted to testing out the effect of his new-found bomb.

You must instruct the older child that, indeed, public masturbation is not looked upon, at the moment, with high favor by
society. To fail to make him aware of this would be to expose
him later to the ridicule of his world. But he should be told, in
action and in words, that masturbation in public is forbidden in
exactly the same manner and the same tone that he will also be
told that such other natural activities as spitting on the floor,
picking one's nose, eating peas with a knife, and going bare-
foot to church are not permitted in our society. And at about
the same age as these other niceties of etiquette are made clear.

To make it more difficult for the child to masturbate in public,
it is certainly permissible to make it mechanically impossible for
him to masturbate by dressing him with so many layers of cloth
and safety pins that *your* psyche is spared. It is not desirable,
however, to hand him a loaded revolver by indicating to him
that his masturbation distresses and upsets you.

By the time the child has become a toddler or a preschooler,
he will have discovered that manipulating his genitalia does indeed produce a different physical sensation from manipulating
his nose or ear. Without such knowledge the race would die
out. You may need to remind a child of this age that the rules
of society insist that he not eat his peas with a knife and that
he not masturbate. It might be wise to add, for the sake of
accuracy, the qualifying phrase "in public." Students of child
behavior have rather well established not that a few, not that
most, but that all children masturbate to some degree at some
time or another. And that this has probably been true for each
generation of children back to antiquity. With the possible exception, of course, of you in your generation.

If we must recognize that childhood masturbation is so commonplace as to be considered "normal," then it is fair to ask
whether it is ever abnormal. Just as any normal activity engaged
in to excess can be considered abnormal, so too with masturbation. But what definition of "excess" is realistic? When a child
masturbates in *repeated preference* to engaging in some other

enjoyable activity, then it is excessive and therefore abnormal. For example, if a child chooses to masturbate in preference to joining his colleagues in a game of tag, or in preference to observing what the teacher is drawing on the blackboard, then it is abnormal. What excessive masturbation may signify is another matter.

A child who masturbates to the exclusion of other activities may be exhibiting a serious enough sign of personality aberration to be worth a visit to the physician. The doctor, can, at the same time, rule out the only other (and uncommon) causes of abnormal masturbation—vaginitis and irritation of the penis. The comforting explanation of excessive masturbation as being due to constrictive underclothing or the like is infinitely more apt to be wrong than right.

Should your child know that some religions frown upon masturbation? Of course he should, regardless of his own religion. If yours is one of such religions, both you and he should know that no religion categorically forbids masturbation, but only under certain proscribed circumstances.

Should your child know that it is *our* society that recoils from masturbation? And that other societies in other times— societies quite as remarkable as ours—considered masturbation acceptable and as natural as eating and sleeping? I believe he is entitled to this knowledge. I know you are.

Bed Wetting

Bed wetting, or nocturnal enuresis, is a subject about which much can be said, and about which perhaps too much has already been said. It is certainly among the commonest problems that parents have in raising their children in this day and age. If a Kinsey Report were available on bed wetting, it would probably say that one-fourth or more of our children endure this problem at one time or another. A full life could be spent reading all the sense and nonsense that has been written in scientific and pseudo-scientific literature upon this one topic.

The attempt to cure bed wetting is perhaps the most unrewarding pursuit in which a parent, a pediatrician, or a psychiatrist can become engaged. And it is this subject which has been the recipient of so much verbiage. On the other hand, the much simpler subject, the prevention of bed wetting, has received, by comparison, little attention and little publicity.

To some extent the presence or absence of bed wetting depends upon how you care to define the word. I would suggest that a child may be a bed wetter if he is of average intelligence, is five or more years of age, and wets his bed more than, say, twenty-five percent of any series of nights.

Essentially there are two types of bed wetting: those of *organic* or structural cause and those of *functional* or non-organic cause. The first of these, the organic, accounts for a real, but very small, percentage of all cases, perhaps five percent or less. Among them are such physical problems as infections of the urinary tract, diabetes, and malfunctions of the kidneys or bladder. They should, of course, be detected early by analysis of the urine and, if necessary, by X rays of the urinary tract. More often than not they give themselves away by diurnal as well as nocturnal enuresis, that is, the inability to hold the urine both day and night. There may also conceivably be some rare families in which the trait of enuresis is inherited over generations.

The overwhelming majority of cases of bed wetting fall into the functional group, in which there is absolutely nothing demonstrably wrong in a physical sense. I am strongly tempted to refer to these cases as being of emotional origin rather than to use the neutral term "functional." This is what I myself believe. The most succinct explanation of these cases that I have ever read is that these children are urinating upon the world about them, in retaliation for the discomforts and tribulations that the world has imposed upon them.

To parents with children too young to have yet had the opportunity to become bed wetters, I address the following plea: the most striking thing to me about bed wetting is that, with the exception of the organically caused cases, no child would ever have been able to hit upon this tactic by his own thought processes. Each child who is a true functional bed wetter must have had explained to him the device and the potency of wetting the bed. And it seems to me that this is usually done inadvertently during the period of attempted toilet training. I commend to you the thought that if you don't tell your child how to wet the bed, he will never find out about it himself. No animal other than man has ever discovered the art of nest soiling beyond infancy.

In the first place, how should you train a child to remain dry through the night? How should you teach him not to urinate while he is asleep? To me it is obvious that you would manage this in exactly the same way that you would teach a sleeping child to speak French or to observe good table manners. I just don't see how you can intelligently expect to teach a child—or an adult either—anything at all while he, the student, is asleep. Therefore, I would not try.

I wouldn't try for other reasons too. There is little enough time in the life of a child to teach him all the truly important things that he must know for the future and which he cannot conceivably learn by himself. I just wouldn't squander time trying to teach my child something that he could not help but learn on his own. And by the same token I have yet to see the job-application form which inquires, "At what age were you dry at night?"

Becoming able to remain dry at night depends not upon any intellectual teaching, but rather upon developing a large enough bladder to be able to hold whatever amount of urine the kidneys produce between bedtime and awakening. "Training" a child to be dry at night depends, then, solely upon leaving him in diapers until he has demonstrated over and over again that he does not have to empty his bladder in his sleep.

On the other hand, actually conditioning a child to wet his bed is accomplished by any one of a dozen approaches. All have one thing in common: they tell the child how to do it, and how important it is to his parents that he not do it; they are roughly equivalent to handing him a loaded pistol with an explanation of how important it is that he not pull the trigger.

One method of training a child *to* bed-wet is to awaken him before the parents go to bed and to lead him to the bathroom. This method is often made doubly sure of success by only half waking the child, carrying him to the bathroom, and then encouraging him to urinate while he is still half asleep. This method is almost sure-fire.

Another effective method is to put the child, who has once, or twice, or never, gotten through the night dry, into fancy pants or pajamas and then to instruct him, silently or aloud, not to wet them. This system could be rendered even more efficient if the child were able to read, for it could then be accompanied by a written statement to this effect: "It just bothers and annoys the heck out of me to have to change your wet clothes in the morning. As your parent, I know I have done many things to you that have annoyed you, such as making you go to bed when you didn't want to, come to meals when you didn't feel ready, and stop pulling the pussy cat's tail. However, now that I have pointed out a good way for you to get back at me, I implore you to stay dry at night."

Another good approach is to have Grandma say, "What, you still wear diapers at night? Why, you're a big girl now. You shouldn't still be wetting at night and causing your mother all that trouble."

Or, with very intelligent children, a successful method of teaching the child to become a bed wetter is to be overzealous in your attempts at daytime training. The really bright child will quickly deduce from your concern that nighttime wetting can be made into a great game also.

Perhaps you yourself have already thought of still other effective ways to suggest to your child how powerful a weapon he has at his disposal.

I will bet you my rights to heaven that, if you don't bother to explain bed wetting to your young child, he will never figure it out for himself and will simply follow his natural instincts, and, provided he does not have a physical problem, will be dry at night by the time he is three or four years of age. Then, and only then, should he be taken out of his night diapers.

I am not saying that the bed-wetting child does so consciously, or that he could stop if he wanted to. Quite the contrary.

All bed wetters punish themselves unmercifully, either audibly or silently, and each desperately wishes consciously to be able to stop. It is the unconscious or the subconscious we are dealing with in the sleeping child, which neither he nor you can control. Have you tried controlling your own dreams recently?

What, then, can parents do whose children are already bed wetters? Well, first of all, be reasonably sure that there is no physical cause by consulting the child's physician. After that, any one of many "cures" might be tried with your doctor's help, but please don't wager any money upon the success of the venture.

I have one objection, perhaps minor, even to trying most of the methods. And that is that the more attention lavished upon bed wetting, the more the child may be convinced that he has a good thing going, and the less able he may be to forget why he started this uncomfortable "habit" in the first place. Certainly one method that avoids this objection that might be worth trying is to put the bed-wetting child back into waterproof pants of some sort—they come in sizes big enough for adults—and tell him with a smile, "Honey, I know you don't wet the bed on purpose, and lots of other kids your age wet the bed too. So to spare you the trouble of sleeping in a wet bed, I am going to give you these waterproof pants, which many other children your age wear, and we'll just forget about it until you are able to go through the night." Then you spend the next three months biting your lips and riding herd on father, grandmother, grandfather, cleaning girl, and brothers and sisters to keep anyone from mentioning the subject of bed wetting in front of the trainee. And when said trainee takes the trouble to report either that he did, or did not, successfully get through a night, you smilingly shrug and say, "That's all right, dear, it's not important anyway."

Other expedients, old and new, tried and untrue: Have the bed wetter hold his urine during the daytime as long as he possibly can before urinating. This may, of course, help by stretching the bladder to a greater capacity and thus make possible a dry night's sleep. The success of this method may be evaluated by measuring, every few days, the volume of urine the child can hold before he absolutely has to go to the bathroom. This may so center attention upon the trainee as to convince other members of the family to become bed wetters too, for a share of the pie.

Or offer the child a bribe for each night that he remains dry. This approach is often spectacular, in that the intelligent child can sometimes parlay the price up to a pony, or a mink stole, in return for each night of dryness.

Or whip and belittle the child each morning that he arises from a sodden bed. This procedure separates the men from the mice. If your child has any backbone, and is made of satisfactorily stern stuff, worthy of his forebears, he will stoically withstand the punishment. If he is chicken, he will give up, and he is probably not worth raising anyhow.

Or try a reasonably new tack: Give him a mild tranquilizer before he goes to bed. This method seems to work occasionally—about one time in three. The only real disadvantage I can think of is that each night, by giving him the pill, you remind him to wet the bed if he wants to, whereas occasionally he might otherwise have forgotten.

Another angle I know of, which is often successful, is this: Send all the brothers and sisters, his competitors, away to Grandma's house. Allow him to stay home from school. Have your husband stay home from work, and you and your husband take him wherever he wants to go, whenever he wants to go, to do whatever pleases him. Fix only the foods that he likes. Have mealtimes at the hours he chooses on the spur of the moment. Forget about bathing. Don't explain to him that a toy that he wants is too expensive. This device is almost sure-fire, but unfortunately only temporarily so. When family living is resumed, the bed wetting is apt to recur.

Or try a conditioned-reflex machine. (Such machines are actually available for purchase or for rental.) This rings a bell and turns on a bright light the instant he starts to wet the bed. As with any conditioned reflex, including Pavlov's dogs, the reaction is not controllable by any higher intellectual centers. Therefore, this method almost always works—that is, unless the child is smart enough to get out of bed, and to sleep on the floor, or to disconnect the machine. But a word of warning. Don't try it on children who are so young, say under twelve or fourteen, that they are apt to substitute some other "habit" which is even more unacceptable socially—as, for instance, masturbating in school or undressing little boys or girls in cellars.

I have one comforting thought about bed wetting. If, in your child, it is the only sign of rebellion, or in fact is only one of a few signs of retaliation, then it is a pretty small escape valve, and a cheap price to pay for all the restrictions we must necessarily impose upon our children in order to make them conform comfortably to the society for which we are attempting to prepare them.

Did you know that many confirmed bed wetters do not wet the bed when they are sleeping at the home of someone who is not a member of the family? Did you know also that there have been very few cases of bed wetting persisting into married life? Take solace where you find it.

Temper Tantrums

Does your child have temper tantrums? Or, more important, does your child have a temper? I certainly hope so, for a child, or any animal, without a temper is a sad, defenseless thing.

But I will admit that temper tantrums can be most annoying and embarrassing. A temper tantrum, of course, is simply a wild display of anger, usually accompanied by throwing oneself to the floor, kicking, screaming, beating with one's fists, biting, or hurling things. It is only fair to add to this definition that a temper tantrum is a wild display of anger by someone not yet wise enough to know a better and more effective way of displaying his displeasure.

How often does your child have temper tantrums? He's never had one in his life and he's four years old? Well, you had better be careful. If you have *never* kept him from doing something that he wanted desperately to do, then you may not be teaching him much about the realities of life. If you have *never* frustrated your child to the point of enraging him, it is possible that you have not taught him much either.

He has a temper tantrum sometimes once a day, sometimes once a month, and he's two years old? That sounds pretty good to me. It sounds as though he's learning a good deal about life and has the spunk to resent it once in a while.

You say he's having three or four tantrums a day, and he's two and a half? Then I would say that you are either pressing him too hard and making too many demands upon him—that is, trying to teach him too much at one time—or else he is being taught in a contradictory or vacillating manner, or else he isn't quite sure who, if anybody, loves him as much as he needs to be loved.

But how do you get across to a child that displaying his temper in an extravagant way is not socially acceptable? Well, he needs to learn that it is not an effective device, and therefore not worth persisting in. Far and away the best way to deal with a temper tantrum is to pretend to be as unaware of and as uninfluenced by it as you possibly can. Since most of us are human and our emotions show through our veneer, the safest thing to do in response to a temper tantrum is simply to walk out of the room. It is most difficult to conduct a temper tantrum successfully without an audience. This method even works on adult temper tantrums.

Of course, if you're in a department store or in the middle of Main Street, a variant in tactics is called for. If you cannot safely walk away, then, with whatever savoir-faire you can muster, and in silence, tuck the screaming brat under your arm and march him to a place of safety, before you put him down and walk away. This method never fails in the long run. How long it will take before the child decides that the tantrums avail him nothing depends partly upon your success as an actress and partly upon his intelligence—in some cases, the more intelligent the child, the more easily he sees through your mask, and the longer he will persist before he hits upon a better method to express his anger, such as thumbing his nose at his wealthy uncle.

Certainly it goes without saying that he also must not accomplish what he was aiming at when he threw the tantrum in the first place. That is, if he had the tantrum because he wanted to play with Grandpa's watch, he should not then be given the watch; or if he threw the tantrum because he didn't want to come in for lunch, then, after the tantrum is over, you must go out and pick him up and bring him in to lunch.

Time-established methods of dealing with temper tantrums deserve to be discussed—namely, methods that call for throwing a glass of water in the child's face or spanking him. I cannot recommend these methods, for the simple reason that they do not always succeed. They are, indeed, more tests of the child's mettle than they are proper teaching experiences. If either of these methods succeeds, you have tested, and proved, at what point your child will become a coward and give up. But all he has really learned is that temper tantrums are not effective *if* someone, bigger and stronger than he, happens to be standing around with a glass of water or with a paddle. On the other hand, if the child persists in the tantrum despite the water or the spanking, then you have proven what a brave child you have. But you haven't really taught him much about the undesirability of temper tantrums, and you have made yourself out to be an ineffective, unreliable teacher.

Dealing with a tantrum by matching the child's uproar, decibel for decibel, with parental screaming reduces the parent to the status of a youngster arguing with another youngster. It may be sporting and in the American tradition to give up your advantage as parent over your opponent in favor of a "fair" fight, but first be certain that you are in robust emotional health.

Offering a calm and logical explanation to a raging child is as effective as debating with the surf. Bribery, whether in the form of a gift or a threat, will offer the tyrant the opportunity to place his own price upon the pleasure of his tirade. You may well discover that he is an expensive bargainer. And deriding the tantrum thrower by laughing at him or by comparing him with his younger sister will have the predictable effect of pouring gasoline upon the fire.

Just a word or two about temper tantrums in the older child, say past four, or five, or six—or ten, or twenty, or thirty. These have exactly the same meaning as they do in the two-year-old; their persistence to this late age indicates either that no one has bothered to teach the child the ineffectiveness of tantrums, or that the older child is intellectually retarded or emotionally disturbed—especially if the tantrums occur at twenty or thirty.

Breath Holding

Infants and young children learn to communicate with, and to control, their environment by trial-and-error methods. Those that prove to be successful they retain and perfect. Those that are unsuccessful they soon abandon in search of a better method.

Among the experimental attempts at communication and control are: crying, screaming, and rage reactions, temper tantrums, biting, kicking, hitting, and spitting, whining, and occasionally breath holding and vomiting. All of these are abandoned to a greater or lesser degree as the child acquires skill in speaking and discovers that this is an even more effective method of influencing his surroundings. The investigation by the child of each method that occurs to him is, in terms of his motives, neither malicious nor bad. Simply ignorant. That is, he is ignorant of their relative efficacy. As he discovers them useful or useless, he pursues or abandons them.

It is sometimes astounding how young an infant may be when he accidentally stumbles upon the device of breath holding to impress his neighbors. Breath holding may be used by an infant even as young as four or five months to bring about a satisfaction of his wants. Any youngster worth his salt can hold his breath at least long enough to become purple, and the most expert can throw themselves into a temporary state of unconsciousness resembling sleep. Since the reaction of his environment will determine whether the child concludes that his method is successful or not, it behooves the wise parent to react to breath holding with studied nonchalance. Here the poker face is in great demand. Nothing is more successful in bringing an end to breath holding than for the child, at the end of the performance, to look up and discover that his mother has strolled out of the room and is humming merrily to herself as she goes about her housework.

Is there the slightest, remotest danger to the child from breath holding? Not by any stretch of the imagination. When was the last time you heard or read of anyone committing suicide by holding his breath? Try it yourself any time you want proof positive. The most you can possibly do is to put yourself lightly to sleep. Once asleep, you no longer are able to cease to breathe, and normal breathing automatically returns.

Note too that breath holding, like bowel moving, eating, and sleeping, is one of the score of things that you are powerless to deal with effectively if you ask or tell the child to stop, and he decides not to obey. Since it is a reliable cardinal rule in dealing with young children not to risk your reputation by asking them to do something that you are not prepared to back up, it is clearly not in your interest to demand or implore that the child stop holding his breath. You will only convince him that he is meeting with success and goad him into using the weapon more often.

Breath holding by a master of the art which results in temporary loss of consciousness should be discussed with your doctor to discover whether the unconsciousness is the result of a mild seizure rather than breath holding. If not, it should be ignored.

Deliberate Vomiting

A small percentage of bright children discover that by deliberately making themselves vomit they can readily control their environment. As is true of bed wetting, it is not likely that a child could work this fact out for himself. Instead, it is probably necessary that it be pointed out to him by an ill-advised adult. What no doubt happens is that, after accidentally vomiting, a child witnesses what is to him a soul-satisfying display of theatrics on the part of an adult; otherwise he would not comprehend the effect that regurgitating can have on nearby grownups.

In any event, if you encounter an expert deliberate-vomiter, next best to not having taught him its effectiveness in the first place is, at whatever the price, to teach him now that it is no longer an effective method of control. This involves expressing unconcern when he threatens to do it, pursuing whatever course it was that elicited the threat, and then not reacting in any manner that could bring him satisfaction when he carries out his threat. An effective maneuver is to put him in his crib immediately following the threat, and then to leave him in his crib for a short time, after the threat is consummated, while you find something entertaining to occupy your time. Then, of course, when you clean him up, do it without comment and without the lecture that is sure to bring him satisfaction.

To those who would prefer to beat the habit of vomiting out of their child, I say, "Good luck." My method can't fail. If your child has any gumption at all, your method has at least a fifty-fifty chance of failure. And if at first you don't succeed, I sure hope you're not my neighbor.

Biting, Kicking, Hitting

Probably because they are instinctive, biting, kicking, scratching, and hitting occur sooner rather than later to all children as a method of persuading other people.

Here is a nice, neat lesson for the interested parent to teach the child, for here is an order you *can* give and be absolutely certain of being able to back up. Upon the first experimentation with any of these methods of communication by the child, the parent should *physically restrain* the child from the act, at the same time indicating that it is wrong. "No!" "Quit it!" "Hey!" or "Damn!" said in the proper tone are effective. Explanations, arguments, appeals to reason or logic are not effective; they serve only to confuse the child and offer him a choice, which he is in no position to make.

Since these are instinctive animal reactions, the lesson will never be learned the first or probably not even the twentieth time. But success rewards patience. Be patient. However, don't think it's cute every fifth time Charlie tries it and display your approval by a friendly giggle; otherwise Charlie will learn *that* lesson a lot faster than he will learn that biting, etc., is neither effective nor permitted.

5

Common Problems
of Older Children

Causes of Abnormal Behavior

When a child acts in a strange, illogical, inappropriate, abnormal way, what accounts for his behavior? In looking for the reasons for strange behavior in a child—or, for that matter, in an adult or in any animal—we can distinguish between intrinsic and extrinsic causes. If a child is depressed and cries beyond reason, if he is withdrawn and secluded, if he is frightened and anxious, if he fails miserably to approach his potential in his school work, if he is aggressive or destructive or disobedient at home, the cause may be looked for either in the child's surroundings (extrinsic) or within the child himself (intrinsic).

In short, abnormal behavior may represent the reaction of a *normal* child to an *abnormal*, intolerable situation in his environment, or it may represent the reaction of a *basically disturbed*, confused, unhappy child to a *normal* environment. We may think of the former as the understandable, logical reaction that we could expect from virtually anyone finding himself in a threatening, unbearable situation. We may think of the latter as representing a personality distortion, an aberration or abnormalcy, resulting in a reaction to a normal environment that we would not expect to produce such strange behavior in the "average" individual.

Another way of expressing it is to consider that every child (and every adult) has a breaking point if sufficient stress is applied. The most battle-hardened veteran Marine will eventually crack if he hits one beachhead too many. All children can be made to exhibit abnormal behavior if sufficient duress is thrust upon them. But we expect a child to be able to deal with, and to manage, a certain amount of the usual pain and unpleasantness that represents normal living conditions. If a child behaves abnormally under unusual pressures, we say the cause of his behavior lies in the situation and is extrinsic in nature. If another child behaves the same way, but because of "usual" pressures in the environment, we say that the cause of the behavior lies within the makeup of the child and that he has an abnormal personality.

With these arbitrary definitions in mind, to what sources should we look for the cause of illogical behavior in a given child at a given time? First we must ascertain that the child is in adequate physical health. Once this is established, then we must examine the circumstances of the child's environment, the pressures to which he is currently exposed. Is there some logical extrinsic explanation of his behavior?

We must search in the three realms of his environment: (1) the school, (2) the neighborhood, and (3) the family. Is he under intolerable social or academic pressures at school? Is he receiving frightening religious instruction at Sunday school? Has he been abused or threatened in the neighborhood? Has a playmate been killed or seriously injured? Is a child in his peer group undergoing the anguish of separating parents? Is someone ill at home? Has his father left on an unexpected trip? Is his mother threatening to leave the family? Is there alcoholism or narcotic addiction at home? Is his father beating his mother? Are there threatening financial problems at home—real or imagined?

Abnormal behavior precipitated by an abnormal environment

is short-lived; that is, it ceases to exist soon after the abnormal situation is corrected. If the illogical behavior continues long after undue external pressures have been rectified, or if no plausible environmental cause is uncovered, then, and only then, are you justified in questioning the integrity of the child's personality.

If this point is reached, from now on you are looking not for a cause of the behavior itself, but for a cause of the personality disturbance. Once again you may consider the three areas of (1) school, (2) neighborhood, and (3) family, but in terms of too little love and acceptance, and too much or too little or inconsistent discipline (teaching), and too much smothering of independence.

Although we have spoken of the differentiation between extrinsic causes and intrinsic causes of disordered behavior in a child, it will be apparent to the reader that outside causes, if they are severe enough or recur frequently enough or continue for a long enough period of time, will sometimes themselves become internal causes. That is to say, if a child with a normal personality is exposed to excessive threats and abuse by his environment, he may sooner or later under this influence become a child with an abnormal personality—so that continuing extrinsic causes of disordered behavior become finally intrinsic causes.

Signs of Abnormal Personality in a Child

When an adult, whether parent, teacher, or outsider, begins to suspect that a child is behaving "abnormally," one of four possibilities must account for this opinion: (1) The adult may be mistaken. The child may actually be conducting himself in a manner normal for his age. (2) The child may be physically ill or physically handicapped. (3) The child may have a normal personality and may be reacting in a normal manner to an abnormal situation, such as the death of a parent or an intolerable situation at school. (4) The child may be in a normal environment, under average stresses and pressures, and may be exhibiting abnormal behavior because of his own abnormal personality structure.

Unfortunately for our desire to come to a useful conclusion regarding the cause of the child's alleged misbehavior, the symptoms produced by the last three possibilities are pretty much the same. If we conclude that the child is indeed acting improperly, we can expect little help from pondering the particular type of undesirable reaction that the child is showing. Regardless of the cause of the problem, the child's bizarre behavior will tend to be the same. By what symptoms a child exhibits his difficulties depends upon the child, and not upon the cause.

What are some of these reactions that should alert the parent?

"Nervousness" in a child is a common concern of parents. Unfortunately, this word has so many different meanings to so many different people that it is virtually useless as a term to describe behavior. Nervousness has been used to denote such varying symptoms as excessive physical activity, unusual fears, tearfulness, sensitivity, sleeping problems, and many others. It is better to discard this general term and to use more precise descriptions in categorizing the behavior of the child.

"Immature" is another frequently used designation. Though it is a more meaningful term, it is likewise too broad in its implications to stand alone, and when the teacher pontificates, "This child is too immature to do good work," it is necessary to inquire, "Immature in what field?" A person may be immature intellectually, which is generally just a euphemism for "retarded," though it may instead suggest impoverished opportunity to learn or a late-developing intelligence. A person may be immature socially, which might suggest an inadequate home environment or home teaching. A person may be emotionally immature, which would simply be a rather obscure way of saying either that he was young, or that he had a personality disorder. He might be physically immature, meaning that his physical growth and development was slower than average or that his acquisition of motor coordination was later than average.

Don't handicap your own thinking by using such vague concepts as "nervousness" or "immaturity." And don't be satisfied with advice from professionals which is phrased in such evasions.

Signs of emotional problems in children, as in adults, often take the form of physical symptoms. Headaches, nausea, vomiting, abdominal pain, diarrhea, frequent urination, a lump in the throat, difficulty in breathing, and rapid gain or loss of weight are perhaps the commonest of these symptoms. These distressing complaints are by no means "faking." No adult who has experienced an excruciating tension headache after a friendly conversation with a motorcycle policeman will doubt the realness of these feelings to the child.

Other actions which may signify emotional distress in a child include: difficulty in learning at home or at school, aggressiveness or passiveness, boastfulness, fear, disobedience, unwillingness to try new experiences, sleeping problems (insomnia, nightmares, sleep walking), overeating and undereating, lack of friends, tics, stuttering, lying, stealing, self-deprecation, irritability, sensitivity, dawdling, procrastination or daydreaming, bed wetting, daytime soiling, masturbation, apprehensiveness, rage, breath holding, unconcern for personal appearance, rudeness, interrupting of adult activities, unusual bashfulness or modesty, preoccupation with sexual matters, and physical overactivity or underactivity. It is readily apparent that all of these forms of behavior may be normal, or may be abnormal, depending upon the child's age and the situation in which they are exhibited, how intensely, and over how extended a period of time.

Sometimes it is practically impossible to decide whether a particular behavior is sufficiently deviant to warrant a firm conclusion that the child does or does not have a significant personality defect. Several considerations must be weighed.

Seldom does an emotional disorder proclaim itself by only one or two types of unusual behavior. A seriously distraught child is more apt to display several or many symptoms simultaneously or in swift succession.

Important personality problems are generally displayed in all three areas of a child's relationships—school, neighborhood, and family. If a young person is reacting peculiarly in any one of these, but is clearly functioning adequately in the other two, the problem almost always has an extrinsic cause, and is not a sign of emotional inadequacy.

Assistance for the parent in judging the significance of "undesirable" performance in the child is to be found in council with his teacher, principal, or pediatrician or with a suitable psychologist or psychiatrist.

Fears

The world of children, like the world of adults, is full of fearful things. Some fears are realistic and based upon fact; others are imaginary and based upon misconception. Some fears are expressed directly as fear, whereas the presence of other fears is made manifest by seemingly unrelated and inexplicable behavior.

Babies are popularly thought to be born with a very few basic instinctive fears. Among these are a fear of loud noises and a fear of the sensation that accompanies falling. A knowledge of the myriad of other fearsome things is acquired by the child from experience with his environment.

A more sophisticated and defensible interpretation of the automatic responses of young infants suggests that they are born free from all fear, and that this emotion is totally a learned one, dependent upon intelligence, experience, and maturity to weigh remote consequences.

A major contributing factor in the acquisition of fear concerning an event or an object is the child's observation of the behavior of others in response to the object or the event. Thus a good deal of the fearfulness of a child depends upon the attitude of his mother and father in a given situation. Clearly a child will become frightened of worms if he early observes that his mother shrieks and withdraws upon contact with a worm. Equally so determined will be his reactions to a strange situation, such as a visit to the doctor's office.

Actually much of the child's distress upon being examined by a doctor is not fear but rather anger at being restrained if he has not already learned submission to some form of restraint in the home. When a mother can truthfully state, "This is the only time my two-year-old ever screams and fights," she is often simply confessing that she has never frustrated the child at home.

But the component of fear that also enters into the child's attitude toward an office visit is quickly either fortified or allayed by the behavior of the adults about him. If the mother directly exhibits anxiousness, or if she conveys a sense of fear by an over-solicitous attitude, the child joins her in categorizing the event as fearful. If the mother remains nearby for support, and demonstrates confidence by the quiet naturalness of her behavior, the child comes to accept his mother's evaluation of the situation as not alarming.

If a child's experiences with doctors have had to include prolonged painful procedures and separation from his parents, only the passage of time, strengthened by the calm support of his parents, will enable the child to overcome his rightful apprehensions.

When a child's fears are based upon reality, you have little difficulty in understanding them and in sympathizing with them. It is not remarkable that the child who has witnessed the neighbors' house burn to the ground lives in fear of fire. Nor that the child bitten by an angry dog shies away from other dogs. It is self-evident that alleviating such fears simply requires sympathetic understanding, a willingness to discuss the facts in a reassuring way, and the healing balm of the passage of time.

A person with a fear is a person without reason, and it makes no sense to throw a child who has narrowly escaped drowning into the water to teach him not to be afraid. Nor to urge him to pet dogs after he has been mauled by one. You might profitably provide a three-inch-deep wading pool for the child who has nearly drowned, to be available for his strictly *voluntary* use. Or you might provide a ten-ounce ball of puppy-fluff for the dog-mauled youngster *voluntarily* to be near. But generally such active combating of realistically based fears is unnecessary.

Many of the fears of childhood are founded on misinformation. Fears of ants, shadows, the dark, and so forth are sometimes hard for adults to fathom. They are, nevertheless, as real to the anxious child as the more obviously caused fears. However erroneously based the cause of the fear, it still is true that a person with a fear is a person without reason. It makes no particular sense to thrust a ladybug at a child who is frightened by ladybugs. There is no conceivable rational objection to a night light in the room of a child who is afraid of shadows. The passage of time, and the opportunity to observe over the months and years that others seem not to be frightened by these objects, serve adequately to dispel the child's anxieties.

It is sensible to inquire into the source of the child's misinformation in order to forestall more of the same in the future. Does Great-aunt Emma shriek at the sight of ants? Is the angelic child next door regaling Junior with horror stories concerning the dark? Are the television programs, or even the nursery tales, scaring the Ned out of Junior? I know of a little girl who was panicked for six months by her apprehension over the falling of the sky in "The Little Red Hen."

Most difficult of all are the fears which are not directly expressed by the child, but which come out in the form of apparently unexplainable behavior. The healthy child who dissolves in tears, or who refuses to leave the house, or who suddenly is unable to eat her meals, may be frightened at the prospect, imagined or otherwise, of an impending separation of her parents. The child who stops doing his homework may be fearful concerning the family's financial situation, or afraid that he has not measured up to his parents' expectations.

Any abrupt change in the personality of a child must always be suspected of arising from a fear based on imagined or real threatened harm. If the threat is directed toward someone or something of vital importance to the child, it will generally not be easy for the child to speak about his fears. He will be able to make known the presence of these fears only by a gross change in his behavior. If questioned, he will not be able to reveal his fears or to admit their existence. To explain his behavior, he will truthfully answer, "I don't know why," or will offer a fabricated reason which bears no relationship to the fear. Often he cannot bear to admit the fear even to himself. High in the ranks of such awesome fears must be placed those sometimes engendered by religious education. It is difficult enough for adults to confront the questions "Why are we here?" "Where are we going?" "Must death be inevitable?" "What is sin?" "Am I guilty?" Often enough a child's first experience with some of the unanswerable philosophical doubts of existence, first presented in the form of religious education, will produce sudden dramatic changes in personality and behavior, based on threatening anxiety, where the cause of the problem is often at first obscure to the observer of the child.

It is when fears are not based upon reality that they assume a quality of abnormalcy. That is, when they are not based upon reality as it appears to the child. Remember that the child's view of actuality may be colored by untruths and misunderstanding, and may not be entirely founded upon facts. Fears that are not premised upon the child's true or false knowledge are abnormal and warn of personality disorder. When they exist, they usually exist both in profusion and in variety.

Stuttering

Stuttering is a fascinating problem that has plagued man throughout recorded history. Only relatively recently have investigations provided any meaningful understanding of the affliction. First, let us agree not to be involved in the semantics of stuttering versus stammering. No two experts quite agree upon the definitions and the differences between these two words. For our purposes they mean one and the same thing. We are talking about the involuntary repetition of sounds in speech, whether they be initial sounds, terminal sounds, or whole words; and we are talking about the involuntary pauses that occur in speech because of difficulties in forming particular sounds.

Recordings of the speech of thousands of youngsters, unaware that they were being observed, confirm the fact that at some point in life *all* children engage to some extent in stuttering. It seems to be simply a matter of thought coming more rapidly than the vocabulary and speech of the child are able to keep pace with. This phenomenon is observed occasionally even among non-stuttering adults, when they are in a situation that calls for more rapid or more serious speech than customary. It is also a matter of observation that one young child never seems aware of the normal stuttering of another.

And it is a fact that the affliction of stuttering is perhaps the single divergence from normal health that is never originally diagnosed by a doctor, but is always first diagnosed by a parent or other lay adult. This fact has enchanting implications which will concern us later.

Speech is one of the several functions of the body that are partly involuntary and partly voluntary. The heartbeat and the activities of digestion are purely involuntary. Throwing a ball, or walking up stairs, is purely voluntary. But breathing, swallowing, and speech are partially under voluntary and partially under involuntary control. You normally breathe without much thinking about it. But to a limited degree you are capable of deliberately not breathing or of speeding up your rate of breathing. The effect of too much voluntary attention to breathing is a matter of common experience. Let yourself become too conscious of how fast or how slowly your breath is coming, and you're in trouble. First thing you know you're taking deep sighing breaths, then rapid pants, in a frantic conscious effort to control what is normally an involuntary process. The same is true of swallowing. Become too concerned with where your food is going, and it invariably heads for the air passageway.

Now this is what is so striking about speech and stuttering. Normally when you talk you are consciously controlling *what* you are going to say, but not *how* you are going to produce the sounds. Focus your attention on the normally involuntary acts of how to move your lips, where to place your tongue, and how to vibrate your vocal cords, and you are immediately in trouble. This seems to be the primary basis of serious stuttering.

If all children at one time or another do stutter, then most of them must get over it spontaneously, because not that many adults stutter. But when a child is going through a normal temporary phase of stuttering, let something or someone draw his attention to his speaking and he is on the path to disaster. Once he starts to obey the commands "Say it this way," "Speak more slowly," "Think about what you're saying," "Try it over again carefully," and so forth, then he is apt to stumble more and more because of the impossibility of imposing conscious control upon the involuntary act of forming words.

The curious observation that stuttering is the one disease never diagnosed first by a physician, but always presented to the doctor with the diagnosis already made by a parent or relative, now becomes understandable. It may well be that the conscientious parent, acutely aware of the "normal" stuttering of the child, causes it to become established stuttering by focusing the child's attention upon it, and then the parent is led to present the child to the physician with the diagnosis already established. The unaware parent does not notice the "normal" stuttering; therefore stuttering does not result.

It follows, then, that the treatment of stuttering at its inception is for those around the stutterer to play poker. No anguished expressions on the faces. No helpful instructions on what to do. No calling of the child's attention to his own stumbling speech.

None of this takes into account the reported correlation between emotional tensions in a child and the presence of stuttering. And there does seem to be some such relationship. It is easy to think of, and difficult to prove, explanations which may or may not be true. It is possible that the type of parent who would quickly be aware of stumbling in his child's speech is the type of critical parent who would also be more likely to have an emotionally tense child. It is also possible that once stuttering appears, it then becomes itself sufficient cause to create tension in the child.

If your child begins to stutter, ignore it. And make darn certain that Aunt Suzy and Grandma Clarabell also ignore it. If the stuttering persists for a matter of months despite your magnificent handling of the situation, seek the advice of a competent speech therapist or speech clinic through your physician.

Don't be misled into embarking upon the stormy voyage of first trying your own methods of speech therapy. The problem will be difficult enough for the professional without the added confusion of your help.

School Phobia

Believe it or not, the normal child *wants* to go to school. Or at least he does not want not to go to school. Of course, there are days when any child may occasionally rebel from attending classes—the day he forgot to do his homework, the day of a frightening exam, the day his friend is going to the circus, the day Grandma is arriving. But when a child repeatedly struggles to avoid school, beware.

At the kindergarten age, a modest percentage of children are not prepared to be parted from Momma for the first few days. If the child has had his budding independence a little stunted, if he has been a little too tied to his parents, if he is not yet quite sure of his place of acceptance in the family, if a newborn sibling has recently come on the scene, if there has been sickness or a death at home, if he is aware of threatening marital friction between his parents, he may well decide that the best place for him is by his mother's side, and not in this noisy classroom. There are two approaches to handling the situation of the screaming, hysterical, anxious child who just doesn't want to cross that first classroom threshold.

The first is the "make or break" approach, with which many learned educators seem to like to gamble. With this method the stern or friendly teacher or principal, as the case may be, forcibly removes the leech from his mother and sends the mother unhappy homeward. This approach is exciting in that, like throwing ice water on the child with the temper tantrum, it either works spectacularly or it fails miserably. Or perhaps a more critical analysis would be that it either fails spectacularly or it fails miserably. In most instances, after the first few howling days, the child submits to the inevitable and remains quietly in school. In these "successful" cases it is rather debatable what becomes of the child's repressed anxieties and what long-lasting attitudes toward school are jelled in his mind. In the "unsuccessful" cases, when the child has the guts to buck the stone wall, he may still be screaming, either literally or figuratively, at the thought of school two or three years later.

A less romantic method of dealing with the situation consists of giving the mother permission to remain in the classroom with the child. There can be no effort on the mother's part to duck out when the child's attention is elsewhere, for the intelligent child is looking for exactly this type of adult ruse. By the end of the third day, or the end of the third week, the child can be counted upon to wonder out loud, "Mommy, why are you staying here in class?" Such is the sagacity of children! For all its unspectacularness, this approach has one small advantage. It has no way of failing.

"School phobia," the fear of attending school by other than beginners, has received a great deal of study in recent years. If the fear continues for longer than a few days, it must *always* be looked upon as a potentially serious manifestation. Occasionally its cause may be as superficial as a threatening bully or a gross mismatch between pupil and teacher. More often it is a warning flag of an important personality disturbance within the child. Professional help is always advisable. But the clarion warning that must be sounded is this: the child must not be allowed to stay home from school while the solution is being sought.

It has been conclusively demonstrated that, if the child is allowed to stay out of school for more than a week because of his anxieties, it will become increasingly difficult for him to establish a satisfactory re-entry into school, even though the cause of the problem may be under correction. It is a mistake for well-meaning doctors, and for well-meaning parents, to provide a written excuse for the child whose abject misery at the thought of attending school is so deserving of sympathy. In severe cases, it may be necessary that the child attend school only symbolically —that is, that he be transported to school in the family car, to remain in a quiet corner of the principal's room or the nurse's station for part of the day, and then be afforded the support of transportation home. But the pattern of *going* to school and *re-*

maining in it must be maintained while the problem is being worked out.

To do otherwise is to confirm in the child his own frightening conclusion, that he is such a failure in life that he cannot compete successfully and safely with his peers. The written excuse from those upon whose judgment he is most dependent for approval, and to whose evaluation he is most vulnerable, says with clarity to the child, "We agree with our son that he is a worthless failure, and we have no hopes that he will be able to measure up; therefore we agree that the best thing for him to do is to stay home from school and to hide himself."

Children with school phobia are not delinquents. A student with school phobia *wants* to go to school but cannot force himself to; a delinquent does not desire to attend. The phobic child is anxious, tense, and distressed by his inability to muster the courage to attend classes. The delinquent child is pleased and at ease when he cuts school; he tries to hide his truancy, but when exposed he is not fearful of the consequences.

Lying

The high value placed by parents upon truthfulness, the "George Washington legend," is purely commendable. But like all lessons that require a well-developed ability to make moral judgments, it is a difficult lesson for a young child to learn, and therefore is often the source of conflict between parent and child, which ultimately leads to unnecessary and unjust harmful criticism of the child.

Most parents approach the subject of lying in the proper oversimplified manner. They first set out to teach the young child that lying is bad, telling the truth is good. This is far from what they really want the child eventually to learn, which actually is that lying is *sometimes* good, *sometimes* bad, telling the truth is *sometimes* good, *sometimes* bad. Scarcely anyone wants his child to grow up to think that it is proper to tell his homely aunt that she is homely, or to tell the announced sex maniac at the front door that, yes, his mother *is* upstairs in the bedroom alone. But once having decided correctly to teach the young child first simply not to lie, the parent sometimes then proceeds to foul up the job.

It's all very straightforward. When your child lies, tell him that *he* personally is a great guy, but what he *did* is wrong. Tell him it's wrong by a cocked eyebrow, a word, or, if you must, a whack. When he tells the truth, tell him he's right, and reward him with a smile or a pat on the head. But remember, reward him, don't bribe. Don't announce the prize in advance. Don't say, "I'm going to ask you something, and I want you to tell me the truth, and if you do or don't I will do such and so."

But it really isn't nearly that simple. Suppose he does tell you the truth and that truth turns out to be that he just threw the neighbor's little girl through the second-story stained-glass window of the church. Well, grit your teeth. You simply have got to tell him that he did well by telling the truth. You don't, of course, have to praise his throwing the girl out the window. But it does have to be quite clear to him that the disapproval and the punishment for his heinous act are much *less* than they would ordinarily have been, because of the fact that he did report truthfully. This is easy advice for me to give, but sometimes almost impossible to follow in the heat of the moment. It deserves an honest effort, however.

Suppose you think he is probably telling you a lie. If your knowledge of the matter is at all secondhand, don't, don't, don't put your head in the lion's mouth. If there is even remote doubt, don't trap yourself into accusing him of lying. You only have to be wrong one out of ten times to be in trouble. If you think he's lying, be noncommittal. A neutral "Hmmm" or a non-sarcastic "No kidding" is a Solomonesque way to get off the hook until you have the facts.

And, of course, you have to keep in mind that, even up to six or seven, the perfectly normal child's mind is full of imaginary incidents and playmates. The line between reality and imagination is not always clear to him. So when you get a great rambling whopper of a fib, don't blow your stack without first wondering whether Junior is an embryo novelist. Much, much better to miss correcting a few deliberate lies than to put in doubt your own reputation as an infallible judge by telling him that he has lied when he knows himself that he has not.

Most children, by the time they are into first grade, have accepted, either from their parents or from the surrounding world, the idea that it is "wrong" to lie. If after this age you find your child lying like a trooper, the only sensible approach is to sit down and ask yourself the inevitable question, "Why?" You can assume the following: (1) He knows it's wrong to lie and (2) it costs him something to lie. But (3) from his point of view it would cost him far more dearly *not* to lie. Therefore (4) he has chosen the path of lesser hurt to himself.

Okay, then why, as he sees it, is it going to cost him so much not to lie? Does he know from past experience that when he tells you the truth you exact from him the unbearably high price of belittling him and of withdrawing some of your love and affection from him? Does his sense of belonging in the family depend, in his mind, upon what he *does* rather than upon who he *is*? Is he so uncertain of his acceptance by you that he is unable to risk his status by confessing a failure, even though his only other choice is to lie? Until you have found to your own satisfaction the answer to the question "Why, in his mind, is he paying a smaller price for lying than he would be paying by telling the truth?" you have no basis for intelligent action. If the answer is not obvious, you need outside help. The value a child places on preserving the necessary three requirements of his personality will invariably outweigh any other values he may have!

Remember that it is *never* a good idea to back any animal, or any adult, or any child, into an inescapable corner, and then to threaten him with destruction. If the individual believes that he is fighting for his very existence, then the most extreme reaction on his part is predictable. If you know your child is lying to you, but his attitude of extreme fright and anxiety suggests that he is being forced to fib to avoid what seems to him to be a destructive punishment, it is certainly a dangerously explosive act to hurl the harpoon by accusing him, at that moment, of lying. Far safer to duck and ignore the lie, and to try to find out, without direct questioning or accusation, what sort of trouble the child *thinks* he is in.

And when a child lies so often, and so obviously, that it seems he is baiting you to respond by deliberately telling you lies, it is also not wise to jump upon him for the lying, but rather to seek out why he needs to invite you to scold him.

I would recommend never asking a child whether he is telling the truth or is lying. Not knowing the value he assigns to the choice of replies you force him to make by such a question, you cannot judge the amount of anxiety and guilt you may be forcing him to experience. Besides, it isn't cricket to ask a man to testify against himself. If you know he is lying, tell him so. If you are not certain, hold your tongue until you have ascertained the facts, discreetly and from reliable firsthand witnesses, not from circumstantial evidence. If you cannot be sure without asking the accused for a confession, drop the subject.

Before leaving the subject of lying, let us consider the matter of the parent lying to the child. Clearly this does not set a good example for the child to follow. But worse, you risk destroying a confidence that the child must be able to depend upon.

Of course *you* don't lie to your child—but what about broken promises, forgotten deliberately or accidentally? No matter how you slice it, these are lies to the child; to me too, for that matter. I leave it to your judgment how high a price you will be willing to pay to carry through on a promise once it is made. But I suggest that the price be realistically high.

Some parents lean so far the other way that in their eagerness never to lie to their children they shrink from such fabrications as Santa Claus, angels, fairy tales, and heaven. They even tell the hurtful truth to the children, such as "No, I really don't love you as much as I do Sally" and "Yes, you are rather homely." I sometimes wonder how many of these parents are so unbendingly truthful in their own self-appraisals.

I like my maturing children never to have to lie for their own benefit or to hurt another, but always to lie to prevent hurt or sadness to another. I like my adult parents the same way.

Stealing

The antisocial behavior of stealing is almost an exact counterpart of lying. The very young child may really not comprehend the distinction between "stealing" and "borrowing." Give him a few years to discover the fine ethical point which divides these two and which even an honest adult cannot always clearly see in a given situation. How do you yourself resolve the question. "Is it wrong for a man to steal from a wealthy criminal in order to provide food for his own hungry family?"

When stealing persists in a child of school age, remember first to understand why. The child pays a price in his own conscience when he steals. Why has he concluded that the advantage to him of stealing is worth the price of having stolen? Does he need material things to try to buy the esteem of his colleagues? Is he demonstrating to himself, and to the world, that he can indeed do something well despite the world's opinion of him as a failure? Is he trying to even the score for the love and acceptance and approval which he feels his family has denied him? Is he stealing so openly as to suggest that he is trying to provoke a reaction, which will bring him attention from his parents or from the school? Until you can clearly see why, from his point of view, it is more to his advantage to steal than not to steal, you cannot possibly begin to help him or to stop the stealing intelligently.

Laziness

Any fruitful attempt on the part of adults to understand the oftentimes perverse and illogical behavior of children must involve trying to see the problem from the viewpoint of the child. This means that the adult must never stop asking the question "Why?" until an answer emerges which is so understandable and simple as to suggest the course that must be followed to change the child's behavior.

A glaring example of a completely unsatisfactory answer to the question "Why?" is the I-can't-bear-to-think reply: "Lazy."

"Why is Martha doing poorly in school this year, teacher?" "Because she doesn't apply herself and doesn't do her work." "But why doesn't she apply herself and do her work?" "Because she's too busy daydreaming." "But why is she too busy daydreaming?" "Because she's lazy." "Oh, now I understand."

Bunk! You don't understand anything more about Martha than you did when you started the questioning. You don't yet have an answer which carries with it the suggestion of some concrete action which could help Martha improve her work in school. "Lazy" explains absolutely nothing from the child's point of view. There still has to be another "Why?" "Okay, so Martha's lazy. But why is she lazy?"

"Lazy" means "inactive, dull, slow-moving, languid, having little energy." Show me the child who's "lazy" and I'll show you a child who is half dead. "Laziness" has virtually no meaning or significance when applied to physically healthy children. The very same Tommy who is "too lazy" to do his homework will spend unending hours playing shortstop. The same Jill who is "too lazy" to practice the piano will burn the midnight oil to finish a favorite book. Jim, "too lazy" to pay attention in Mr. Green's classroom, will work to his limit in Mr. Gray's.

What are some of the things that may make a child act in such a manner that to adult eyes he appears "lazy"? When "he's just lazy" seems to be the explanation of a child's behavior, what might be the answer to the more probing question, "Okay, but why is he lazy?"

A "lazy" child may be a physically ill child. A trip to the physician should eliminate this possibility.

Laziness may be a masquerade for boredom. If Martha's intellectual capabilities are being narcotized by the teacher, she may well become "lazy."

If Martha is preoccupied with concern over a volatile home situation, she will be "lazy" concerning her school work.

If Martha is puzzled by a reading difficulty, or by a gap in her knowledge of basic arithmetic, she may feign lack of interest and be labeled "lazy." Most of us are "lazy" about engaging in activities in which we have little skill and of which we have inadequate knowledge. Most of us are enthusiastic about things we do well or comprehend fully. I am very lazy about playing golf because I don't know how to play golf. I am very enthusiastic about playing tennis because I consider myself an expert. I am very lazy about speaking French because I don't much understand French. I am very enthusiastic about discussing mathematics because I am very knowledgeable about mathematics. So with children. Those things they do well they do with enthusiasm. Those things they do poorly they are "lazy" toward. One quick way to find out whether Martha has learned to read well is simply to note whether she does it spontaneously and with enthusiasm. If she is "lazy" about reading, the chances are good that she doesn't yet know *how* to read skillfully.

"Jeremiah is too lazy to go out and play ball with the boys." "Why is Jeremiah 'too lazy'?" Jeremiah doesn't know how to play ball worth a hang. Or Jeremiah knows that if he sets foot outside the door the local bully is going to bash his teeth in. Or Jeremiah is so lacking in self-confidence that he's not going to risk being ridiculed if he makes an error playing ball. Or Jeremiah has had so many of his decisions made for him by his overprotective mother that he hasn't acquired the independence necessary to go out and engage in competitive activity with the other boys. But in any event Jeremiah is not "lazy."

When you are satisfied that the reason for your child's annoying behavior is "laziness," please go back and start over again to find an answer that makes some sense.

Second cousin to the evasive explanation "He's lazy" is the readily misused conclusion "Because he has a short attention span." Perhaps he does. And if so, he needs professional help. But does he really have a short attention span? For every activity? No matter what you try to interest him in, does he promptly tire of it and wander away?

Or does he rather have a short attention span merely for those things which he doesn't understand? Or which bring him grief, such as his father criticizing him or the teacher belittling him? If he has normal attentiveness to some activities—if he will sit for hours before the television screen, or play hopscotch all afternoon with the gang—then he doesn't have a short attention span, and some other explanation for his lack of concentration must be uncovered if he is to be helped.

Posture

One of life's little frictions that can expand into a major conflict between parent and child arises from the subject of posture. Every parent understandably desires an erect posture and a proud carriage for his child. But before trying to alter the posture of a young person it is important to consider what we know about the subject.

Posture is not a simply determined thing, but rather is dictated by many diverse influences. Among the more important factors influencing posture are the emotions. It is a matter of everyday observation that a person's posture varies with his feelings of the moment. The man who has just been promoted, has just received a raise, has just been flattered by his boss, walks down the street differently than does the very same man after he has been discouraged and belittled.

Over the long term, the person who finds himself continually defeated and derided assumes a posture of permanent dejection, as contrasted to the person who more frequently tastes success and who feels himself to be worthwhile. Strikingly so with the child; the sagging shoulders, forward-thrust head, and heavy gait sometimes reflect nothing but the child's evaluation of his own worth. For this reason it is important that parents not attempt to improve the posture of their children through constant "reminding." Frequently repeated friendly reminders soon deteriorate into discouraging nagging. And the parent who constantly suggests to his child that he stand or sit straighter is unavoidably the parent who is thereby just as constantly reminding his child that he, the parent, finds the child unacceptable.

Posture is one of the many areas in which it is not possible for the parent to correct the child's actions without simultaneously being critical of the child himself, for, after all, the child's posture is the child's body, which is the child. It should be clear, therefore, that parents should not try to improve their child's posture by constant vigilance and harping.

In some respects, posture is largely a habit, and, as with any other habit, two things are necessary to change it: (1) motivation and (2) a method of remembering. In order to alter a habit, it is first necessary that the person have some desire to change. It is also necessary that the person have some method of remembering that he does wish to change. To make this clearer, consider the excellent posture that universally marks the upperclassmen of the military academies. The entering classes at Annapolis, West Point, and the Air Force Academy are composed of ordinary men of ordinary posture. But they are strongly motivated to acquire, among other things, a military posture. They all *want* to look like officers. Thus the first requisite for changing a habit is present. And they are *reminded* a dozen times a day, month after month, of their desire to change their habit by the "friendly" upper-classmen. Mind you, they are reminded not by their parents, but by outsiders. They are reminded by persons whose opinion of them is not so important to their sense of being accepted.

These analogies point the way to successful methods of cor-recting the posture of children. In the first instance, perennially poor posture calls for an evaluation of the child's personality, and specifically of his sense of worthwhileness or self-confidence. Sec-ondly, direct efforts to improve the posture must come from sources outside the immediate family, sources who are knowl-edgeable in motivating the child and who are capable of fre-quently reminding the child of his own desire to change. There are available in many areas of the country "posture clinics," which are often inexpensive and effective. Similarly, instructors of diving, fencing, ballet, voice, tennis, musical instrument, charm, etc., are capable of both motivating and reminding the child of good posture—often, of course, without even mentioning the sub-ject of posture.

There are also certain special influences on posture. Very commonly the young girl entering puberty who has not been "sold" by her mother on the beauty and desirability of the female form tries, in embarrassment, to conceal her budding shape by hunching her shoulders and dropping her head. Sometimes the tall adolescent girl resorts to slouching if she has not been adequately convinced beforehand of the statuesque attractiveness of the professional model. (Incidentally, did you know that it is becoming more and more commonplace to halt the growth of a girl prior to puberty if her ultimate height is predictably to be near or in excess of six feet?)

Another important aspect of posture is the ever-present factor of imitation. The child whose parents habitually exhibit poor posture is himself far more likely to adopt an unflattering posture too.

One final major contributor to posture in children is their state of health, both general and orthopedic. It follows that poor posture should be investigated by a thorough physical check-up.

And one eminently successful treatment of poor posture in a boy is a tall girlfriend.

Obesity

Children who are overweight seem to be among those subjects that were long ago thoroughly and exhaustively investigated and studied by the experts, but whose problem and treatment remain a complete mystery to many parents.

Of course, even the definition of the word "obesity" is to a certain extent subjective. Whether or not a child is "overweight" depends partly upon the preference of the observer and, in the case of the older child, partly upon the mode of the moment and opinion of the child himself. It is a fairly safe generalization, however, to say that babies, until they have been walking for a few months, tend to be chubby naturally, while the child from two years to puberty tends to be normally slender. During and after adolescence, "overweight" is largely a matter of contemporary style and personal preference.

What are the causes of obesity? The common cause under two years of age is the specific caloric value of the food eaten. A young child tends to eat until his appetite is satisfied. His appetite is satisfied when his stomach is full. But he has no built-in mechanism for calculating calories. His appetite is just as well satisfied by a stomach full of skimmed milk as it is by a stomach full of cream; indeed, it would be satisfied by a balloon inflated with air. Therefore, in dealing with overweight in the very young, one generally offers the same quantity or volume of food but attempts to choose foods which contain relatively few calories.

In older children, some cases of obesity may be considered simply a perpetuation of family customs and habits in eating. The fat mother and father whose national background features hearty meals of high-calorie foods are apt to have overweight children merely through imitation and family custom. A few older children become obese on account of physical malfunctioning, either because of an endocrine disorder or through enforced inactivity due to disabling diseases. A few children become obese from drugs.

But we know from the superb investigational work of Hilde Bruch that the overwhelming number of obese children in the United States owe their overweight to emotional causes. The emotional cause may be simple boredom and in-the-house inactivity with a ready availability of snacks to combat the boredom. Or it may be overeating by a child with a very poor self-image who considers himself a failure in most endeavors and sets out to be a success in the one thing he does best, eat. Or it might be an emotionallly distraught child striking back at an unacceptable mother who abhors obesity in children.

The first step in treating obesity is to eliminate the possibility of a physical cause by a thorough physical examination supplemented by whatever tests, if any, the physician requires.

The importance of recognizing the commonness of emotional causes for obesity lies in the application of this knowledge to the treatment of the fat youngster. It is *never* appropriate to try to "encourage" or to shame an overweight child into reducing. Obviously, if you recognize the possibility of an emotional factor, it will not help to ridicule, but may serve to aggravate the weight problem by increasing the child's emotional distress. It can be equally disastrous to remind the child constantly that he intends to reduce; whatever you call it, this is a euphemism for nagging. For the same reasons, it often is not appropriate to help or to urge a child to reduce through the use of a diet. When one member of a family is placed on a diet, eating differently or drinking differently according to an announced plan, this can hardly avoid serving as a constant reminder to the child that "You are the fat, ungainly, ugly, unwanted-as-you-are, different member of the family." Furthermore, any child (and any adult) on a diet feels like a martyr, forgoing at some sacrifice the things he wants. With rare exceptions, the weight lost by a child on a diet is therefore quickly regained when the diet finally comes to an end, because every day he has been reminding himself of the good things he has been going without and which he has looked forward to with intense anticipation.

In my experience there are only two successful ways to help an overweight youngster if you hope to make the weight loss permanent. The first method begins and ends at the checkout counter of the local grocer. The mother must bring home and must prepare only enough food for the immediate needs of the family. It is generally possible to say to a child, "I'm sorry, that's all there is for dinner. I guess I didn't prepare enough," or "I wish I could spare you a glass of milk, but there's just enough there for tomorrow's breakfast." It is not generally possible to say successfully, "Yes, there's plenty here, but I don't think you should have any more." I don't suggest that this is an easy method, for it requires careful shopping, constant planning, and shrewdness on the part of the mother, but it is a successful method for those who feel the goal is worth the effort.

The second successful method is for the doctor to prescribe mild, carefully selected anorectic medication (appetite killers) under regular and careful supervision, while telling the child that he may eat as much as he wants whenever he wants to. With this approach it is often possible to shed about two pounds a week with no harmful side effects, and since the child is not martyred during the experience, there is somewhat less chance of the weight being taken on again as soon as the treatment is terminated.

The parent of the obese child may often protest, "He eats like a bird; much less than any of the rest of us!" No one doubts this for a moment. It is all too clear that, because of the differing metabolisms of different normal persons, a group of any ten people eating exactly the same food and taking exactly the same amount of exercise will end up with two of the group gaining weight, two of them losing, and the remainder staying unchanged. But it still boils down to the fact that the obese child is eating more than he needs.

Calories consumed in the form of liquids are often the hidden culprit in the case of the fat child. Most juices and soft drinks contribute nearly as many calories per ounce as does milk. Each four ounces consumed, say between meals, are equivalent in fattening power to a slice of bread.

So accurately balanced is the relationship between the intake of calories and the expenditure of calories for energy and growth that as small an excess as one hundred calories per day beyond the needs of the child will result in the accumulation of about six pounds of fat each year. Since one hundred calories are found in one half slice of bacon, or five ounces of milk, or one pat of butter, or one orange, or four crackers, or two tablespoonfuls of ice cream, the fact that not all Americans are obese is an accolade to Nature.

Efforts to reduce overweight by increasing physical activity are pathetically misdirected. In the first place, it requires tremendous muscular effort to burn up even the calories in a glass of juice. Further, in most children the more active they are, the "better" their appetites become. "But my little fatty only loses weight when he is kept active all summer at camp!" Sure, your little fatty loses weight when he is kept active and away from readily accessible food at camp.

Sissy and Tomboy

Little boys and little girls, initially no different in their behavior, normally grow up to be big boy boys and big girl girls. Why? Well, really for two reasons working in conjunction. First of all, they both spend years observing the female role their mother plays and the masculine role their father plays in the everyday activities of the family. So, just as they both grow up knowing their religious affiliation, almost by osmosis, the boy grows up sensing that he is to emulate the father, and the girl the mother. Secondly, they grow up to fulfill their appointed mission in life because their year-after-year relationships, which form their personalities in a normal manner, make them willing and unafraid to mature into manhood and womanhood.

Conversely, the boy may have difficulty attaining a properly sexually oriented manhood if either of the two essentials goes awry. If his mother is domineering, aggressive, unfeminine in manner and dress, and wears the pants in the family, while the father is retiring, soft, unobtrusive, and milk-toastish in managing the family, the boy may have difficulty in identifying clearly his own role in life. Secondly, if his childhood experiences contain enough destructive factors to interfere seriously with his development of a normal personality, he may also veer away from accepting the role of manhood. Precisely the same two diversions from the normal path of development may influence the girl.

It is an interesting fact that in our society, in contrast to other societies of a different age, effeminate boys are castigated at the drop of a handkerchief, while masculine girls are affectionately called tomboys and treated with easy acceptance.

The truth is, of course, that a ten-year-old boy playing with dolls, sewing, and cooking, unless these are his sole diversions, is a perfectly normal boy. Just as a ten-year-old girl with a bat over her shoulder, in blue jeans and spiked shoes, is a perfectly normal girl. So too is the fourteen-year-old boy who occasionally likes to experience the soft comfort of silk or fur.

The completely masculine teenage boy and the completely feminine teenage girl will often develop strong and normal attachments to, and friendships with, young persons of their own sex. None of this need frighten or offend the anxious parent. The attainment of normal sexuality is further considered in Chapter 9.

The physical sex of a child is determined at the instant the sperm penetrates the ovum. If the father contributes an X chromosome to the union, every cell of the developing child will be a female cell with two X chromosomes, and the individual will have the physical contours of a girl. If the sperm carries a Y chromosome, each cell in the body of the conceived infant for his entire life will bear the male genetic configuration of XY. Thus the physical sex is fixed throughout the body from the very beginning, with every cell stamped "his" or "hers."

Not so the emotional sex.

There are no intrinsic factors—not chemical, not physical, not hormonal, not inherited—which influence the emotional development of a child in the direction of maleness or femaleness until the sexual hormones begin to act in the early pubertal period. But boys and girls do begin to behave differently long before they approach adolescence. They show preferences for types of toys and play activities. They react in vigorous or in gentle ways; they strut or they demur. What accounts for these developing differences in mental and emotional behavior?

Before ten or twelve years, all the differences in behavior between boys and girls are determined solely and exclusively by their environment! So potent are these learned patterns that even after the full maturing impact of the male and female hormones at puberty, the emotional reactions of boys and girls along sexual lines are still largely guided by their earlier and continuing contacts with their environment.

This is to say that little boys and girls learn to act like little boys and girls from what they observe about them—or they do not, as the case may be. The early, and indeed the late, sexual behavior of a child depends, then, upon the opportunities he has for learning inappropriate or appropriate behavior from those about him.

In terms of heterosexual activity, up until kindergarten years boys and girls show no preference for playmates of one sex or the other. Their friendships are quite neuter. Exceptions are the result of superficial circumstance. For example, a boy may play exclusively with girls because he lives in an all-girl neighborhood. Or he may prefer boys because they have toys of the sort he is familiar with and possesses himself. But essentially his peer activity is asexual.

During the school years, friendships become firmly homosexual, and boy shuns girl and girl shuns boy. This is completely learned behavior. Partly, children of this age tend to associate with peers of like interests. Mostly, they are told, directly or indirectly, to feel and act this way. Boys' bathrooms and girls' bathrooms. Boys line up here, girls there. YWCA and YMCA. Boy Scouts, Girl Scouts. You play these games, but you play those. Books for boys, books for girls.

Since all these causes of behavioral differences are external, variable circumstances may cause quite different responses in completely normal boys and normal girls. As at an earlier age, Tom may associate with girls and Joan with boys simply because they are the only ones available in the neighborhood.

Bob may prefer girl playmates because he has not learned to play baseball or because the available boys show more aggressive behavior than his gentle-family experiences have prepared him for. Sue seeks boy companions because she is athletic or is more comfortable with the boisterous activities of her brother-rich family.

All these, and infinitely more, variations are normal sexual conduct arising from rational experiences.

Identical behavior may be abnormal if it is dictated by developing personality faults. Jack may shun male playmates because his self-image is too vulnerable to risk competitive defeat. Emily may seek boy companions because she is surfeited with female rejection from her mother. These variations then foretell possible future unhappiness, but of a form which will not manifest itself as sexual confusion unless the causes are of the specific types discussed later.

At physical maturity, which comes over a wide age range in both boys and girls, heterosexual friendships begin to supersede, but never to supplant, the homosexual companionships, partly because of hormonal influences but still largely from environmental teaching. A slowness of interest in the opposite sex to develop to a stage of active pursuit is never abnormal. On the other hand, a continual avoidance of even casual social contacts with the opposite sex by mid-adolescence is often significant.

Sometimes young boys of about three to six show marked preferences for their mothers, and girls for their fathers. Emphasized as the Oedipus and Electra complexes, these learned responses do not occur in all children, do not need to occur, and indicate an unbalanced family relationship only when they occur in exaggerated degree.

It is frequent, but again not necessary, for young boys and girls to show a preference for the mother, for the child from four years to pre-adolescence to prefer the parent of the same sex, and for the adolescent to favor the parent of the opposite sex.

The essentials of the formation of normal sexual orientation in the child are two: normal personality development and observation of a normal male-female relationship between mother and father. Given these ingredients, sexual deviations cannot develop. Deprived of them, some children nevertheless still manage to acquire satisfactory sexual orientation.

What are the types of childhood experiences that result in homosexuality in later life? Not all, not even a small fraction, of personality distortions result in sexual deviation. And while the observation of abnormal husband-wife relationships may handicap the establishment of fully satisfactory sexuality, it only unusually results in homosexuality. There are certain specific parent-to-parent-to-child insults which nurture sexual deviations. Several of the following situations must prevail in order for the male child to be directed toward adult homosexuality:

The mother shows a preference for the son over her husband and her other children. She arouses him by immodest exposure and seductive physical contact. She shares her bed with her son; the father sleeps in another room. She stifles his independence and is overly protective. She interferes with his friendships with girls. She is openly contemptuous of her husband and aggressively dominates family decisions.

The father spends little time with his son, and that is spent in belittlement. He prefers his other children, particularly daughters. He continually defeats his son by setting impossible goals for him. He denigrates his wife and avoids family decisions by passive withdrawal.

A daughter may be directed toward lesbianism under analogous conditions:

The father and mother are mutually derogatory, and he plays the passive, conciliatory part while she assumes the aggressive, forceful, decisive role.

The father adulates the daughter in preference to other siblings and to his wife. He stimulates her by physical exposure and by passionate caresses. He may lie beside her, and he disrupts her male peer friendships. He subverts the normal maturing of her independence.

The mother contributes by surrendering her bed place and by absenting herself physically or in spirit from the daughter. She shows marked preference for male children, and she defeats by criticism the daughter's efforts to emulate her.

These are the commoner of the particular learning situations which produce homosexuals, who number one to two percent of the population, and bisexuals, who are somewhat more numerous.

What Is a Child Psychiatrist?

This book is devoted to the development of a normal personality in a child. But since this goal is not always the easiest thing in the world to attain and some parents may find themselves in need of a child psychiatrist, perhaps we should try to understand a little better what this strange genus, called a child psychiatrist, is.

As in all fields of endeavor, there are good and bad, better and worse child psychiatrists; and in about the same proportion that you might expect to find good and bad doctors, good and bad lawyers, good and bad painters. When dealing with any service group, it usually is a good idea to inquire around to try to find the best. Perhaps there is a slightly higher percentage of screwballs in this specialty than in some other fields, but most of them are reasonably sane people, just as you and I. There are still a few die-hard pure Freudian child psychiatrists in the woodwork, but they are fortunately becoming extinct and you need not worry much about meeting one.

A good child psychiatrist is an ordinary guy, tall or short, fat or thin, old or older (they age prematurely), who by reason of some amount of training, some amount of experience, and some amount of interest has acquired about as much knowledge and understanding of children and their problems as you would inevitably acquire yourself if you fathered and raised several hundred children. He is endowed with no really magic powers, but he has learned to say more or less the right thing to children at more or less the right time, and to gain thereby their confidence and trust.

He is keen enough to let them know that he likes them and approves of them. But not foolish enough to let them think they can do anything they want to without meriting some disapproval, though always of their action, never of themselves as people. In other words, he has the knack of being a nearly perfect parent—with your child, not necessarily his own. Thus he is often able to "establish rapport" with a child and to help the child to see some solutions to his problems.

As a general statement, children under the care of a child psychiatrist enjoy and look forward to their visits with him, with occasional exceptions when they are beginning to recognize that in some ways the fault is partly theirs. The progress made by a child psychiatrist is generally somewhat less speedy than that achieved by penicillin in a case of pneumonia, and the first meetings may seem particularly unrewarding from the paying parents' point of view, because, as you have proved, it is not all that easy to establish a friendly and trusting relationship with a child. Nevertheless, and particularly as compared with adult psychiatry, the favorable results on the child are not that long in starting to become apparent. Usually before the second mortgage becomes a reality, the parent begins to see signs that the psychiatrist is not a fraud after all.

Child psychiatrists, Hollywood notwithstanding, do not practice psychoanalysis in the sense of a couch. They also are not high on the list of people expert in communicating with parents.

Part of this is deliberate, of course, because it would not do for the child to feel that his trusted friend was divulging his secrets to his parents. But if you find the weeks of silence becoming boring, or too anxiety-provoking, you have the utter right and need to telephone for a report.

Many child psychiatrists find it helpful to have one or the other or both parents receive some guidance and help in handling and understanding their child. This form of adult education is usually accomplished through some form of expert other than the psychiatrist himself. It is a relatively painless experience for the parent, provided he decides in advance to sit back and enjoy it. Not too much more agonizing than third-year Latin or advanced algebra.

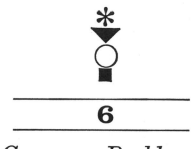

6

Common Problems of Family Relationships

Most of the situations in this book apply equally to all children in all families. They represent conditions and potential problems that are inherent in the parent-child relationship itself.

There are, in addition, many special factors that bear upon the personality development of some children. There are atypical—though common enough—intrafamily stresses that affect the child. They may arise from unique characteristics of the child himself or from peculiarities of the family composition.

For instance, the order of birth may expose a child to special family circumstances. Adopted children or handicapped children may arouse unusual conflicts within the parent. An unnatural family structure, as when the parents are divorced, creates its own distinctive relationships.

The elementary family unit, basic to the interplay between parent and child, exists in its simple form only in the three-member family, composed of one child, a mother, and a father. Concentrate for the moment upon this trio and consider that the child quickly becomes aware of his total dependence upon these two others for subsistence and later for love and guidance. The parents thus represent to the child (1) the only objects whose threatened loss can fill him with instant panic and (2) the only persons who can contribute to or detract from his self-image through the essentials of love, discipline, and independence.

Now, still considering this simplest family group, we can begin to appreciate through the child's eyes the immensity of meaning that minor events assume.

For example, he overhears a routine marital argument, accompanied perhaps by violence, perhaps by threats of dissolving the household. Or maybe he is witness to intercourse, which he interprets as abuse and physical attack. The threatened loss of a parent produces anxiety, made more intense if he believes himself guilty of having caused the fight.

One or even several husband-wife tirades will never destroy a child, if on balance the parents' compatibility is clear to him. But frequent wrangling can make him cripplingly uncertain of the continuation of his only source of love.

The normal personality of the child therefore requires that a degree of love exist between the parents. The *quality* of the love will only influence his own ability to give love, since it is the sole example upon which his early teaching is based. But the relative *absence* of marital love will have a direct and more fundamental harmful effect upon his personality.

Equally, the illness of a parent, or a suspicion of the impending death of a parent, factual or imagined, will threaten the child's personality structure. Of particular interest, and of great practical import, is the fact that the sudden death or disappearance of a parent has much *less* impact upon the child's personality than the departure of a parent after a long-drawn-out period of illness or threatened leave-taking. Especially is this true if the child is led to feel no self-blame and is reasonably assured that the remaining parent will not follow a similar path. The developing personality requires love from parents present, but not from parents departed, if the departure is final. The same mechanism explains the child's emotional tolerance of divorce under the proper safeguards and his intolerance of a spite-filled marriage.

It is a striking fact that sane parents are not necessarily required for the development of a normal personality in a child. I have seen several instances of deep psychoses in both parents, which, since they did not happen to interfere with the requirements of love, discipline, and independence, had no harmful effect upon the child's attaining a sound personality.

Examining further the family of three, it is self-evident that such conditions as adoption and physical handicaps can hamper personality development if they prevent the parents from tendering appropriate love, discipline, and independence.

If one of the parents is an alcoholic, the child is in double jeopardy of witnessing the threatened loss of a parent and of being deprived of the comfort of acceptance and of supportive teaching from the affected parent. He is especially vulnerable so long as the unneurotic parent persists in trying to hide or to minimize the presence of emotional illness in the family. Children have strength and compassion to face difficult facts. They cannot deal with mysterious threats to their self-confidence. When the alcoholic's behavior is confronted, with the honesty of the other parent, as a sickness for which no other member of the family is to blame, the child's feeling of rejection can be made tolerable. The informed child, even at an astoundingly early age, can attain an understanding of and a degree of acceptance toward a family burden so long as his image is not left defenseless by ignorance.

Let us now leave the "simple" dynamics of the family of three and enlarge the number of persons in the home. Add first other adults—say, a grandmother and grandfather. "Two" is not a sacred number to the child. He can respond to more than two "parents." But it is more complicated. Given two additional adults in his intimate environment, does he receive full acceptance from all four parents? Or does a substantial fraction love him when he's "good," berate him when he's "bad"?

God knows, it's hard enough to follow one set of rules in

learning to grow up. Does he now encounter confusion and defeat in two or more interpretations of the regulations? Does he
thus surrender to the conflicting teaching or does he deduce
from it the unreliability of *all* his teachers?

Grandparents have a vital role to play in the child's life. They
are exemplars of dignity, compassion, fulfillment, tolerance, and
appreciation of the more durable values in life. They no longer
qualify as parents. Once to a customer. Their enjoyment of, and
contributions to, the child cannot readily come from their continual presence within the household.

Now further complicate the family relationships by adding
other children.

Aside from their normal jealousy reactions, older children
sometimes also adopt the role of supernumerary parents. Pre-teen
siblings can duplicate all the mistakes of the natural parents—
smothering, contradictory discipline, bribery, and so on. Make it
clear to older children that you don't appreciate their playing
mother and father until they are old enough to have their own
offspring to ruin. You will be able to make plenty of mistakes on
your own on this one, thank you.

Older brothers and sisters naturally tend to set standards that
cannot be met by the younger child, not only in school achievement, social expertise, and athletics, but in daily activities—dressing, running, eating, sleeping (not sleeping), leering, destroying,
fighting. For all the reasons that older playmates can mislead a
child, so too can older siblings. Youngsters grow on peer contacts; they become disoriented by constant competition with
superiors.

Younger siblings play dirty pool. They usurp the gushings of
aunts and grandparents and neighbors, if not of Mom and Dad,
while simultaneously provoking parental exhortations upon our
hero to "grow up." It's like taking away a guy's shield while smit-
ing him with a longsword.

"My children's constant bickering and fighting drives me wild.
How can I prevent it, Doctor?" I wonder what the veterinarian
at the zoo tells the distraught mother lion to do about her quarrel-
some litter of cubs? As for avoiding fights among human siblings,

by nature somewhat less civilized than young lions, I can only offer a few equivocal suggestions. Choose from among them.

1. Take "the pill" regularly after the birth of the first child.

2. Lodge siblings in opposite wings of a large house, introducing them only at mealtimes, seated at opposite ends of a banquet table.

3. Direct each of them toward different achievements amidst different groups of friends.

4. Employ armed guards—"mother's helpers"—on rainy indoor days.

5. Look the other way, with cotton-plugged ears, when no antagonist is armed with anything worse than fists and nails.

6. Buy Mace.

7. Practice and practice and practice establishing your own reliability in the minds of your children with action-backed commands and avoidance of entreaties, explanations, bribes, nagging, and unenforceable requests. Then when you order, "Quit it, damn it!" you will effect a temporary cease-fire.

8. Avoid constantly demonstrating to them—and thus misleading them—your own violent, physical solution to a disagreement. If you discipline them in kind by an angry cuffing onslaught when they are involved in a ruckus—or if you perpetually solve your personal problems by enraged belligerence —you offer them no mature, more socially acceptable pattern of behavior to imitate.

9. Above all, remember that, short of physical or emotional mayhem, it's normal.

Mommas, and occasionally poppas, wonder how to encourage brothers and sisters to "love" one another. I think the word misleads you. The need to receive love in terms of acceptance is instinctive. The desire to give and to get love at the adult heterosexual level is instinctive and hormonal, modified by learning. But love between siblings is simply peer love—not love at all, but an inconstant urge to avoid hermitage and boredom and an instinct to be a group animal (social, if you prefer). Sibling love is, in a way, myth and propaganda—that is, it is mainly socially acclaimed behavior learned by hearing of it so often that it becomes an accepted concept through familiarity. It becomes adopted, provided of course that you don't first learn its disadvantages.

Fundamental to the preservation of balance within the family is the maintenance of the sanity of the husband-wife relationship. You chose each other for better or worse. You didn't choose the rest of this mob. Your wife's contentment and your husband's satisfaction come first, by any moral or biological rule of priority. Be a husband and a wife; then be a parent. After all, everyone else in the family is replaceable. The kids will survive, even profit from, some judicious neglect and from some satanic mishandling. They won't survive the collapse of their father's lover or of their mother's suitor.

Jealousy

Jealousy is a topic on which we are all experts, for at one time or another, and in some form or another, we have all experienced it. It exists in an infinite variety of forms: jealousy of the lover toward his rival, jealousy of the son toward the father or of the daughter toward the mother, jealousy between the parents. But the type of jealousy that we are specifically concerned with here is the jealousy among brothers and sisters. Jealousy among siblings is a potent force in the personality development of the child, because it may touch upon all three of the major influences: love, discipline, and independence.

The first-born child has the glorious uniqueness of living without sibling rivalry. If one were to extol the advantages of a one-child family, this would be among the foremost.

But a once-in-a-family situation automatically arises upon the birth of a second child. For the advantages of giving up his only-child status, the first-born accepts the disadvantages of acquiring a competitor for the love and affection and time of his parents. Only the first-born experiences the distress of first being the sole recipient of his parents' maternal and paternal love and then suddenly needing to adjust to a situation of sharing. Love is not exactly a commodity that you easily reconcile yourself to sharing.

To appreciate the first child's position when the second child arrives home from the hospital, consider a simple analogy. Suppose you, the mother, arrive home from the maternity hospital to find your husband comfortably ensconced with another woman. And he hands you this placating explanation: "Darling, I have been so pleased with *you* as a wife that I have taken a second wife. I want you to love her and to help me make her feel at home. She will be a fine companion for you." This is rather specifically what you imply to the first child when you present to him his new brother or sister. Now, honestly, would you say to your husband, "Great, buddy, just what I've always wanted"? Or would you, rather, consider yourself justified in fighting back by any means, fair or foul, to avoid sharing your husband's love? You see, love is *not* a commodity that is readily shared.

It is rumored that in bygone days, in certain polygamous sects, the wives lived happily together. I have it on good authority by personal communication that "t'ain't so," but rather that the first wife usually lived out her life resentful of those that followed.

Is it normal, then, to expect Junior to be jealous of the newborn, or will he be jealous only if he is a nasty, selfish brat? Well, in my opinion, if he's not jealous he's a fool. I just don't think one can expect a first child not to be jealous of a second. The goal is to make him as little jealous as is reasonably possible—that is, feeding him this bitter pill in as small doses as possible, until he at least has a chance partially to adjust to the intolerable situation. It doesn't seem reasonable to me to walk into the house with a new baby and say to the oldster, "Look at the pretty little brother I brought you." Nor to say to him later on, "Let's go diaper *our* baby" or "See how nicely *your* baby brother takes his bottle." It strikes me that, if I had a rival, the less I knew of him, and the less I heard about him, the less it would bother me.

On this premise, I would propose that the second baby should enter the home as unheralded as possible, certainly not in the arms of the mother, and should be tucked into a distant corner like the vegetable he is, while the mother and father reacquaint themselves with the first-born. And, thereafter, the less the first-born sees and hears of the newcomer, the better. He obviously can't help discovering the awful truth. But it might at least be gradual. There's no point in calling his attention to every feeding, and every diapering, and every bathing, and every cuddling that the baby gets. Of course, I don't suggest that you push the older child out of the room or out of the house. When he must watch, or wants to watch, he is gladly included. But when he is happily lost in television, or in taking apart Daddy's watch, don't call him in to rub his nose in the presence of his rival.

It goes without saying that the baby doesn't take his predecessor's crib away from him, and that Grandma and Grandpa don't brush him aside in their exuberance to enthuse over the newcomer.

Suppose the first-born child is only a year old when his sibling arrives into the world? Surely he's too young to understand. Not on your life! At twelve months he's as sharp as a steel trap, and it will take him about eleven seconds to figure out that his mother is squandering some of her time and love on an interloper. "But he's seen me handle other babies a hundred times!" Okay, so then it will take him twenty-two seconds to discover that this one's different; this one has come to stay.

"But my older child is twelve years old. Certainly he can't be jealous of the baby!" Of course not. You wouldn't mind if the second woman your husband chose were twelve years younger than you, would you?

A nice, normal, understandable jealousy should be fully expected in *any* first child when the second child enters the family. Perhaps things are a bit worse if the event occurs when the first child is between one and five years of age; but better or worse, no matter what the age difference, the same potential situation exists.

How will the first child express his jealousy of the baby? Well, if he's the appealingly direct type, he'll step on the baby's fingers, or poke a finger into an eye, or jump up and down on him in the crib, or simply throw a skillet at him. Needless to say, it doesn't pay to allow this to happen too often. On the other hand, in the interest of the first-born's psyche, it doesn't pay either to keep pulling him away by the scruff of the neck and screaming at him, thus demonstrating to his satisfaction that you really do prefer the newcomer. Better to keep the baby in a safe place, even if it means buying or making a completely enclosed crib, in order to avoid both the maiming of the baby and the traumatizing of the older child.

If he is the more subtle type, his jealousy will be expressed in more indirect activities. He may try going backward in years and reverting to methods that he formerly found to be successful in capturing your attention. For instance, he may become untrained, or he may demand a bottle again, or he may take to waking up at night, or he may ask to be fed or dressed. This calls for an approach on the parents' part which accomplishes two goals. First, the child must come to observe that these undesirable regressions do not accomplish their purpose of buying his mother's attention. In other words, the mother must respond to them in whatever manner gives him the least amount of her time. The second goal is to convince the older child that he does get attention, either when he is being good or when he is being nothing in particular.

For example: He temporarily becomes untrained. Wrong method: Jump up and down, scream and threaten, and whack him a few times. Wrong because it gives him too much attention and takes too much time. Second wrong method: Explain to him at some length that big boys and good boys don't do such things if they love their mother; remind him repeatedly during the day that he's your big boy and you know he won't soil himself. Wrong for the very same reasons. Right method: When it's convenient, quietly change him *with no comment,* and go on about your business.

Example: You're feeding the baby and the older child screams that he wants a bottle too. Wrong method: Either scream back at him or explain patiently that big boys don't drink out of bottles. Wrong method: Let him keep screaming for the bottle while you try to ignore him, until your twitching nostrils and clenched fists convince him that he's really got your attention. Right method: Hand him the bottle in your hand, *without comment,* and go fix a second bottle for the baby.

Example: He starts waking up at night and screaming for company. Right method: Peek in to be sure he's not dying. Wave in a friendly fashion from the doorway. Close his door and go back to sleep, with cotton in your ears if necessary.

Example: He wants to be fed or dressed, though fully capable of feeding and dressing himself. Correct method: Feed him and dress him quietly, quickly, and *without comment.*

If he's really the ultra-sophisticated type, he will show his jealousy in the most guileful ways. Being advanced in his thinking, he will quickly figure out the best way to recapture your attention. He will kiss, pat, fondle, and fawn over his adorable baby brother. Sure-fire way of getting mothers and great-aunts to pat one on the head and say, "What a fine boy." Or whenever the baby whimpers or frowns, he will run to you and demand that you take better care of his baby brother. Or he will suddenly become the angelic child, responding to your every suggestion and need almost before it is expressed. Wrong solution: Come to the conclusion that the doctor was all wet and that, really, the child couldn't be less jealous. Let down your guard, and give him more and more reason to be justifiably jealous of the little monster. Right method: Praise God! Pat him on the head and say, "I love you anyway." Redouble your efforts to convince him that you value him more than ever, and far more than you could ever admire this squirming little thing. Then praise God again. You're getting off easy. But don't assume that next week he won't take a hatchet to his little buddy.

Does it sound pretty cynical? Really, it's not. If I were a mother or father and brought a second child into the house and saw no jealousy on the part of my first-born, I'd be a little hurt and insulted that he really didn't care that much about his parents.

Do I imply that he won't like his little brother? Lord no, I insist that unless you really go out of your way to botch up the job, he will indeed grow fond of, cherish, and defend his brother;

but, even while laying down his life for him, he will occasionally have pangs of normal jealousy.

Second, third, fourth, fifth children never have quite the same urgent need to be jealous of a subsequent newborn. But that just means it's a little easier for them. They will be jealous. They merely don't have quite as good a reason, and it will be less difficult for them to adjust. But nobody readily and willingly subdivides his share of his parents' affection.

Does it help to prepare a child in advance, during your pregnancy, for the fact that he is ultimately to have a rival? Certainly it helps, about two cents' worth, and mostly the mother. Go back to our analogy. Would it help much if your husband told you about his plans for the second wife in advance? Mostly it would give you a little more time to plan the subtlety of your attack. It's rather like preparing the child for his visit to the doctor. It all sounds great until the poor child actually confronts the ogre.

Sibling rivalry, of course, doesn't begin and end with each homecoming. It probably goes on throughout life, until all the brothers and sisters have grown up and have died. After that I'm not sure. But good habits are more easily continued than are bad habits broken. Develop the habit of *not* referring to one child when addressing another. This simple knack will keep you in later years from telling Susie how much better Johnnie does something than she does. Just as you won't tell your husband that that man you could have married does something better than he does.

An important tool in minimizing jealousy among brothers and sisters is an outgrowth of not calling number one in to watch you diaper number two. To the degree that it is possible, let each child develop his talents in a different direction, so that Bud is competing with strangers in the academic field, and Tommy is finding his field of competition in sports, and Anne is making music her own arena of competition. Connive to see that each child operates within his own sphere of friends, and not in a group which contains one of his own brothers or sisters. Again, I don't imply that you keep them so well separated that they are strangers. No more than I would say to a child, "No, you can't come watch me feed the baby." But I suggest that competition among siblings is best taken in small doses at all ages.

First Child, Middle Child, Last Child

In a way, it is misleading to think of the first child in a family, or the middle child, or the youngest child, as having personality problems that are his and his alone. Each child is exposed to influences which in the long run relate to the basic requirements of love, discipline, and independence. All problems that arise with the first child might just as well occur with the second, third, or twentieth child. All the problems of the youngest child might just as well be encountered with the middle or oldest child. An oldest child might have typical "middle child" problems. A middle child might have classic "youngest child" troubles. The easy tendency to say, "Oh well, he's a middle child," or "Oh well, he's a youngest child," or "Oh well, he's the oldest child, and his problems are therefore only natural, so what else can you expect," leads to fuzzy thinking. Nevertheless, in discussing the personality problems of children, it is worthwhile to recognize that the child's position in the family does make it somewhat more likely that he will be under different influences from those experienced by the other children in the same family.

Dr. Benjamin Spock astutely observed that no two children ever have the same parents. This is both important and terribly true. With each passing year, parents change in their attitudes and accumulate more experience. A baby born in 1968 to Mr. and Mrs. Jones is born to a different set of parents than the child born to Mr. and Mrs. Jones in 1967. Even twins are in a sense born to different parents, because it is virtually impossible that parents should feel exactly the same toward any two persons, including their own children. It is equally true that no two children are ever born into the same family, because the presence or absence of older or younger brothers or sisters makes the whole family structure different.

The first-born child in a family has the great disadvantage

of being the noble experiment. He is the first cake the new bride bakes. Unfortunately, he cannot be discarded when he falls. He provides the training ground for the uninitiated, amateur parents. He serves to correct their mistakes in child raising, but only after the mistakes have been made—on him. He gives his mother and father the opportunity to learn that what they had considered the normal behavior of a four-year-old is in truth more nearly the behavior of an eight-year-old. Efforts to push him into independence, which fail, demonstrate to his mother and father that independence is achieved by a child and not thrust upon him.

But the first child pays for the lessons learned by the parents. The oldest child in a family tends to be the child who is "nervous," tense, overly pressured, overly motivated, perfectionistic, self-demanding, unself-confident, unsociable, rebellious, stuttering, bed wetting, nail biting, materialistic, and malcontent.

Knowing in advance the self-punishing icebreaker role that the oldest child is destined to play, it is reasonable to offer him whatever compensation for his trials is available. He has the right and the need to be granted the privileges of the heir apparent, so that the stresses that naturally are his are minimized.

He needs such tangible evidence as the privilege of staying up fifteen or thirty minutes later than his younger brothers and sisters. He needs *not* to be pushed toward independence, *not* to be told that he is a big boy and should "act his age."

When children outnumber bedrooms, he should be the one who does not have to share his room with a sibling. When there is one extra piece of cake, or one extra pat on the head available, it should be offered to him. When there is a fracas of undeterminable origin between him and a younger brother or sister, it should be assumed that he was the victim and not the culprit.

He deserves parental protection from teasing and abuse by his younger siblings. In short, he needs the opportunity to see for himself that the higher price he pays for being a member of the family is at least compensated for in part by some preferential treatment. He should taste some of the advantages of growing up to soften the disadvantages.

The youngest child in the family sometimes faces burdens that are in some respects the opposite of those of the eldest. It has become apparent to the parents that babies are babies for too short a period of time. They may tend, therefore, to resist the development of independence in the youngest. He occupies a crib until he is four or five. His efforts to give up the bottle, to feed himself, to dress himself, to climb, to make decisions, may be met at every turn by too helpful a hand.

He may have not just two, but four or five or six "parents," depending upon how many older brothers and sisters he has. This leads to a variety, and therefore an inconsistency, of teaching, which adds up to no effective teaching at all.

The thrill and challenge of teaching and disciplining have become old hat to his adult parents, and their time for such activities is now spread thin. He may therefore have learned little of the realities of life by the time he reaches school age. The youngest child tends, in sum, to be influenced in the direction of overdependence, of an unrealistic appraisal of his own station in society, which will expose him to hurtful experiences outside the family circle.

The problems of the middle child are those peculiar to the state of being the second of three children, or the second through the nineteenth of twenty children. These are the problems of nowhere to go, neither up nor down. The oldest child is accelerated into adulthood too soon; the youngest is maintained in infancy too long; the middle child finds his way upward challenged and his effort to hang back frustrated. He finds it difficult to measure up to the standards set by the child ahead. At the same time he cannot tarry in his childhood, nor easily back up a few steps for the reassurance that the nest is still there and available to him, for the nest is being usurped by an onrushing rival. Therefore he has the best of neither world. There is too little love and support, and there is too much likelihood of failure by comparison, if he should gather up the courage to try.

The sex of a child may qualify him for disadvantages that are not appropriate to his numerical standing in the family. The firstborn male with three older sisters may find himself subjected to many of the pressures and unrealistic expectations that would have been his lot if he had been the oldest child.

The second girl in a family may be treated as the youngest child all her life, even though six brothers may follow her in order of age.

Again it should be stated that the same requirements are present, and the same mistakes are to be avoided, in the case of each child regardless of numerical position in the family.

Twins

Twins are an enchantment and a delight to raise. But they present greater challenges and difficulties in the area of personality development.

In order to develop and to preserve self-esteem, each child needs to feel himself an individual—and a worthwhile individual, in at least some small way different from and superior to and more lovable than any other individual in the world. This sense of uniqueness and acceptability is just as important to a twin as it is to any other child. How distressing it is to feel that there is someone, particularly someone near you, who is, in every way, just as good as or better than you. Even as with other siblings, but here more so, the parents of twins should seek to establish and to develop individual differences between twins, rather than to stress their similarities. They should not be dressed alike, or encouraged to develop similar interests, or to travel in the same group, or to attend the same class.

The feeling of competition between twins is often more intense than that between other siblings. If one twin is a little stronger, a little brighter, a little prettier, or a little better coordinated than the other, it is altogether too easy for him to emerge as the perennial victor, while the other accepts the role of loser. As with other children, success begets success. The role of underdog is too easily assumed, to the permanent detriment of the personality. It is sometimes necessary to manufacture opportunities for success for one twin, while forbidding the other twin to engage in the same activity.

These observations, of course, are completely valid for identical twins, almost as valid for fraternal twins of the same sex, and only a little less valid for fraternal twins of opposite sexes.

Impossible Goals

Have you ever been impressed by the fact that so many famous, eminently successful leaders in life have had such little luck in successfully raising children? It may well be that statistically these successful people have as good or bad a batting average as parents as do other people. But even this, it seems to me, would be thought-provoking. Why shouldn't they do far better than average? It has seemed to me also that parents who think themselves to be terribly successful people, or who pretend to think so, likewise often have an unusually difficult job of raising normal children.

This is, of course, mostly speculation. It is safe to assume that children learn much of what they know simply by observation and imitation. Therefore, children will generally act and talk and think and react and dream and strive and set their sense of values more or less as their parents do. It also seems safe to assume that people who have been unusually successful, or who think they have been, may set their own standards of acceptability somewhat higher than average. We know that a young child who finds at every turn that his efforts to accomplish something meet with defeat, sooner or later learns to protect his own opinion of himself by refusing to expose himself to further defeat. He feels so certain of losing that he thereafter refuses to try, often pretending to be uninterested.

If all these things are true, it might account for the difficulty that unusually successful people have in helping their children to develop healthy personalities. For if a child is allowed to leap repeatedly for the goals established by the parents, whom the child wishes to imitate, and if the child continually tastes the rebuff of failing to attain these impossibly high goals, he would understandably be unable to develop an adequate self-image to sustain his own personality needs.

It may recommend itself to people who have attained considerable success in life, and who have then become parents, to be willing to allow their children to glimpse whatever few human frailties and failures might possibly exist in the parents, and thus to permit the child to have at least a few goals in life which he might easily be able to achieve.

If I were certain that there was not the remotest chance that anyone would ever read this, I guess I would put it more bluntly. I would say that if you are a parent and are a pretty great guy, eat your guts out, even lie if necessary, to let your children think they have *some* chance of successfully imitating you.

Similarly, some parents are handicapped by having themselves exceptionally high IQ's. These poor souls have a built-in intolerance which requires special forgiving compassion on the part of children and spouse. Hard to live with is a brilliant child. Harder still is a brilliant parent.

If you are unfortunate enough to be an intellectually gifted adult, you must force yourself constantly to consider that your offspring and your mate are literally not capable of the swift, sharply logical, unerring, analytic thought processes that are natural for you. No intellectual giant would ever deliberately belittle, or make impossible demands of, a companion with only average powers of rationalizing. Not sporting, you know. Einstein was a gentle man who never annihilated his inferiors with his genius.

The Adopted Child

The adopted child has certain special needs. But I would like to have you see their true magnitude in proper perspective.

The fact is that 99 percent of his requirements are not the least unique, but are precisely the same as those of the natural son or daughter. And 99 percent of his personality problems are caused by relationships and misunderstandings that are standard for all children and not at all derived from his adopted state.

He needs the same type of love, the same measure of discipline, and the same quality of independence as do all children.

He learns to trust or distrust authority by the same testing and probing of the dependability of the teacher. He values the preservation of his self-image above all other concerns and subordinates all other learning to this primary end. He is to the world of adults alternately an obnoxious, unreasonable character and a lovable child, in the same degree as a natural son.

The needs of the adopting parent, too, are largely the same as those of any parent. But these needs may indeed be magnified by the circumstances that lead up to and accompany adopting.

All thoughtful parents experience doubts and frustrations arising from their inadequate preparation for the infinitely complex assignment of guiding a child. The adopting parent is likely to have been made even less confident because of belittling experiences that may have preceded adoption. Intellectually it is easy to recognize that being a capable parent and being a satisfactory mate and being a masculine man and a feminine woman bear no relationship to the ability to procreate. In fact, as one looks about, it is tempting to defend the very opposite relationship—that is, to conclude that the more unsuited the parent, the more fertile. But, however rationally aware, the adopting parent is sometimes handicapped by an emotional sense of inadequacy.

All parents are at times hindered by the love they have for their children. Adopting parents may have had their desire for children so exaggerated by years of denial that they lose sight of the other needs of the child—needs in addition to adulation.

The average parent has understandable trouble reconciling himself to the inevitable angry outbursts from his child: "You don't love me," "I hate you, I hate you, I hate you," and "I wish Mr. X were my daddy." It is not easy to remember to translate these messages properly as: "Would you mind telling me again that you love me?" "It sure is tough to learn all the things I need to know," and "Can you bear to reassure me that you're glad to be my father?"

It takes even greater self-control on the part of the adopting parent to avoid misinterpreting these normal, coded questions and accepting them as true denunciations. Only a parent prepared well in advance will be able to reply to "I wish I had my real daddy instead of you" with the appropriate answer, "That's okay to feel that way, but I sure am glad that *I'm* your daddy."

It can be hard for any parent to realize that it is normal for him to be annoyed, or resentful of, or hostile toward his own flesh and blood at times. But after all, what normal adult deliberately invites five- and ten-year-olds to a dinner party with thoughts of having an enjoyable evening? The adopting parent is even more susceptible to wondering guiltily whether he is a "normal" parent when he discovers that the child he is committed to cherishing is sometimes a pain in the neck.

Thus it is that the relationship between any child, natural or adopted, and his parents consists in the main of the same situations. The adopting parent, however, is especially vulnerable if he is not fully prepared for his role.

The wishful fancy that the coming of children can restore a crumbling marriage is fortunately losing popularity. The exact opposite is more apt to be the case. The arrival of a son or daughter places stress on any marriage. The added demands upon the man and wife come as close companions to the joys. Increased financial burdens, the necessity of sharing each other's attentions with a newcomer, mounting responsibilities, the need for increasing personal sacrifice, all test the maturity of the married couple. Far from binding wounds, the adoption of a child may shatter a faltering household.

Equally unsound is the adoption of a child for the purpose of providing a companion for and "helping" the personality development of an already present son or daughter. If you plan adoption because you and your spouse have a great surplus of parental love, fine. If you consider adoption so that your older child can profit from the experience, forget it. He too will pay a price. And companionship may be a small recompense.

How much will the adopted child reflect the influence of your family? How much of his developing abilities are predetermined by his genetic background? Some potentials of physical characteristics, skills, intellect, personality, and disease susceptibility are present at birth. But with rare exceptions the development of these potentials is totally dependent upon the environment

—upon you. You have the privilege of claiming the finished child as your masterpiece. Likewise you have the privilege of recognizing that any developing deficiences have originated from you too. To do otherwise is to forgo, in the name of predestiny, the opportunity to look for and to correct the cause of personality problems, learning difficulties, and physical disorders.

Since most of us prefer to duck unpleasant assignments, it is a temptation to consider withholding from the child the possibly hurtful knowledge that he is adopted. Whatever clever rationalizations you may summon to justify this course, be certain to put temptation firmly behind. The adopted child must grow up fully aware of his status.

The possibility of hiding forever the fact of adoption is remote. A slip of the tongue, an informed outsider, a challenge to the probate of a will, may drop a bomb at any age. Then you are faced with refuting the obvious inference, "There must have been something hideous or shameful about my origins, else why would you have kept the facts from me?"

Better to let the adopted child know before he is even old enough to comprehend, and as casually as you would let him know his name or his religion, that he is a selected rather than a biological son. Children love those who love and protect them, not those who spawn them.

Children revel in hearing oft-repeated stories of their infancy. Cherished recollections make good bedtime and rainy-day stories that the child can grow up with, starting perhaps before his second birthday, when belief is complete and doubting unknown. The details of adoption can be as spellbinding as the recollections of a natural birth. How eagerly the arrival was expected. How Daddy stayed home from work. How grandparents telephoned. How proud Mother was. The yellow blanket. The immense eyes. The tiny fist. The happy tears at the agency. The drive home.

It seems to me charming to emphasize the careful selection of the most winsome child—"We personally chose you"—as contrasted to the potluck, take-what-you-get method of biological birth. This can give the adopted child a special significance, and can supply a ready reply of "You're jealous" to any later taunts of "You're adopted." But be careful to emphasize that he's special just for being himself, and not special in that he has to perform up to expectations in order to justify his having been picked. He was chosen because he was irresistible, and not because of something he did, or because of promise of future brilliance or goodness or ability.

Another way of letting a child grow up knowing by osmosis that he is adopted is to mention the fact in his presence in routine conversations with other adults. "It was a great satisfaction when we adopted Junior." "Remember how it snowed one month after the adoption?" The word should be associated in his young vocabulary with warmth and love so that it cannot be used later by malicious peers or adults with a connotation of rejection.

You will not, of course, make a weekly fetish of laboriously discussing the adoption. And there is no particular purpose in meticulously spreading the gospel. He need not be introduced to all comers as "my adopted son, John." Nor it is especially natural to notify teachers and neighbors and playmates that "he's adopted, you know."

It is perhaps judicious to let a fiancée know the facts. It is certainly preferable to separate out the bigots before, rather than after, the wedding ceremony.

Siblings should be informed as casually as they would be told the name of the hospital at which a natural brother had been born. But taunts of siblings directed at the fact of the child's adoption are no more permitted by parents than are taunts directed at freckles or at curly hair or at plumpness.

The acceptance of the naturalness of adoption is epitomized in the two sisters speaking to their teacher: "One of us is adopted, but we can't remember which."

Even if there is no sense of shame associated with being adopted, sooner or later the child will ask questions. The exact intent of the question should be clear before an answer is ventured. If need be, you inquire, "What is it you want to know?"

"If you're not my real mother, will you leave me someday?" may be based on nothing more poignant than that the governess of a playmate down the street quit her employ, and may invite the reply, "Darling, I'll never leave you" rather than an enthusiastic dissertation on the personalities and motivations of biological versus adopting mothers.

Questions concerning details of the natural parents usually start around the age of six, and are inquiries prompted by curiosity, not charged with emotional longing. Answers should always include the assurances that (1) the baby was not surrendered because of rejection or hate and (2) he was not the cause of his natural parents' problems.

Adolescence can be the wonderful age when all the hard work of the parent comes to fruition. When Mom and Dad can, if they put their minds to it, enjoy the ebullient companionship of a young adult. When they no longer have to tolerate the presence of a dependent, semiliterate child who usurps so much of their time. When the burdens of parenthood can be reduced simply to a guardianship of moral issues.

But the adoptive parent must guard against misinterpreting the normal rebelliousness which is so essential to the proper fulfillment of adolescence. The preparation for adulthood requires wearing the cloak of independence. If your son or daughter reaches maturity with complete docility and no questioning of authority, you have failed somewhere. Don't misjudge the normal rebellion of your teenager as an indictment of yourself as a parent, and particularly not as a condemnation of yourself as an adoptive parent.

A familiarity with the facts of sexual relationships, with some understanding of the motivations and circumstances that influence them, is valuable for all teenagers. Sex education for the adopted child may need to be particularly comprehensive. Few adopted children escape the information, as they grow up, that many "unwanted" babies are illegitimate. The oversimplification that "bad" people are promiscuous and "good" people are continent leaves the adopted child in a moral stew. An understanding of the foibles and confused values of some human sexual behavior allows him to escape the stigma of "bad" parentage and at the same time enables him to set his own standards toward less self-hurtful behavior.

Adopted teenagers usually have an *intellectual* curiosity of small proportion concerning their biological parents; they have a strong *emotional* tie with their adopted parents. However, it is reported that an occasional older adolescent will insist, against the advice of his mother and father, upon searching for and knowing his real parents. This has never occurred in my personal experience, but if and when it does it may well signify an important emotional disturbance. Certainly an adopted child insisting upon such a demand should first have the advantage of professional counseling before undertaking the quest.

You see how little advice there is specifically for adopting parents. Most of the knowledge they need is exactly the same as that which all parents need.

The Handicapped Child

Parenthood itself is, by whatever yardstick, the most intricate job undertaken by man. Add to this the special demands for wisdom placed upon the parent of the handicapped child. How to guide him to the attainment of a normal personality which so often escapes the grasp even of a "normal" child?

What exactly does one mean by a "handicapped child"? There are so many different kinds of handicaps, we might start by sorting them into groups. One classification separates the problems into hereditary and acquired handicaps. Hereditary conditions are those which are transmitted through the genes of the ovum and sperm, and include some forms of deafness, diabetes, asthma, cystic fibrosis, rheumatic fever, bleeding, severe anemias, and mental retardation. All conditions that are not hereditary are therefore acquired.

Since the parent of the handicapped child is likely to be burdened with a sense of guilt, it is well to know that with rare exceptions hereditary abnormalities are carried by recessive genes. For this reason, both parents must have contributed a causative gene, and neither side of the parentage can bear the sole blame. Even in those cases where the condition is known to exist in one family and not in the other, the fact is that both sides had to have contributed equally. The apparent absence of the problem on one side of the family means only that it was hidden, but present in a carrier state.

Another grouping divides defects into congenital and non-congenital—that is, present at birth and developed after birth. Cerebral palsy, heart disease, missing or paralyzed limbs, deafness, mental deficiency, and other defects may be congenital or they may be developed during childhood.

A third classification of handicaps separates them into (1) physical, (2) intellectual, and (3) emotional.

1. Physical shortcomings may be clearly discernible to the observer. These may be purely cosmetic handicaps, such as portwine birthmarks or misshapen features, or they may be functionally crippling. such as a missing limb, a club foot, blindness, muscular dystrophy. Some are both cosmetically and functionally handicapping, such as cerebral palsy. The invisible physical deficiencies do not, of course, detract from one's appearance but may be very disabling. Included among these are deafness, heart disease, asthma, fibrocystic disease, sickle cell and Cooley's anemia, and diabetes.

2. Intellectual handicaps or mental retardation is always relative, but usually implies an IQ of under 75. On the other hand, an IQ of 100 in a family whose average intelligence is exceedingly high can be disabling if there is poor understanding and acceptance.

3. Emotional handicaps are rarely congenital, usually developed, and result from a destructive environment. They range in severity from totally disruptive true psychoses to minor personality distortions.

As with any such system of classification, there are mixtures of, and interactions among, these three groups. Physical and intellectual shortcomings often result in emotional problems. Emotional upsets may masquerade as intellectual retardation or deafness. Speech inadequacies may be partly physical, intellectual, and emotional. Invisible handicaps may beget discernible problems such as grossly altered behavior patterns.

4. To this standard classification I would add a fourth group—imaginary handicaps. I refer not to psychosomatic disabilities, which are properly classed as emotional, but to crippling nonexistent disorders. The typical instance is the child cardiac invalid; the child who is forced to lead a restricted life because of a meaningless murmur in a normal heart. Other cases involve fictional kidney disease, imagined endocrine disorders, nonexistent anemias, and so on.

I have set forth above a thumbnail sketch of the standard text on the handicaps of children. It is at once clear that these vary in degree of severity—a little hearing loss, total deafness; a missing finger, four extremities gone. It is also apparent that a particular handicap will burden one child very little while severely warping another. But instead of passing along to a standard explanation of and standard advice concerning children with handicaps, let me suggest to you a somewhat unstandard point of view. Perhaps parents of handicapped children and parents of normal children can learn by rebutting what I will have to say.

I may not know you, and I may not know your children, born or unborn. But I can tell you this for certain. You and your children are handicapped people. And each of you has not one but many handicaps.

Your family may, of course, have some of the few handicaps mentioned above. They don't? Okay, how about these:

A child who is exceptionally bright, say with an IQ over 150, has to overcome a handicap. If he is with his social and emotional peers, he must sidestep intellectual boredom or condescension. If with his mental equals, he will almost surely be regarded as a social baby.

If either of your child's parents is brilliant, he may be inadvertently crippled by the built-in intolerance of the genius parent for the lesser ability of the child's average mind.

Does your child have parents who quarrel and denounce each

other frequently in his presence? Or who have too many important things to do to have the time to let him know how much they love him? Here's a real handicap.

Do his parents live out their own shortcomings by urging him to greater and greater efforts toward unattainable goals?

Is his skin color proper? His religion correct? His education adequate? Handicaps of note.

Is he too tall, too short, too fat or thin?

Are those whom he must emulate lacking in sexual maturity, ethical values, social deportment, ambition, responsibility, morality?

Enlarge this partial list yourself and you will begin to see the obvious conclusion. There are not handicapped and non-handicapped children; all children are handicapped. Each has his own list of handicaps, and each has his own strong points.

What helpful understanding might you develop from such a concept?

First, I think the handicapped child should be raised from infancy with this outlook: The only thing remarkable about his disadvantage is that it is different from the handicaps of his peers, visible or invisible. Each boy and girl has his own list of impediments.

We all know of famous handicapped people—Einstein: poor student, reading disability; Churchill: stammerer, uneducable; Booker T. Washington: black son of a slave; Franklin Roosevelt: cripple; Napoleon: epileptic dwarf. But it is more effective to learn to see the handicaps—emotional, intellectual, physical, attitudinal, moral, and so on—of your own peers.

Second, it is helpful for parents (as well as teachers, siblings, and friends) of handicapped children to have this concept to orient themselves in the role they have to play. What *is* the parents' curriculum?

As with all children, the vitally important need of the handicapped child is self-confidence—an acceptable self-image. The attainment of this is the parents' responsibility—they who have almost sole control of the matter during the child's early years.

Love and acceptance are the starting point. Love for who the child *is,* not for what he *does*—nor for what he doesn't. Love because he's yours, not because of his handicap, not despite his handicap. I love you because you're lame, or I love you despite your lameness, is no way to court a woman or to be a parent to a child.

Thoughtful discipline is as essential to the handicapped child as to the so-called unhandicapped. How much do you teach a disabled child? As much as he can learn, as fast as he can learn it. Pity which masquerades as discipline is an unacceptable substitute. When parental compassion slips across the line to pity, list all of your child's handicaps and then look closely at his peers to see who among them have shorter lists. Get yourself off your own child's list of disadvantages.

Independence develops spontaneously in the handicapped child—if you don't in your contrition try to coerce it and don't in your self-conscious guilt smother it by overprotectiveness. Your job is to let him be hurt—a little at a time—through his efforts, and to prevent him from serious harm to himself or to his surroundings, people and things.

It is often difficult for any parent to permit activities which allow the child to develop and to mature, especially if they entail an element of threatened harm. To avoid overprotectiveness requires a deliberate effort. The problem magnifies itself in the presence of a handicap. Often, too, the physician and the educator, focused on the vulnerability rather than on the whole child, permit or extort too much protection. Generally physical risks are better to take than emotional risks. Few physical injuries cannot heal or be repaired. Rarely are emotional hurts short-lived or rescindable. Treat the handicapped child as different, and he will grow up different.

For example, all children with diabetes, seizures, missing extremities, deafness, asthma, and unilateral blindness should be permitted full participation in all sports and other extracurricular activities. They should not swim without careful observation, or be exposed to dangerous heights without protection. But then neither should any other child.

Children with heart disease, kidney disease, controlled hypertension, paralyzed limbs, cystic fibrosis, scoliosis, should be allowed full activity also, with the exception of highly competitive sports. Under normal conditions the child will rest from his exertions short of harm. In competitive team endeavors, he may persist beyond exhaustion out of loyalty or dedication.

Only activities which the doctor foresees as *likely* causes of permanent and serious damage should be denied the handicapped child. Not activities which might *conceivably* be injurious, and not those in which the child runs the risk of minor correctible injuries.

"Shall I concentrate on teaching him in areas in which his disability handicaps him, to show him that he can overcome? Or shall I steer him toward interests regulated to his disadvantages?" Neither. Or better, both, but with different goals.

The basic need, without which nothing can be well accomplished, is a normal personality. Helpful to attaining this is the child's observation that he can succeed. Now there's not much sense in steering him toward the taste of success by directing him toward areas in which he has the least chance of succeeding. As with any child, for the purpose of building self-confidence, the handicapped child should be encouraged to direct himself toward goals for which his talents and abilities most suit him. It would be absurd, in an effort to build confidence in a child, to encourage him to try first those tasks in which he is most likely to fail.

Just so with the handicapped. The success he needs to bolster his image should be sought in accomplishments which are least affected by his weakness. Limitations in mental functioning would suggest challenges in the physical fields. Physical impairment recommends tasks in the intellectual category.

One can and should confront, with the child, his handicaps. Mind you, *after* his self-confidence is blossoming. And in ways that will not reduce his confidence. Success achieved with difficulty of course encourages a child. But repeated failure in attempting to reach impossible goals is destructive. Challenges in difficult areas are warranted only upon the foundation of an already established satisfactory self-image.

"Today's failure becomes tomorrow's success" is a favorite

slogan to encourage parents of disadvantaged children to try, even in the face of a severe handicap. The statement becomes true when qualified by adding "if yesterday's attempts in other fields were encouragingly successful."

All help should be offered the child to minimize his handicap. Medical, educational, psychiatric, and physical-therapeutic resources should be utilized to their fullest availability. But until the child's confidence is strong, no element of competition or failure should be permitted to enter these efforts.

And remember this: effort and success are important to the personality; they are not essential. If, in your eagerness to help a child overcome his handicap, you convey to him that your acceptance hangs in the balance, you have purchased a small prize at an intolerable price.

If you do not have a child handicapped in the usual definition of the word, but can believe in the "aren't we all, in many ways" concept, you might extract many analogies applicable to helping your own child to adulthood. Handicaps, formal or informal, succumb to the same approach.

Relative family values have a way of coming unstuck sometimes when unfamiliar weights are thrown onto the scale. And the needs of a handicapped child can represent just such an unfamiliar unit of measure to a mother and father. Each additional child always represents a family's willingness to reapportion its resources for the sake of a new member to be loved. No family has endless resources, so each member, in a way, sacrifices his share in the amount necessary to meet the needs of the others. A handicapped child needs a little more of the family time, a little more of the family money. But how much more?

In the case of acute illness, the entire family effort may be diverted temporarily to the demands of the one in need. But a handicapped child may have extraordinary needs for years, and the rest of the family cannot serve as human sacrifices.

If the handicap is severe, it could easily utilize 100 percent of the mother's time and attention. To acquiesce in this might be a valid personal decision for the widow with one child. Otherwise, does the mother of a handicapped child have the right to sacrifice her husband's wife and her other children's mother to the needs of the deficient child?

If each living child has, as I suggest, a list of handicaps of his own, how much can you add to the lists of your other children before they exceed the burdens of the handicapped sibling?

What I am saying is that it can mature and ennoble members of a family to sacrifice for a handicapped member—but not to an unlimited degree. At some point the value to the less fortunate member is far less than the price exacted from the other members. The harm done to the sum of the members of the family outweighs the good done for the handicapped.

I make this obvious point in rebuttal to the unqualified propaganda of families of unlimited resources—money, plus time purchased through hired help—who urge, through the media, all parents to keep their handicapped at home, as though there were no relative values to be considered.

And as rebuttal to the unprincipled group who allow thousands of family hours to be devoted to one child without evaluating the cost to the other children in the family. To put it another way, how much future happiness could be bought for the unhandicapped children in the family if these same thousands of family hours were spent on their unlisted handicaps, were spent strengthening their personality weaknesses?

Don't write me letters. I don't know any absolute answers. But let me illuminate the opposite side of the coin so you can better judge for yourself.

Too many marriages have become mockeries, too many children have been emotionally bled to the point of being lifelong cripples because the family's total store of money, feelings, and time was poured into the needs of a handicapped member. Or because the defective one was kept at home when he needed placement outside the family.

Mothers and fathers are human, with human limits to their abilities and strength—though I don't hear many people say so. Their energies and talents are often strained by the demands of raising ordinary children. In the handling of a severely handicapped child, strain the reserves of the community, of the state, of the government—I can't imagine *them* cracking up. But don't ask the impossible of my mothers and fathers. I can't spare them.

Absentee Fathers

Much has been written in recent years about the harmful effects of the absentee father on the personality of the growing child. This is the father who is so busy with his work or so dedicated to his avocation that he spends little or no time at the job of helping to rear the children.

There is no doubt that handling children is a difficult and complex task, hard enough for two parents working in concert, almost impossible for a mother struggling alone. It is tempting to think that this is too well known a point to be worth belaboring. But week after week a practicing pediatrician meets educated, knowledgeable fathers who profess to honest ignorance that their child's problems may in part have arisen from their own failure to assume any responsibility in the guidance of their children. This being so, I wish to add my own voice to emphasizing that raising and educating children is a difficult two-person job, and no wife can reasonably be expected to deal with the situation without the full cooperation of her mate.

This is not meant to suggest that fathers need be companions to their young. Companionship and "buddyism" they don't need. But love, acceptance, discipline, guidance, and the furtherance of their independence they do need.

It is most practical for the parents to have a weekly or monthly meeting of the minds so that each may know whether he or she is acting in accordance with the wishes of the other and so that problems and differences of opinion can be discussed and reconciled. It is far better for the child for parents to act in accord, even though perhaps both are wrong, than it is for each parent to be right but to handle the children in contradictory manners.

In my opinion, the actual physical presence of the father is not nearly so necessary as the presence of his strength and his backing of the mother. A father whose business requires that he travel, or that he work such long hours as to preclude his spending much time with the family, can nevertheless make it quite clear to the children that his wife speaks with the voice of two. When the necessity of business requires it, I think this works out relatively well. On the other hand, when the father has free time and obviously prefers to devote it exclusively to pursuits not involving the family, I think the average child quickly sees through the ruse and decides that the father is completely uninterested in his world.

To a large extent it is more the quality of the time the father is able to devote to his children than it is the quantity. Nonetheless, there are scores of things which the mother, regardless of how much backing she receives from the father, cannot, with rare exceptions, teach either the daughter or the son. The father with limited time must accept the responsibility of seeing that these lessons are accomplished.

Speaking entirely from the point of view of the welfare of the children, I would say that the prime demand upon the limited time of the absentee father is the need for him to spend time with his wife in the presence of his children. As discussed elsewhere, the meaningful education of the children in matters of physical love between the sexes begins at an early age, probably before the age of two. The attitudes and moral values developed by the boy and the girl toward heterosexual love are based to a major extent upon the relationship they have observed during childhood between their mother and father. The greatest loss for the children of absentee fathers may well be their failure to have observed over their formative years the consideration of the one parent for the other, the glance of admiration between them, the wholesomeness of physical contact, the respect and support shown by one to the other. These form the firm foundation for normal sexual love which the child will need to have learned by growing up in their presence.

Most of the other lessons that are peculiarly the responsibility of the father to teach may satisfactorily be delegated to other males. But it is the obligation of the absentee father to see that a suitable substitute is provided. For instance, it is of some importance that boys and girls be taught certain physical skills.

Not so that they will become "well-rounded people," for the Lord knows we probably have too many well-rounded people in the world today already. But rather so that they will acquire the necessary skills to provide them with some enjoyment of leisure time and so that they will avoid the derogatory jibes of their peers. I have in mind the ability to have a game of catch, to roller-skate or to ice-skate, to turn somersaults, to work with elementary gymnastic equipment, to swim, or to bowl.

The self-confidence of children is protected and nurtured by the acquisition of one or more physical skills around the same time as, or preferably a few months earlier than, their peers.

The absentee father who properly feels the chagrin of not having the opportunity to provide his offspring with these skills will find it simple to procure a father substitute from among the other males in the community. There are scores of ex-college athletes as well as talented and empathic teenagers who have a fondness for children and who, at a modest price, can teach the child the necessary abilities.

Similarly in the field of academics. If the absentee father cannot guide his children in their formal education, he can at least provide appropriate tutorial services when they are needed. This is not to suggest that all academic and athletic tutors are suitable teachers. You must choose those who are capable of encouraging a child to an enjoyment and knowledge of the subject.

The most surely destructive of all absentee fathers is the one who places upon his wife the sole task and responsibility of guiding and managing the children and who then berates and derides her for her mistakes and for the ultimate shortcomings of the children. This may indeed be the most assured path to the destruction of the wife, the children, the family, and the marriage.

Divorce

To a young child his parents are his fortress, his defense against the awesomeness of the outside world, and infinitely his most valuable possession. The merest hint of losing either parent inflicts paralyzing anxiety upon a child. Separation or divorce is a fearsome burden for a child to be exposed to. On the other hand, a divorce is less destructive to the personality of the child than is the continuance of a bickering, hateful marriage.

The intense anguish of the child who lives in a home steeped in marital hatred and distrust is visible to all. Visible to all except the parents, preoccupied with their own problems. It is not enough that he exists with the continual fear of losing a parent. In addition, he must bear the feeling of guilt that he, somehow, is the cause of the strife. He must try to behave in whatever artificial manner he imagines will appease both parents. He must suffer the efforts of each parent, deliberate or unconscious, to alienate him from the other. He must tolerate the loss of attention from each parent, whose own emotions are too focused upon preserving his own image to have time to consider the child's.

All of these pressures upon a child are well-nigh unbearable. He much more easily could adjust to the death of a parent.

The legally acceptable substitute solution is divorce—the death of the marriage. Divorce, properly managed, is far less harmful to the child than is the continuance of a bad marriage.

"We would have left each other long ago, except for the children." Find a better excuse for your cowardice if the failure of the marriage is being daily made obvious to the children.

On behalf of children, it must be clearly stated here that no two completely normal people ever get divorced! For the proper ingredients of a divorce to be present, at least one of the marriage partners must be emotionally abnormal! Indeed, since people with personality defects of handicapping proportions tend to be attracted to one another for reasons of mutual security, it is frequently true that both members of a dissolving marriage nurse emotional deficiencies. For these reasons, second marriages by divorced partners carry higher actuarial risks.

If couples contemplating divorce would recognize this fact, even if each were to insist that it must be the other who was abnormal, and if both would agree to accept competent professional psychiatric and counseling help for a year or two, many divorces could be happily postponed. At worst, with proper counseling the terms of the divorce could be made least destructive to the child.

It never ceases to appall me that so many books and so many organizations devote so much time to counseling and instructing parents on how best to deal with their children *after* they, the parents, have been divorced. The assumption is clearly that these advices are given to emotionally normal, thoughtful, self-sacrificing adults. And, beyond understanding, it is assumed that this good advice is received and acted upon in good faith. What in God's name brings sudden thoughtfulness to an adult upon the awarding of a decree? If a fraction of this advice could be given, and could be accepted by the partners of a failing marriage, before the court's decision, how many of these marriages could be satisfactorily repaired?

When divorce or separation does occur in the presence of adolescent or younger children, there should be generally no visiting privileges awarded to the spouse not having custody of the children! With no exceptions that I have witnessed, visiting privileges with the parent not immediately responsible for the guidance of the child result in nothing but confusion and anxiety —sometimes less, sometimes more, but always present!

This is even so in the not rare instance when the custody of the children is awarded to the less competent, less normal parent. This opinion would generally impose a penalty upon the father, for men are seldom given their children even when they are glaringly the more competent of the two parents. Nonetheless, until divorce courts become more humane, I would prefer that children living with an inadequate divorcée be spared the rack of visiting a superior father.

In the best of all possible worlds, this would be horrible advice. That's not where we live. Let me give you contrasting examples of "enlightened" and "unenlightened" divorcing parents.

First we have Mr. and Mrs. Jones. Six years ago, after a year of courtship, during which they came to find each other indispensable, they were married. By mutual agreement they conceived their first child, John, now four years of age.

Both Mr. and Mrs. Jones were reasonably whole adults emotionally, and each adjusted at first to the new responsibilities of parenthood, without diluting their love for each other. Recently, however, they have discovered their marriage to be unsatisfactory. There are religious conflicts. Or there is a disagreement about financial goals, or about in-laws who must be supported, or about the location of the home or its upkeep, or about young John's upbringing. In any event, Mr. and Mrs. Jones have decided to seek greener fields apart.

But they are mature, responsible adults. So they have been careful to keep their disagreements out of their relationships with John. They are sophisticatedly agreed that their innocent child should not pay for the death of their own love. They have continued to share the same bedroom in order not to upset John. Heated discussions, if any, have been carefully guarded from his ears. Each has attended to his role of parent as though he had no personal emotional dilemma.

The divorce is consummated in a civilized manner, without any wrangling in court. John is "awarded" to his mother because of his youthfulness. But Father is allowed to have his son, who needs a male image of course, every weekend and one month of the summer.

Mrs. Jones speaks to John each day concerning how fine a man he has for a father.

Over the years Mr. Jones unfailingly shows up on time for visitations and devotes himself to guiding his son toward a happy manhood. He speaks of John's mother as a kind, devoted mother, of whom John may well be proud. He never dreams of buying John presents which make Mother's gifts seem insignificant.

Ultimately Mr. Jones remarries. But he never neglects his visiting privileges with John. And his new wife is mature and unjealous; she eagerly accepts John as a young boy whose first love is properly directed toward his mother. The new wife is warm and uncritical of John and of John's mother.

Now we have the second example, the failing marriage of Mr. and Mrs. Smith. There are a thousand variations to this example. In life, the roles of Mr. and Mrs. may be reversed, and only some of the conditions will be present in one given family, but the pattern remains.

Mrs. Smith had been first attracted to her husband by his personality and his looks. He was attentive, thoughtful, and gay. Their courtship was romantic and brief. True, he was a little careless about his expenses. And he was very devoted to his mother, to whom he always looked for guidance in making important decisions. His religious background was different from hers, but his religious dogmata never governed his actions. And she, Mrs. Smith, was certain she could help him to learn to make mature, independent decisions after they were married.

The honeymoon had not quite survived the first year. For some reason Mr. Smith couldn't seem to follow the logic of Mrs. Smith's patient explanations of the role of responsible husband—and her efforts almost began to sound like nagging.

So Jimmy was conceived. His coming would please Mr. Smith, who spoke boastfully of his son-to-be, and fatherhood would quickly bring him to responsibleness and would smooth the waves of the marriage.

But somehow Jimmy never quite measured up to his father's expectations of a son. Mr. Smith beamed and lavishly rewarded Jimmy's successes, and sulked over his failures. He continually set goals a little higher, a little higher to "encourage" Jimmy to strive. Mrs. Smith, to "support" Jimmy and to "help" him please his father, constantly reminded Jimmy that he was a gifted child and that he could do as his father desired if he would only try a little harder.

Meanwhile Jimmy listened nightly in silent terror to the voices that warned him by their tones that he was on the brink of losing one or the other parent.

Mrs. Smith thoughtfully left her husband's bedroom to sleep in a room with Jimmy so that her son would be spared the sound of as many arguments as possible. This arrangement heaped guilt upon Jimmy's anxiety.

The divorce arrangements were humane, because Mrs. Smith was dedicated to sparing Jimmy's feelings. The judge was even urged to ask Jimmy which parent he chose to live with. And Jimmy would never, never forget the necessity of patricide.

The visiting arrangements were fair and equitable. For the first four months Mr. Smith almost always arrived on time, and only occasionally forgot to come altogether. Somehow Jimmy never quite got used to the torture of "will he show up or won't he?"

The game of punishing Mrs. Smith through Jimmy was enough to jog Mr. Smith's memory at first. It was only fair that Jimmy see all the facts in their true light. How his mother was really selfish. How she pretended love for Jimmy to serve her own ends. How she had forced her own husband out of his home. How she was even now running after other men. And many, many facts that Jimmy had a right to know.

Mrs. Smith, on her part, was aware of Jimmy's growing confusion. But she was emotionally mature and she knew that she had to help Jimmy retain a good image of his father. So she soothed Jimmy and extolled his father, and she told him what a fine father he had, who loved him very dearly.

And she helped Jimmy to admire his paternal grandmother, to whose home his daddy had returned. And Grandma helped Jimmy by frankly revealing to him his mother's shortcomings.

So Jimmy grew up with a fine father image, in constant, terrifying dread. He knew his "good" father had left home. What in heaven's name then could dissuade his "bad" mother from leaving home too.

And when his father reopened the application for custody, Jimmy was again allowed, in the name of kindness, to choose his guardian. And now, "wiser" for knowing the facts, he chose his "good" parent.

Play your own variations of this theme. No matter who performs the parts, the final chord comes out the same.

You see, my years of experience are all filled with bias. All the Mr. and Mrs. Smiths show up at my office. All the Mr. and Mrs. Joneses go to the experts who write the books which give counsel on divorce.

Whenever Mr. and Mrs. Jones show up in my practice, with their mature emotions, and their love for their child, and their considerateness, they turn out not to be contemplating a divorce in the first place. With their emotional maturity they are either already making a success of marriage and parenthood, having adjusted without help to each other's weaknesses, or they are seeking help to resolve their differences with no thought to the surrender of divorce.

My experience forces me to say that the children of my knowledge would always have been better off emotionally if there had been a sharp break, as with death, instead of the duress of visitation privileges.

And I would advise mothers and fathers that it is not the duty of the parent in charge to defend or to praise the absent parent. The child is frightened and worried by the demonstrated fact that a parent is perfectly capable of walking out of a child's life. This is an absolute form of rejection which the child's personality can scarcely survive. It is all too clear to the child that if one parent can desert, then so, logically, can the other! This over-hanging fear that his one remaining anchor may also be cut loose is the major concern that will continue to plague the child of divorce.

The only defense against this anxiety that can be provided by the remaining mate is the frank admission that the absent parent was different, strange, atypical, sick, and not in any way representative of parents in general.

The deserting parent may have been a "good guy," or a "nice person," or "fun to be around," a man with certain or many admirable qualities and traits. But with it all he must have been not normal, not well, and above all not a parent. It is too much for a child to have to consider, "One of my good parents left me. My other good parent is still with me. But what is there to assure me that what one good parent has already done the other good parent won't feel free to do tomorrow or next week?"

Please don't tell me about all the authoritative books by experts on divorce with whom my advice disagrees. I tell you very briefly my own experience with children of divorce. If you would read further, I commend to you *Children of Divorce,* by Dr. J. Louise Despert. The author would not fully agree with my viewpoint. But among the dozens of volumes available, her contemplation of children of divorce is worth your while if you face such a problem.

7

Education

The effects of a child's school experiences upon his personality orientation are important and direct. His relationships with teachers and with his peer group, his acadamic achievements and failures, all influence his self-concept and his attitudes.

More important, however, is the interplay between child and parent which arises from and is focused upon his attainments in the various aspects of school activities. Schools often serve the incidental role of fulcrum for the leverage exerted, whether for good or for ill, by the parents upon their offspring. This chapter considers some of the bases of both misunderstanding and support that education stimulates in the parents' relationship to the student.

Nursery Schools

Nursery schools of all sorts are playing an increasingly prominent role in the education and personality development of American children. Yet often the pros and cons of sending a child to nursery school are not fully enough considered by the parents before they makc a decision.

To send or not to send is commonly resolved solely upon the grounds that the child "needs companionship," that he needs to be with other children his age in order to learn to get along with his peers. This concept is almost pure tommyrot, and has little or nothing to do with whether nursery-school attendance will be desirable or undesirable for a particular child. It is clear that companionship with his peers is *not* one of the essentials for the normal development of the three- or four-year-old's personality. A properly oriented child will have plenty of time to learn to be socially adaptable during his kindergarten year, and will have little difficulty in so adjusting, even though he might never have seen another child before.

There are two major disadvantages in deciding to send a youngster to nursery school. First of these, and of no small consequence, is the cost. For most children the advantages of nursery school are not important enough to warrant unbalancing the family budget.

The second major disadvantage is the absolute certainty that the child attending nursery school will have far more illnesses than if he were to stay at home. In many instances the nursery-school child will contract a new illness on the average of every two weeks. The notion that this frequency of disease is no greater than would be experienced in any case when the child enters kindergarten is fallacious. In the first place, with each year of age the child is better able to cope with an illness and suffers less serious consequences from it. Furthermore, the exposure rate to sickness is far higher in the average nursery-school class than in the average kindergarten class.

There is one supreme advantage to attending nursery school. Few, if any, normal adult mothers are capable of entertaining day after day a four-year-old child, even their own. And still fewer normal adults, mothers or otherwise, can survive the constant companionship of a four-year-old. Imprisonment with a child of this age will eventually drive the sturdiest mother to distraction, if not worse. And if she is a normal human being, she will sooner or later react like a normal adult, to the detriment of her mother role with the child. The man who raises and trains alligators needs occasionally to get away from alligators. The mother who is involved in raising and training four-year-olds needs occasionally to get away from four-year-olds. This is the big advantage of nursery schools, to preserve the sanity of the mother.

Considering just the two disadvantages and the one advantage mentioned above, it is obvious that there is a better solution than nursery school. Companionship with one or two or three other children of a like age in the neighborhood affords the same advantage with neither of the disadvantages. Sometimes, however, there is a scarcity of qualified companions. Not a day passes in the life of a pediatrician without his hearing at least once, "But there aren't any children his age in the neighborhood!" All over this country there are countless thousands of mothers sitting at home with their preschool children, each certain in her mind that she is the only one in such a fix. Visit the nearest playground, walk three blocks in each direction from your home, inquire of church groups or P.T.A. gatherings, and you will uncover another suffering mother as eager to find your four-year-old as you are to discover hers.

How about the child who needs nursery school to learn independence? Or who needs to learn social maturity (that is, to learn to obey and to respect the rights of others)? Or the child who needs to feel that he is a worthwhile person, appreciated and loved? In short, what about the child whose personality traits are off to a bad start? To the degree that the teachers in the nursery school are capable of responding to the needs of the child better than are the parents, nursery school may provide one source of help. This is a legitimate therapeutic use of a good nursery school, and it is receiving increasing attention as a means of helping disadvantaged families.

However, if the nursery school chosen is less capable of understanding and of meeting the needs of the child than the parents are, it follows that attendance will be disadvantageous for the child. And the extreme variations that exist among nursery schools suggest that the schoool should be selected with great care. For the overly pressured youngster, the rigidly organized school will be of little value. For the child unmindful of the meaning of authority, the unstructured school will offer little.

For those mothers who need to work, either for financial reasons or for reasons of personal emotional idiosyncrasy, nursery schools may be a necessary evil unless someone can be found to serve as a governess. Fortunately, children survive necessary evils, though not always without cost. And the family may properly decide that the loss to the child of attending school is less than the loss to the family from his remaining at home.

Beginning Formal Education

Somehow or other the subjects taught a child in school make up the "formal" education of the child, while all the far more important subjects taught at home are called his "informal" education. It would be interesting sometime to investigate the rationale behind this terminology.

Many parents agonize over the question of when to begin their child's "education." "When shall I start to teach Dorinda to read or to write or to figure?" Certain preliminary truths are obvious. (1) Nobody really knows. (2) It doesn't matter so much when you start as how you start. (3) The rate at which you proceed for the following twenty years is more important than when you start. (4) The answer is different for each individual child. With these reservations in mind, let us work toward an approximate answer.

In the first place, a child at any particular age can be expected to learn only just so many things at one time. And there really isn't enough time in a lifetime to learn all the things one *ought* to know. When the child is two, is there enough time in his day to bother about teaching him reading or writing or arithmetic? Or are there infinitely more important things with which he had better be occupying his mind and time? For instance, should he be learning not to climb on the furniture with his muddy shoes, how to get along amicably with the two-year-old babe across the street, how to drink his milk without getting more than half of it in his lap, and so on? At age three or four or five, has he learned enough of the other important things in life so that he can hope to fit fairly well into society, and so that we have enough spare time to devote to the three R's? The answer is yours, because it involves relative values which only you can assess. But I cannot refrain from biasing your answer by noting that I have known remarkably few parents who were able to indoctrinate their children with even half the important things they needed to know by their fifth birthday, without squandering time on arithmetic or composition or reading. Remember that you have sixteen to twenty years to mold this masterpiece; take first things first, and spread the work evenly over the full sequence of years.

We know that a child of three can learn to play a simple piece on the piano with, say, ten hours of instruction and practice. The same child at age six would achieve the same proficiency with perhaps four hours of effort. At age nine he would require perhaps one hour. And at twelve years of age he could acquire the same skill in fifteen minutes. The point is, the older a child, the more intellectually developed and muscularly coordinated, the more rapidly he is able to learn a given set of facts or master a given task. How much more would a young adult of twenty know regarding the subjects of formal education if his attention to these subjects were to be started at three years of age as compared to, say, six years of age? You don't know, and I certainly don't know. However, it seems highly likely that he might know only a very small fraction more by having had the earlier start.

Whether we agree with it or not, it is a matter of practical fact that our public-school system, and that of most private schools, currently operates on the assumption that a child's formal education is best begun at age five or six. For our present purpose, we need not argue the validity of this assumption. The fact is, this is the available system. How much profit is there in having Herkimer know the first-grade equivalent of a subject before he gets to first grade? It depends.

It depends upon whether the first- and second-grade teachers are going to be masterful enough to let him move along at his own rate, or whether they have twenty-five other little charges to occupy their time and are going to let Herkimer be bored to tears, so that his initial reaction to school is: "I hate it."

It depends also upon whether Herkimer is going to be in class with children much smarter or with children much duller than he is. If Herk is pretty dull, it's probably just as well he got a little head start. If he's pretty bright, his head start may only help him to realize that he can get along with very little effort on his part, and he will therefore develop poor study habits earlier than do most children.

It depends also upon whether the people who taught him his subject before he reached school were knowledgeable enough to have used roughly the same method that he will follow in school, or whether he's going to be totally confused to discover that there's more than one way to approach the subject of reading (or writing or arithmetic).

All of us, I am sure, would agree that Josephine should be allowed to learn to read at age three or four only if she showed herself to be interested in, and happy at, the task. Scarcely any parent would be foolish enough to pull Josephine by the ear and sit her down crying before a book in order to "stimulate her interest" in reading. But how do you know that what you are observing is really *Josephine's* interest in learning to read? Josephine is no fool. It takes her four seconds to discern what pleases her parents. And she already knows that by pleasing her parents she feathers her own nest. So perhaps little Josephine is one step ahead of us. "But she just loves to read." How do you know? "She goes and gets the book herself. She makes me sit down and teach her to read!" Well, it's still not clear to me what motivates Josephine. Is she really interested in reading? Or is she buying her mother's praise? And if the latter, at what age will she say, "Oh, the heck with this pretense. It's not worth the effort. Guess I'll give up reading."

At what age, then, should formal education be started? I'm not sure anybody knows. But I do know which side I would prefer, for safety's sake, to err on. I would wait until the system I had chosen to furnish my child's formal education thought the time to start was ripe; rather this than to risk starting too early. At least the cog would fit into the machine more smoothly.

It is interesting to consider whether a child who shifts into high gear early in the formal educational process is generally able to maintain the pace through high school or college or post-graduate school without inevitably letting down. Certainly there is always the possibility that if the effort put by the child into learning is the least bit excessive over the years, the point is apt to come, before the end of the race, when the whole wonderful machine may stop to reconsider what it is getting out of life— and at what price—and may decide that it just isn't worth it.

It would seem to me rather a safer policy, if the machine is going to change speeds along the way, to have it shift into high gear at junior-high or high-school level. If you yourself had missed third grade altogether—that is, had stayed home from school during that particular year—how much less prepared to face life successfully would you be now? With due apologies to all third-grade teachers.

What about the other side of the coin? Suppose Junior has finished kindergarten, and you or the teacher suspect that he is rather a "late bloomer" and may not be quite socially mature or emotionally mature or intellectually mature enough to find first grade his cup of tea? Would it be better for him to repeat kinder-garten, or better for him to try first grade regardless? This, obvi-ously, is an individual question that cannot be answered except with knowledge of the particular child involved. The answer must be arrived at by a meeting of the minds of the teacher, the parents, and perhaps the principal or school psychologist. In cases of real doubt, the added aid of an outside expert might be sought.

The point I wish to make is that if there are any grounds for suspicion that Junior may not be ready for first grade, please be convinced of the infinite wisdom, and of the tremendous ultimate rewards, of giving him an extra year to develop his skills so that he may profit from his next sixteen years of education, rather than insist that he drag himself through year after year of agony, never quite understanding why the others in the class are doing better than he is. It is no disgrace, but rather a tremendous advantage, to be a year or two more mature in your attitudes and judgment than are your colleagues by the time you reach college or postgraduate school. Every shred of evidence from our experience with postwar G.I. students cries out in testimony to this fact.

How about the private schools that start children at whatever age they seem ready and let them progress at their own rate? Surely for the slow child they are magnificent. They permit him to learn as fast as he can while preserving his dignity and self-esteem. For the bright child, the advantage is not so definite. It seems to me a mistake to contemplate starting a child in a system such as the Montessori schools if you have any intention of attempting to transfer him to a standard public-school system halfway through. If you are committed to following through with this method of education, and if the high school is geared to accept the child whose formal education may be at a different level from that of his classmates, then, given these circumstances, I doubt whether anyone really knows whether this system produces in the end a better or a worse citizen, having started with above-average raw material.

Since this method, though admittedly in an imperfect way, was formerly mimicked in part by public schools which "skipped" bright students, we do have knowledge of some horrible examples of socially distraught pre-teenagers completing high school. Perhaps not representative, they nonetheless had acquired considerable knowledge at the cost of peer isolation and without possessing judgment or emotional maturity.

The Roles of Parents in Schooling

Since school is a major arena for the development of a child's personality, the parent should learn as much as possible about the local educational system in order to understand its formative impact upon his child.

The schools in the United States are as varied in their abilities and concepts as are the citizens of the country. The policies of each school, public or private, are to a major extent determined locally by the virtually autonomous boards of education, super-intendents of schools, and (in the case of private schools) school directors. Only a minor degree of uniformity is imposed by the states in the form of minimal academic and curricular require-ments. Because of the resulting tremendous variation among schools, no comprehensive conclusions concerning your child's school could be completely valid in any general discussion. The conscientious parent, concerned with his own child, will find it advantageous to know as much as he can about his own school system.

Information concerning individual schools is available from a wide variety of sources. Visits to the school, consultations with teachers, counselors, school psychologists, and principals, and visits with your child's general practitioner or pediatrician will all provide information concerning the local school situation. It is well to keep in mind, too, that every university in the country is ready, willing, and able, for a fee, to supply information on and to help you evaluate the local elementary school, junior high school, high school, and the special schools available in your neighborhood.

To what extent is it the responsibility of the parent to check up on and to concern himself with the formal educational process of his child? Should the parent help in (interfere with) the classroom experiences of his own child? These are moot and sometimes emotionally charged questions, the answers to which depend upon the individual parents.

Educators in general are, understandably, quietly or vocally fed up to the gills with "interfering" parents who trespass upon the professional functioning of the teacher. The educationally amateur parent who knows better than the professional teacher how Esther should be taught, and the overzealous, overcompeti-tive parent who would have the school push and pressure Albert beyond his abilities and into an emotional frenzy, are the bane of the educator. The resultant reaction has tended to be: "You do your job as a parent at home, and I, the teacher, without your interference, will do my job here in school."

The other side of the coin has its proponents. Are there parents who are capable and parents who are inadequate, while there are only superior teachers? Of course not. Just as there are good and bad plumbers, so there are good and bad parents, and good and bad teachers. In fact, a realistic definition of a *very* superior school would be one in which less than half the teachers were below the level of mediocrity.

If in the field of teaching (discipline) it is possible for a child to have too much or too little, then in the case of a school child we might reason thus: He is being exposed to pressures from two sources, home and school. It is the sum of these pressures upon him which must, at any given time, be considered too great or too little. If the classroom teacher of the moment is strict, demanding, and perfectionistic, the pressures at home, in compensation, must be kept to a minimum. If the teacher is casual, undemanding, and notably permissive, then it might be desirable that the pressures and demands at home be increased in compensation. Who but the parent, cognizant of his child's progress in school, can be responsible for these individual adjustments?

If the parent is a poor parent to start with and the school is a good school, it is not possible for the school to undo the errors of the parent in the few hours of the day it has control of the child. If the parent is a good parent and the school is a poor school, it is the responsibility and the right of the parent to oversee and to enhance the education of the child. If the parent is a good parent and the school is a good school, they will work together, each sharing and using the knowledge of the other to complement the child's total learning experience.

Schools are populated by people dedicated to children. The good school needs, and welcomes, the knowledge of the parent in deciding which teacher is best for which child, and which manner and plan of teaching is best suited for which pupil.

The good school needs and deserves the support of the parents at home. Just as the young child who observes early in life the ineffectiveness of the authority of his parents, and thereafter learns little from the parents, so the school child who hears at home the ability and integrity of his teacher discussed in derogatory terms is handicapped from the start and learns little from that teacher.

In the final analysis, it would seem clear that the prime responsibility for the child's education rests squarely upon the parent and cannot be delegated to the school. With your interest and cooperation most schools can do an excellent job. If, despite your cooperation, the school seems to be failing your child, outside professional advice should be sought from the child's physician or pediatrician or from the local university.

Evaluating the Child's Academic Progress

In general, we—that is, we the parents and we the teachers—estimate Johnny's ability by an overall observation and assessment of him and then judge his progress in school by noting whether he does as well as we have led ourselves to expect he will. But there are also rather more exact methods of measuring both his ability and his achievement.

The famous and infamous, much maligned and much misunderstood IQ test is worth some understanding. There are now many different tests used to measure what is called "the IQ." Some of these tests are administered to children in groups and some are administered individually.

What exactly does the IQ, or Intelligence Quotient, measure? Theoretically it evaluates your child's native or inborn intelligence. But we have long since given up the thought that this is exactly so. From a technical point of view, it does measure how many correct answers your child was able to give to a set of questions on a test as compared with how many correct answers to the same questions hundreds and thousands of other children (sometimes of all ages, sometimes of the same age) all over the country were able to give. In fact, what it actually estimates rather accurately, and the *only* thing it measures, is how your child *should* be able to do academically in our American educational system. It appraises, and therefore predicts, how well your child *should* be able to learn in *our* school system. Indeed, a more accurate name for these tests would be "academic aptitude tests."

If the IQ suggests that Robbie will be able to learn in school at an average or above-average rate, and Robbie falls far below average in his learning, then one should be alerted to look for the causes of the discrepancy.

IQ scores obtained by group tests are significantly more affected by a student's reading ability than are individualized IQ test scores. That is, group testing gives a much heavier weight to reading ability than does individual testing. A child who is an unusually good reader may score as much as 15 points higher, or a poor reader as much as 10 points lower, than children of otherwise comparable "intelligence."

Is the IQ score accurate and reproducible? Yes, it is accurate and will reproduce within a few points—if the child was physically well and was not tired when he took the test, if he was not emotionally upset, if the test was properly administered, if the test was properly scored, and if the child was properly motivated. The scores of tests administered individually (Stanford-Binet and Wechsler) are more reliably reproducible than are scores of tests administered to groups.

If on a single individually administered test your child scores an IQ of say 110, you could reasonably conclude that his true IQ is probably between 105 and 115, is very probably between 100 and 120, and is almost certainly between 95 and 125.

Actually to test a child's native intelligence, it would be necessary to administer the test shortly after birth. This of course is impossible. What the IQ test generally succeeds in indicating is inborn ability in certain skills which are necessary for success in our educational system, as these skills have been influenced and strengthened or weakened by the child's experiences up to the point of taking the test. Therefore, the score is affected by the social and cultural background of the child.

What does the IQ not indicate? It does not evaluate, or even comment upon, any of the other important attributes of the child. It does not measure or predict his worthwhileness as a child or as an adult. It does not assess his talents or his artistic gifts. It does not indicate his ability to contribute to or to detract from the progress of the world. It does not consider his personality, or his sense of values, or his motivations or his future abilities as a wife or a husband, as a mother or a father. It does not foretell his out-of-school achievements. It does not weigh his "common sense." You do not choose your mate or your friends or your employees upon the basis of their IQ's. Babe Ruth's IQ, Churchill's IQ, Raphael's IQ are of no particular interest to us.

Nevertheless, a reliably administered intelligence test is not meaningless, and is of considerable value in helping to decide whether a child's progress in school is measuring up to his predictable ability. Virtually all school systems, at least during the elementary grades, administer one or more intelligence tests to each pupil to help guide the teachers. It is my firm conviction that all parents should be informed of the results of these tests. Indeed, I believe that parents should ask for the results of these tests. But only after they have fully understood what the results mean and what they do not mean. Not so that they can judge their children as worthwhile or worthless, for this has nothing to do with IQ. But rather so that they can intelligently help to decide whether their children are learning at a rate commensurate with their ability.

Because the IQ does approximate the potential ability of the child to succeed in our educational system, and because some vocations require many successful years of schooling, the IQ can help us to establish realistic occupational goals for any given child. Roughly speaking, an IQ of 110 or 115 is helpful to survive the rigors of college; perhaps 120 or 130 is necessary for the more exacting colleges. Roughly 120 to 130 is needed for postgraduate studies. Therefore, a child with a dependably determined IQ of, say, 90 to 100 would be ill advised to set his sights on the study of law, for example. On the other hand, a gifted child with an IQ of 150 is not necessarily going to succeed in college, for success, educational or otherwise, depends upon many other facts, including motivation and emotional stability.

An IQ score may sometimes indicate that a child should not be in a particular elementary school—if his score, for example, is far out of line with those of most of the other children in the school. A differently oriented school might predictably offer him more comfortable educational facilities.

There are other important tests besides the IQ which help us to judge whether a child is succeeding in school according to his ability. These, called achievement tests, measure not the child's potential to learn, but what he has actually learned in any given subject up to the moment of the testing. Achievement tests are given in many school systems approximately every two years right through high school. They are subject to the same errors as the IQ tests. In order for them to be valid, the child must be physically well and emotionally undisturbed, and the tests must be properly administered and properly graded. Within these limitations, they are of considerable help, when compared with the IQ, in concluding how well the child is profiting from his educational experiences. Like the intelligence tests, the marks are expressed in terms of comparison with children all over the United States or with children within a group of private schools or with children in a particular school or school system. It follows, then, that if your child has an average IQ and is being educated in an average school, he should, if all is well, obtain an average mark (50th percentile) on his achievement tests.

If his IQ is in the 90th to 99th percentile (upper 10 per cent) and his school is an average school, his achievement scores should also be about the 90th to 99th percentiles. If his IQ is at the 60th percentile (40 percent from the top) and he is in a truly superior school system, his achievement tests should be above the 60th percentile. If his IQ is at the 30th percentile (70 per cent from the top), and his school is an inferior school, his achievement tests might well be below the 30th percentile.

These figures must always be taken with a grain of salt, for they are not mathematically precise. The child, for instance, may have had a bad headache when he took a certain achievement test, and this would have adversely affected his score. Nevertheless, parents should be aware of the results of their children's achievement tests and should be satisfied that they are reasonably in line with the child's predicted potential, for if they are not, the parents should look about for an explanation.

Consecutive achievement scores for a particular student in a given subject over the years should remain within the same range. For example, if a child scores 60, 55, and 62 two years apart in reading and on the next achievement test scores a 20, it is a good sign that something must be amiss. Similarly, a disparity of scores in different subjects—such as marks of 75 in math, 82 in grammar, and 30 in reading comprehension—is suggestive of trouble.

Conversion tables are available for comparing various IQ scores with achievement-test scores. For instance, with the revised Stanford-Binet Individual Intelligence Test (one of the more widely used in this country), an IQ of 140 or over is comparable to the 99th percentile on an achievement test, 130–139 to the 97th percentile, 120–129 to the 91st percentile, 110–119 to the 78th percentile, 100–109 to the 58th percentile, 90–99 to the 34th percentile, 80–89 to the 16th percentile, 70–79 to the 7th percentile, 60–69 to the 4th percentile, and below 60 to the 1st percentile.

Apparently on the theory that the average parent is unable to comprehend numbers and percentiles, IQ's are often reported in "more understandable" but infinitely less meaningful and less useful terms. One such system of reporting translates the IQ as follows: "very superior" (140–169), "superior" (120–139), "high average" (110–119), "average" (90–109), "low average" (80–89), "borderline defective" (70–79).

As I have mentioned, periodically administered achievement tests may warn of a developing educational problem if the student's percentile score falls significantly from one test to the next. Obviously this is at best a warning, and another test should be given to check the validity before any remedial action is taken. The built-in errors of virtually all of these tests result in too low a score; very, very rarely are the scores too high.

A deteriorating series of IQ scores always is suggestive of a worsening emotional problem if physical illness is excluded.

Helping with School Work at Home

Ah, here's a ticklish barrel of eels! Should the parents help Junior with his homework? The wrath of the P.T.A.'s notwithstanding, in my opinion the answer is a resounding "Yes!" That is, they should if they are qualified to do so.

It is the right and privilege and joy of any parent who feels so inclined to pass on to his children all the skill and knowledge which he himself has acquired through years of trial and error. One of the many better ways to express tangibly to your child your acceptance and love is by *properly* helping with homework. Unfortunately, one of the better ways to express concretely your hatred and rejection of him is to help him *improperly* with his homework. If you are not suited and not qualified, beware; if you are, and are honest in your appraisal, hop to it.

Are you qualified? One requirement is academic ability. If you have been through grade school, and if your child is not twice as gifted intellectually as you are (most children are only one and a half times as smart as their parents), then you *are* academically qualified. Don't be put off by the "New Math." The New Math is composed almost entirely of (1) a new vocabulary for the same things you learned, and (2) a tendency to introduce topics in a different order from the way you learned them when you went to school. Six times six is still thirty-six in the New Math (base ten), but you may well find something that you would have learned in second year of high school popping up in Junior's second grade of elementary-school homework. In any event, you can read Junior's textbook just as meaningfully as he can, and there are available short, comprehensible paperback do-it-yourself explanations of the New Math which should dispel any sense of inadequacy you may wrongly have. Just be foxy enough to find out first how the teacher is teaching subtraction and division before you show Junior the "better" way you learned thirty or more years ago.

For all subjects there are "teacher's guidebooks" which go with each student's textbook and workbook. These help the teachers stay one jump ahead of the kids. They are available through any large bookstore or direct from the publisher, and can easily serve the parent as well as they serve the teacher.

Are you qualified personality-wise? Well, you're certainly not if you can't remember that when you tell Alphonse something is wrong you must be careful to make it clear that you are criticizing *what he has done* and are in no way criticizing Alphonse. You may consider yourself qualified personality-wise to help your own child with his homework if you can believe in the rules listed below, and can remind yourself of them before each teaching session.

Rule 1. A good teacher can successfully teach his subject to anyone, for a good teacher can always think of some way to explain a fact in words that will be meaningful to and understandable by his pupil. That is, if the good teacher explains something very carefully and very clearly to his student and the student responds with a blank look and a "Huh?" the good teacher looks for other ways of explaining the fact so that it will be comprehensible to the student. When the good teacher says something six different ways, each way terribly clear and terribly brilliant, and the student is still befuddled, the good teacher's silent reaction is automatically: "How come *I'm* so stupid as a teacher that I can't think of a way to explain this so that he will instantly understand it?"

If you are going to help Junior successfully with his homework you must learn this automatic reaction of the good teacher. When you have explained in four different ways, each one more magnificently conceived than the others, that you simply carry the two over to the next column, and Junior still looks as though you were discussing the Special Theory of Relativity, you must be prepared to say not: "How can you be so damned stupid!" but rather to yourself: "How can *I* be such a lousy teacher that I can't think of a better way to explain this?"

Rule 2. A good teacher knows and appreciates the value of demonstration in teaching. Demonstration is a tremendous tool for learning. But too many teachers, and particularly too many parents, are afraid to use it. In fields of advanced education it is intuitively accepted. When the master plumber wishes to instruct the apprentice in threading a pipe, he has the apprentice silently watch him do it a dozen times before he offers to let the apprentice try his hand. If the novice says he doesn't understand, the master demonstrates a dozen more times. When the surgeon wishes to instruct the intern in the technique of doing an appendectomy, he allows him to stand silently by, observing through a dozen operations, before he offers to let him try his hand. If the intern says that he still doesn't feel capable, the surgeon simply demonstrates another dozen times. This same method of teaching is remarkably well suited to parent-child instruction.

For instance, Junior needs help with addition. Demonstration method: "Well, you sit here beside me at the desk and just watch what I do. See, I always start with this column on the right, and work down. Six and four, that's the same as four and six—so that makes ten. Ten plus this next number, three—that makes thirteen. Thirteen—well, now I write the three here under this column, and I put the one in this next column, and add it to this first number."

Contrast this approach with the "You Do Your Own Thinking" method: "What! You haven't learned to add a simple problem like that yet? Sit down at the desk and I'll stand behind you and help. Where do you start? No, stupid, not with the left-hand column. Don't you know yet that you start to the right? How much is six and four? Think! My God, you're just like your mother." Do you get the point?

The method of demonstration, provided the child is watching and listening at least half the time, provides the same information and the same opportunity to learn, but in an atmosphere of calm in which the child can think and remember, and at the same time it inherently prevents the teacher from venting his spleen upon the pupil. And, believe me, it is a method that works.

How many times does one have to demonstrate? I haven't the slightest idea. But it should be continued at least until the student offers his willingness to try it himself. People learn some things easily and some things with difficulty. After years of observing, for instance, I wouldn't want to try out my skill at an appendectomy upon you. But the doctor down the block watched only twice and he's a whiz at it.

Another example for the sake of clarity. "Dad, how do you look up a word in the dictionary?" Demonstration method: "Well, let's go find the dictionary first; I think it's under the waffle iron in the kitchen. Now, let's see, that word begins with an 'r,' so first we look for the 'r's.' Well, I'll be darned, this book is arranged alphabetically! So all we've got to do is say, 'm,n,o,p,q,r,' and here are the 'r's.' Now, let's see, the second letter is 'e' so we've got to thumb through here till we come to 're-.' And the third letter is 'a.' That's good, 'cause that's one of the first letters in the alphabet and we get to it quickly. Here's a word that looks like the one we're looking for! No, it's a little different at the end, see? Oops, here's the word! Now, let's see, it says 'an instrument for measuring the intensity of the sun's radiation.' What the heck does that mean? I guess it means 'a thing for telling how strong the rays of the sun are,' don't you think?"

"Think, You Dope," method: "You wanna know how to use the dictionary? Don't they teach you anything in school these days? So go find the dictionary and bring it here. Okay, now look for the word. What the heck are you doing looking in the front part of the dictionary? Don't you know 'r' comes way down in the alphabet? Why, of course, the dictionary is arranged alphabetically! What's your teacher's name anyhow! Of course that's not the same word, idiot! Can't you spell? No, I'm not going to help you find it! How can I build your character if I baby you? Well, sure, that's the right word, can't you see? What do you mean, 'What does it mean?' It means just what it says! It's an instrument for measuring the intensity of radiation of the sun. What else?"

Rule 3. A good teacher always leaves his pupil feeling a little more important at the end of a lesson than he did when the lesson started; never feeling that he, the student, is an incompetent.

Rule 4. A good teacher always ends the lesson with himself and his student feeling a little bit more friendly toward each other than they did when the lesson started.

If you believe, and can remember, these principles of good teaching, then you can and should help your child with his homework. But sometimes with the best of intentions even good teachers forget themselves and act like human beings. If you find yourself pounding the table, or wondering at the top of your voice how come *he's* so stupid instead of how come *you're* so stupid, better conclude the lesson and both go have a Coke.

Do these methods of helping a child with his homework make him dependent upon the parent? Do they rob him of the independence of standing on his own feet? Of learning to take the initiative in his studying? Do they prevent him from developing his own skill in approaching a problem? Of formulating his own good work habits? Do they interfere with his developing a sense of responsibility for his own work? Most emphatically they do not.

To the contrary, they do help him to become independent by building confidence in himself to the point where he is able to risk independence. By helping him achieve a measure of success comfortably, they encourage him to seek more success. They assist him in developing good work habits by example and demonstration. They show him how to approach a problem and give him the confidence to feel that he can succeed. They enhance his sense of responsibility by improving his self-image, by equipping him for independence, by indicating to him that those who love him are ready to help him, and by showing him how natural it is for someone to help others.

You say you have always offered to help your child with his schoolwork but he never wants help? Well, good. Maybe he never needs help. Perhaps he has no school problems, no difficulty doing as well in school as his abilities allow him. Certainly not all children need parental help with their homework.

But are you fairly sure that your child hasn't discovered that, when you offer to help, what you really have meant in the past is that you are offering to criticize him, to nag him, to belittle him, to frighten him into wondering whether you love him? And that in his eyes what he is turning down is not help but rather abuse?

Do you start off a "helping" session with angelic intentions and then discover to your dismay that you are really human like the rest of us? Do your good intentions too quickly vanish in anger? Then perhaps you'd better employ an outside tutor when necessary. Or perhaps you could read the rules over a few more times and get your wife or husband to help you—to help you by remaining within hearing distance and by calling you to come have a coffee or a beer when she hears the good intentions start to crumble.

Have you ever watched the face of a child whose parent says to him, "You do *so* know the answer. Think harder"? The child's every thought is instantly concentrated upon how best to escape the parent's criticism. He can no more think of the answer than he could fly. Ask him now his own name and he will have trouble remembering it. He is panicked into a state of imbecility. How well do you solve an algebraic equation while someone you love is pushing you out a tenth-story window? This is why most wise educators do not favor parental help with homework. If this is the way your personality drives you to "help" the children with their studies, don't do it.

If you can't separate the role of loving, protecting, proud parent from the role of critical, threatening teacher, please don't try to play both parts. You're certain to mess up not just the one role, but both.

A General Approach to School Problems

So you suspect that Isobel isn't doing as well in school as she should be, particularly since she takes after your side of the family. Or maybe she's just not that happy about going to school altogether. What to do about it?

First, talk to the teacher. But do it with an appointment, and at a time reasonably convenient for her. No success in finding the answer? Request an audience with the principal—or the helping teacher, or the counselor, or the school psychologist. Still no solution? Try the child's family physician or pediatrician. If, after a thorough physical and after listening to all the facts, he too is perplexed, he may suggest, or you may request, further investigation by other experts. This is sometimes available locally through clinics or through private testing psychologists, but if not, it is always available at the nearest medical center or university.

When do you conclude that you have found the answer? Only when it is spelled out in such simple, direct terms that you clearly understand, and believe in, the explanation, and only when the steps to be taken to correct the problem are so precisely stated that you can easily follow them. Otherwise, you keep asking, "Why, why, why?"

"Why is Clara doing so poorly in school this year, Miss Smith?" "Because she's lazy." "Okay, but why is she lazy?" "Because that's just her way and she doesn't work hard enough." "Okay, but why is that just her way and why doesn't she work hard enough?" "Because she and I hate each other's guts and we don't get along, that's why," or "Because she sits in school all day and worries her head off about whether you're beating your wife at home or not, that's why," or "Because she has a splitting headache in class every day, that's why," or "Because she's a crazy mixed-up kid and needs to see a psychiatrist, that's why." These answers, finally, are concrete, simple, easy to follow up, and may or may not be true. But in any event, you have finally found an answer.

Follow up and correct all four of the answers if they all seem plausible to you. If none of them corrects the problem to your satisfaction, you still have to go back to asking "Why?" of the best expert available until you have the answer.

Reading Problems

There is one particular school problem which is so common and so important that it deserves the attention of all parents. This is the so-called reading problem. It is a fact that a fair percentage of children (2 to 10 percent) have a particular and specific difficulty in learning to master the art of reading. These children must be looked for, sought out, and helped early enough with their problem to prevent serious adverse effects both upon their personalities and upon their total school work.

Some children have difficulty learning to read because they have poor mental equipment for coping with our educational system (low IQ). Some children have difficulty learning to read because of physical disabilities, such as poor eyesight, poor hearing, or recurrent or chronic illness. Some because they are worried, distracted, and emotionally upset. Some because they have a poor teacher. Some because their classroom is chaotic and riotous. But all of these causes tend to retard the child's ability to learn in all fields and not just in reading. These are not reading problems in the sense that we are discussing.

If by the time your child has finished first grade, and certainly no later than second grade, he seems to be having trouble in learning to read, and particularly when compared with his ability to learn other subjects, you should entertain serious suspicions that he may have a specific reading problem. How do you decide that a child is not satisfactorily learning to read? Partly by his report card, partly by consultation with the teacher, partly by his achievement tests, but especially by attention to his attitudes toward reading at home. By the end of first or second grade, a child who is satisfactorily learning to read will be showing an active and spontaneous interest in books of a suitable nature. A child who shows no interest in reading is a child who is not learning how to read!

Just as some people are color-blind and cannot tell red from green, so there are children who, without any correlation with their intelligence, are "reading-blind." These children are simply not able to learn to read by the ordinary methods of teaching in use in our present-day schools. Some schools are acutely aware of this situation. Some schools appear oblivious to it. All schools, no matter how aware, occasionally overlook cases of reading difficulty. It therefore, as always, devolves upon the parent to be aware of this possibility and to be alert to it in his own child not later than the end of the second grade. These children are perfectly and fully capable of learning to read well if special methods of teaching are employed. If the school is not able to provide such special teaching skills, it is imperative that the parent seek out qualified tutors in this field from other sources. Special reading tutors can be found by consulting the school authorities, the child's physician or pediatrician, or a nearby university.

Just as a color-blind individual can learn to tell perfectly which traffic light is on by remembering that the top light is red and the bottom green, these children can be taught to read well by a variety of techniques. There may need to be special emphasis upon phonics. Comprehension of, and practice with, spatial relationships may need stressing. Auditory reinforcement of each letter and word seen and written or tactile reinforcement through tracing the letters with a finger can be the key. The development of physical coordination and of rhythm may help. But it is the technician skilled in testing and in remedial reading who can best determine the presence of a reading problem (word-blindness, dyslexia) and choose the method of correction.

It is of course important to remember that difficulty in reading may not be a specific reading problem, and sometimes the child's physical health and emotional stability should be looked into.

And remember, too, that books of interest to a child may not be the books *you* choose. In the early reading years, literary content is less important than practicing reading skill. Comic books, if not monstrous or salacious, are suitable and sometimes attractive. And publishers of juvenile books annually issue more books than you would care to count, catering to all tastes. So your child should have no difficulty in finding something attractive to him—if he is given the choice.

Handedness

Is your child right-handed or is he left-handed? Or is he truly ambidextrous, preferring neither side to the other? And does it make any difference after all? Handedness is a fascinating subject about which we know little and speculate much.

We know that everyone's brain has two cerebral hemispheres and that the right hemisphere controls the movements of the left side of the body while the left controls the movements of the right side. We know that each hemisphere contains all the structures that the other contains but that in most people one side appears to be dominant; most people from early life seem to be more proficient with either the right side or the left side. We know that, in certain instances, when one side of the brain is injured, the opposite side can learn to take over the functions of its damaged mate.

We suspect that in the young child the naturally dominant hemisphere should be allowed and encouraged to dominate the brain's activity. There is evidence to show that some children who have had their natural laterality changed (that is, who were destined to be left-handed but were forced to become right-handed, and vice versa) and some children who have grown up without ever establishing a definite laterality (that is, who seem truly ambidextrous) have more than their share of learning problems, especially in the fields of reading, writing, and spelling.

It is generally agreed that the preservation of a natural dominance avoids conflict and confusion between the two sides of the brain and is more likely to head off problems of learning, or at least is unlikely to cause problems.

Some children who have had their natural laterality changed (and some children who haven't) tend to mirror-write or -read. They confuse "saw" for "was" and "on" for "no." (To gain some insight into this problem, try the following experiment. Stand before a blackboard with a piece of chalk in each hand. Starting from the middle of the board, try writing the same sentence simultaneously from left to right with the right hand and, in a mirror fashion, from right to left with the left hand. You will find that, with little or no practice, you can, with surprising ease, write simultaneously in both directions.)

A child's natural tendency to be right-handed or to be left-handed is usually evident by the end of the second year and virtually always by the end of the fourth year. Before this age, I would suggest that instruments and utensils, such as a fork and spoon, pencil and crayon, cup, or toy, be placed more or less directly in front of the child so that he may, without pressure, elect to use the hand he prefers. Once he has clearly demonstrated a preference for one side or the other, he should thereafter be encouraged to use and to practice with the dominant side, by having objects placed in a position more available to that hand.

By the time he is four, and certainly before he has had much teaching in reading or writing, if he has not manifested a preference for one side or the other, an effort should be made to determine whether one side or the other is truly dominant. This is usually accomplished by testing to see which is the dominant leg and which is the dominant eye, for obviously if the child is left-legged and left-eyed he is probably also meant to be left-handed. Assigned the task of running after a ball and repeatedly kicking it, without any explanation of what is being looked for, a child will tend to kick the ball more often with his dominant leg. Or if he is given the job of going up a short flight of stairs over and over again, the dominant leg will tend to take the first step up more often than the recessive leg. Told to hold a cardboard tube at arm's length with both eyes open and to aim the tube (still with both eyes open) at a distant object, a child will tend to sight with his dominant eye. Which eye is actually being used to do the sighting can be determined either by having the child aim the tube at the nose of the observer, who has seated himself across the room, in which case the observer can see the child's dominant eye down the tube, or by covering up first one and then the other eye after the child has aimed the tube and thereby ascertaining which eye was doing the sighting. Assuming that the sight in both eyes is normal and that both legs are normal, if the child has a clearly dominant right leg and a definitely dominant right eye, it is a relatively safe conclusion that he is intended to be right-handed.

Once the determination is fairly certain, thereafter he should be encouraged to prefer that hand. In the rare case in which a child is truly and naturally ambidextrous, it is generally considered proper to urge him to become right-handed, at least for several years, before permitting him to return to ambidexterity. In general, psychologists with special skills in testing are usually assigned the task of determining laterality in cases of doubt.

For the parents of sufficient age to remember the disadvantages incurred by the left-handed child learning to write in school, let me hasten to say that in most modern elementary educational systems the lefty is nowadays taught to write in a manner as comfortable and graceful as the right-handed student. And if you want your son to be a big-league pitcher. . . .

It is provocative to note that in reading and writing and spelling, despite all the fastidious theories, there is nothing instinctive about proceeding from left to right for either right-handed or left-handed people. Children of either laterality can simultaneously learn to write English and Hebrew. Yet Hebraic mirror writing, of course, is the converse of English mirror writing.

Clumsiness in traversing from left to right, and from top line to next line below, can be alleviated by practice just as can clumsiness in pegging from third base to home plate. Play exercises that emphasize arranging blocks, garments, toys, and symbols from left to right and from above down improve this skill. That is, they do provided they are not so unartfully presented as to repel the child.

It is also apparent that mirror reading is the companion of poorly developed spatial awareness and not solely a consequence of mixed laterality. Children who are too young to comprehend clearly such relationships as "in front of," "behind," "above," "nearer," "to the left," and so on are ready participants in mirror reading.

As there are children too young to grasp relative positions in space, so there are older children whose spatial concepts are late to develop or are actually permanently deficient. These young-sters will have reading and writing difficulties whether they are right-handed or left-handed. They, too, through exercise and practice can develop and improve their comprehension of spatial relationships.

These and other causes of mirror-writing weaken the argu-ments of those who stress the significance of handedness.

There are reading readiness tests, usually administered at kindergarten age, which predict with frightening accuracy the child's preparedness for reading and writing. And there are short texts, available to the parent through the kind graces of kindergarten and first-grade teachers, which detail games to help develop in children spatial awareness and left-right orien-tation. Even better are the specially trained tutors learned in these skills.

Underachieving

One responsibility and privilege that parents may rightly claim is the enjoyment of seeing each child achieve according to his full capabilities. And one favorite complaint and concern of both teachers and parents is that "Frankie isn't working up to his full capacity." In a recent investigation of several hundred American public-school children, it was discovered that, in the opinion of either the schoolteacher or the parents or both, over 80 percent of the children were considered to be underachieving compared with their estimated abilities. What a waste!

A waste? Nonsense! If the judgment of these sampled parents and teachers is correct, this might herald the coming of the most emotionally stable and productive generation of American adults yet seen. Do you honestly want your child at five or ten or fifteen to be working to the full extent of his capability? Do you drive yourself, day after day, to the greatest efforts of which you are capable? Or do you coast along, doing perhaps 75 per-cent of the things you could do if you worked at full steam, only now and then, when the occasion calls for it, working for a short time at the highest pitch of which you are capable?

The child who, year after year, through elementary school, junior high school, and high school, felt compelled to drive himself at such a pace that he achieved, without let-up, to the fullness of his ability would worry me. I could hardly believe that at some more important episode in his life (college, business, or marriage) he would not throw up his hands in despair, turn off his racing motor, and decide that it just wasn't worth all the frantic effort.

Like a long-distance runner loping at a comfortable speed across the country, saving his full bursts of power for the hills he will meet, I imagine a child would be more certain of attaining his final goals in life if he worked most of the time at less than full capacity, reserving his supreme efforts for those moments which deserved them. The human machine, driven at full tilt, sooner rather than later requires repairs. A child who underachieves to a modest extent through most of his childhood is likely to be the unneurotic adult who can and will safely pull out the throttle to meet the demands of higher education or of a vocation.

Is your child an "underachiever"? Good! Unless he is markedly so, you may be a successful parent!

"Brain-Damaged"

Here is a subject that deserves some careful thought. Particularly, here is a term, "brain-damaged," which demands close inspection. To me it is a hatefully inaccurate word which would have been better buried before it was born. In the past ten years, it has become fashionable in educational and medical circles for the usual reasons; it sounds learned and at the same time conceals monumental ignorance.

Certain facts about personality are commonly known. Each newborn child has certain physically determined personality potentials. But, with rare exceptions, these potential gifts are capable of being influenced, either to be encouraged or to be minimized, by the child's environment. In the recent past, astute observers have noted that a fair percentage of children seem to have an inborn tendency to develop certain characteristic traits: physical hyperactivity, emotional lability, short attention span, and poor motor coordination. In other words, these children seem to have a natural tendency to be very active physically, moving about constantly and scarcely able to sit still for longer than a few moments; they seem to have less than average control of their outward emotions and range quickly from joy to rage and back; they have a difficult time focusing their attention upon any one subject for longer than short periods; and they are physically somewhat clumsier than the average child of the same age.

In a very small proportion of children with these characteristics, one could demonstrate to a limited degree that some area or another of their brains did not seem to be functioning in quite the same way that other children's brains do. Thus arose the designation of this type of personality syndrome as "brain-damaged" and of such children as "brain-damaged children."

Scientists have known for many years that the brain is composed of thousands and thousands of so-called centers. Each center, or small collection of cells, concerns itself with the ability to perform a specific act or function. For example, there is a center which controls vomiting, one which controls breathing, one which controls the motion of the right forefinger. There are, similarly, centers which control seeing, smelling, tasting, and hearing. There are, likewise, centers which are concerned with the more subtle of man's faculties, such as his emotions and attitudes.

As a simple example, there is a center in the brain which is concerned with man's ability to comprehend mathematics. Have you ever joked about your wife's endearing inability to balance the checkbook? Well, your wife's mathematics center is not up to snuff. Therefore, by this terminology, your wife is "brain-damaged." Do you have a friend who for the life of him cannot distinguish the color red from the color green? His color-perception center never developed properly. Therefore, he is "brain-damaged." So perhaps you will begin to see that "brain damage" doesn't quite mean what it sounds like; it doesn't really mean that there is a hole in the person's brain.

The concept is that children with the previously mentioned personality traits are born with a missing or malfunctioning center or centers in their brains, which accounts for their somewhat unusual behavior. The trouble with this concept is that it just ain't necessarily so. Undoubtedly in some cases it is true, but it also makes a too handy wastebasket to dump children into, and to no particular purpose.

I would like to have a dime for every child who has erroneously been labeled "brain-damaged" during his first year of school, and I would gladly kick back twenty-five cents for each child who was with justification so labeled. Not that I would condone the label. Let's say they could have been just as properly labeled: "children with certain identifiable personality traits which were present, not because of some influence of their environment, but because of predetermination at birth." This title would be far closer to the truth: that is, that we know that *all* children are born with more or less developed aptitude potentials.

How are these children, the so-called brain-damaged, identifiable? Well, a careful neurological examination may reveal some measurable deficiency in some part of the brain. For instance, a mild weakness in a hand might be detected. The trouble is, in most of the children there is no such demonstrable neurological deficiency, and many other children in whom there is such evidence do not exhibit characteristic personality traits.

It is also very popular for someone to suggest that an electroencephalogram be performed to demonstrate abnormal electrical brain-wave activity. And some of these children do actually demonstrate abnormalities in their EEG's. On the other hand, so too do 10 percent or more of otherwise completely normal children and adults walking about on the streets with no thought of being "different."

Another way of identifying such children is by the administration of a battery of psychometric tests. In the hands of a capable testing psychologist this is certainly the most reliable method. And here, too, there is room for error, errors of over-diagnosing and of underdiagnosing.

We know full well that children who conclusively do not have any "brain damage" can exhibit any or all of these typical personality traits. For example, children who have been raised for five years with inadequate teaching at home, with totally lacking or with totally ineffective discipline, will exhibit exactly these four personality traits, and to the same degree. And only the most astute psychologist can make even an educated guess as to whether these children are, or are not, "brain-damaged."

Of considerable interest is the fact that "brain-damaged" people seem not to be identifiable in the adult population. Or, in other words, these peculiar personality traits, if they are physically (organically) caused, seem to disappear as a person passes through adolescence. Other, more sophisticated, centers must obviously come into play, which supersede the activities of those centers which had predisposed the individual to these particular personality traits.

Now, a "brain-damaged" child, with his overactivity, emotional lability, short attention span, and physical clumsiness, can be more than a bit annoying to the adults with whom he comes into contact. Furthermore, his personality traits may make it difficult or impossible for him to learn in the average educational situation. But there is no sure correlation between these personality traits and the intelligence of the individual. He may be far more intelligent, or far less intelligent, than the average child, just as any other child may be more or less intelligent than average.

If these children are handled medically and educationally in the special manner which they require, they learn well and they behave tolerably, and, most important, they become useful, productive, happy, unidentifiable adults. But by this time they have been thoroughly and completely labeled "brain-damaged" —a term which conveys to strangers, and even to educated parents, an understanding of the situation which is cruelly and harmfully fallacious.

In some states this foolishness is compounded by absurd legislation. It is necessary, because of the existing laws, actually to name and to stamp these children "brain-damaged" in order for them to be able to enter the special educational classes that they need. The laws are so ridiculous that many children who have special educational problems, but who are not "brain-damaged," must, with tongue in cheek, be called "brain-damaged"; otherwise they would not receive the necessary specialized instruction.

Wait, it gets worse. Do you know any delightful and highly successful adults who are so poorly coordinated that they can't repair a defective lamp and who seem to trip over their own shoestrings when they enter a room? Well, they're lucky. When their counterpart, the delightfully clumsy child, now passes through his first three years of school, his poor coordination may be duly noted and recorded, and sometimes even reported with a quaver to his now bewildered and anxious parents. Is his handwriting still poor and childish when he reaches fourth grade? No matter what his ability in math or reading or social studies, he must get a D in handwriting on his report card, he must practice to the point of emotional tension to improve his penmanship, and both he and his parents must be made acutely aware of the fact that he is "different." Sometimes one longs for the old days of ignorance, when this child would have been labeled "probably going to grow up to be a doctor; no one can read his handwriting."

Is Susan unable to sit still in her seat in second grade long enough to understand what the teacher is saying? Well, maybe she's "brain-damaged." Sure, maybe she is. But also maybe there are eighty other more common causes of her problem, and if we get touted away from looking for them we will never find them.

Fortunately the pendulum of enthusiasm for "brain damage" seems to be swinging back a little. Perhaps, hopefully, in the coming decade the term will be relegated to obsolescence.

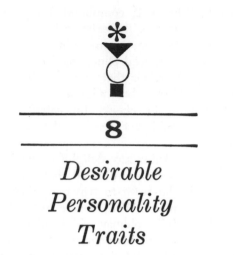

8

Desirable Personality Traits

The alleged intent of this book is to help parents foster the development of a normal personality in their children. But a normal personality does not necessarily require any particular "desirable traits." In any case, who is to say what traits are pleasing? Pleasing to whom? If a person found that certain traits in himself were contributing to his unhappiness or interfering with his functioning in society they would be to him highly distasteful—regardless of their so-called desirability.

It is not my purpose to influence parents in their selection of the attitudes and values they would like their children to acquire. My sole concern is that the finished product have a normal personality. Only upon such a base can any ethics be erected by parental guidance.

Nevertheless, there are popularly cherished traits which many parents expect their offspring to develop, and to the extent that the parents, in their efforts to inculcate these traits, warp the normalcy of the child's total personality, these traits, then, fall into the purview of this book.

The attitudes and values adopted by a maturing child are formed largely on the basis of the things he sees happening about him, particularly within his immediate family. What makes most children ultimately emulate their parents' attitudes whereas a few adopt the very opposite of their parents' views? I presume to suggest that to the degree that a child's personality develops toward normalcy, he tends to accept the values of his parents; to the degree that it departs from normalcy, he tends to reject the views of his parents. Perhaps it is that the more he esteems his own self, the more he reflects his parents; the less satisfactory he finds his self-image, the more he rejects his parents.

In any event, the hard fact is that imitation (or rejection) of what he observes within his own family is the important educational force in determining a child's character traits. To a lesser degree he is influenced by what he overhears of the family's attitudes. Only to a minimal extent are his values influenced by direct efforts on the part of the parents.

Direct efforts to teach values and attitudes (lectures, "man-to-man" talks, arguments, preachments, assignment of duties) have little effective teaching worth. On the other hand, a sound child-parent relationship is of critical importance. The nurturing of a normal personality in the child is also of great value. Commonly the overenthusiastic efforts by parents to force attitudes and values on their children merely result in long and destructive harangues and angry denunciations. These squabbles both wreck the child-parent relationship and warp the personality structure of the child.

It would be a foolish investor who would risk a possession of great worth in a needless effort to obtain something of lesser importance. Particularly if the less valuable thing could be better attained without any risk at all.

So, in the interests of a better understanding of children, it may be of some worth for us to think carefully together about a few of the commonly desired character traits.

Bravery

A common cause of concern among parents, as brought to the attention of a pediatrician, is that their young son is not showing signs of becoming manly enough or brave enough. "I just can't teach him to hit back, Doctor." Or "He won't fight for his rights when the other kids pick on him." Or "He runs crying home to me when a smaller boy pushes him down."

Misdirected efforts on the part of parents to force their son to "be brave" sometimes result in all sorts of unnecessary and astounding conflicts between the child and the parents.

The desirable quality of "braveness" in an individual is intimately related to a complicated structure of ethical decisions. These decisions are far too complex for a preschool child to be able to handle and master. The point is, in exactly what way do you want your under-six-year-old to be brave? At his age he is capable of learning either to be physically aggressive or not to be physically aggressive. He can learn, if you want, to strike, to scratch, to bite, or to bludgeon a rival whenever the rival gets in his way. Or he can learn the opposite, that physical aggressiveness is not a socially tolerated way of solving every problem, but rather that the problem should be reported to the authorities, generally to the parents. The choice between these two alternative ways of responding to an antagonist is relatively simple, more or less black or white, and certainly can be taught even to a two- or three-year-old.

But does this have anything to do with bravery or cowardice? Is it bravery to have learned to lambaste a little girl who annoys you or to go after the corner policeman with fists and feet when he thwarts you?

The question of the propriety of physical self-defense involves a series of complicated rules which concern themselves with *when* it is proper to be aggressive, when *not*, against *whom*, and *for what reasons*. No preschool child is capable of such judgments. The three-year-old who has been taught to retaliate when his legitimate rights are threatened by another three-year-old is hard-pressed to see any reason why jumping up and down on one-year-old Suzy's stomach is not also permissible, particularly after she has just maliciously destroyed his block fort.

As with the teaching of any behavior that involves fine moral decisions, the initial teaching concerning physical aggressiveness in young children must be oversimplified in favor of the most often acceptable behavior. Refinements can be added later when the child is intellectually capable. The preschool child should learn that physical aggressiveness is frowned upon, regardless of the provocation. Incursions on his privileges or imagined rights are to be resolved at this age by recourse to the wisdom of the courts, namely his mother and father.

The meaningful acquisition of bravery depends upon the confluence of several factors:

1. The child learns to be brave, and to defend his rights, in large by observing and imitating the behavior of his parents. It is a difficult subject to learn. When is it proper to be brave, and when is braveness merely foolhardiness? What price is it appropriate to pay to defend what rights?

2. Bravery also depends upon the secure knowledge that there are people who believe in you and who will still love you and support and defend you, morally and spiritually, if you get in over your head or are severely defeated. In other words, bravery depends upon an adequate self-esteem.

3. True physical bravery in a child, as opposed to an anxious braggadocio, must generally await the development of a true sense of time relationships. To a young child, the past and the future are vague concepts, whereas the present is all-important. "Not now, Sammy, I'll do it for you in five minutes" has almost the same meaning as "Not now, Sammy, I'll do it for you next year." "It happened last month" and "It happened the day before yesterday" are pretty much the same to a young child. The present is the only reality, and it goes on forever.

Therefore, it is impossible for a young child to comprehend that pain has a limited duration and may be borne with the knowledge that it will eventually cease and be forgotten. Try explaining to a four-year-old that an injection will hurt for only a few seconds. A few seconds is now, and now is eternity. All that can adequately register is the fact that it *will* hurt. Much adult bravery is based upon the knowledge that, whatever the pain will cost us, this pain will eventually end and will fade into the forgottenness of the past. The young child has no such sustaining concept.

Somewhere about the age of nine or ten or eleven this relative sense of time begins to be fairly well developed. The twelve-year-old whose father says to him, "So what? All he can do to you is punch you in the nose and that won't hurt forever," gets an entirely different message than the four-year-old whose father delivers the same words of wisdom.

An interesting aspect of bravery as it relates to the willingness or ability to cope with pain is the observation that adult women, in general, are able to bear pain and discomfort better than adult men. The pain of wounds, of hot utensils, and of physical sickness is on the average far better withstood by females. The "little boy" reaction of the male to the discomforts of physical illness is common knowledge. What explains this difference? Customarily the little girl who falls down and scrapes her knee, or who cuts herself, runs unashamedly to a parent for help. In this haven she receives comfort, sympathy, and a willingness to share her woes. She is permitted to cry and to express her fright. There is no stigma attached to her being "soft" and delicate. She learns that, when things get too bad to bear, there are loved ones who will support her without ridiculing her. The little boy, on the other hand, suffers the same accident, runs to the parent, and receives the admonition "Oh, you're not badly hurt. Be a big brave boy!" He grows up in doubt concerning just how much he has to take before the reinforcements will come to his rescue, and in doubt as to his own ability to perform this role of stoicism to the satisfaction of his parents and ultimately of the world.

This cause-and-effect relationship is, of course, unproven, but it is consistent with other well-known aspects of human behavior. The hero of the moment, whether in war or in peace, is not so apt to be the tough, aggressive, table-pounding braggart, but rather the melt-into-the-crowd guy around the corner who feels confident that those he loves will support him and believe in him regardless of whether he fails or succeeds in his effort to meet adversity.

Let your child achieve braveness through maturity, establishment of self-esteem, confidence of support, and emulation. Don't try to thrust it upon him by exhortation or by belittling denunciation or by pushing him into premature combat.

Sportsmanship

All fathers and most mothers urgently desire to instill into their sons and daughters a personality trait glowingly referred to as "good sportsmanship." This is a praiseworthy goal, but only if the parent fully understands just what it is he is aiming at.

If sportsmanship suggests to you the quality of enjoying being defeated, then I am against it. In any even mildly competitive society it would be self-destructive to encourage the habit of deriving pleasure from being bested.

If the "good sport," who leaps over the tennis net to shake his conqueror's hand, proffering a smile and a congratulation, is not enjoying having lost, what then is he doing? Lying. With lack of sufficient forethought, teaching a child good sportsmanship may result in nothing more than teaching him that, after he has tried as hard as he can, after he has wanted to win but has lost, then he must force a smile, pretend that he couldn't care less, and lie through his teeth: "Congratulations, old boy. You played a great game and you deserve to win."

How old should boys and girls be before they learn such sophistry? Well, if they learn too young to understand exactly what they're doing, they may learn instead that they are truly supposed to enjoy losing. It is better for a young child who is still learning the demands and rewards of competition to continue to cry when he loses, and for you to comfort him for having lost. The age of ten or twelve or fourteen is soon enough for him to start practicing to be a professional diplomat.

If the aspect of sportsmanship that enthralls you more is the quality of not taking unfair advantage of a handicapped opponent, you don't teach this by unsupported lectures. Your child acquires this behavior from observation.

From the fact that you restrain his younger brother from tormenting him when he himself is defenseless to retaliate because you will hold him guilty as the older brother who "should know better."

From the fact that you scrupulously avoid cutting her to bits with verbal denunciations, of which you are the master, she the unskilled novice.

From the fact that you do not use your superior strength in confrontations with your wife.

From the fact that you do not take advantage of the weaker or older or slower or unforewarned pedestrian or driver or servant or delivery boy or bus boarder or grocery shopper or golf companion.

With such a magnanimous teacher, how could he fail the lesson of sportsmanship?

Let your child see his parents fight the good fight, impartially observe the rules of the game, refrain from cheating and from taking unfair advantage, and you can safely save yourself the valuable hours of nagging and scolding on the subject of playing fair.

Appreciation of Athletics

Lest I be accused of being against fatherhood, let me make it clear that I am all in favor of physical fitness for our children. Sports and athletics are strong factors in the proper personality development of the child—sometimes.

Sportsmanship is an admirable trait that might just possibly be developed by participation in athletics. On the other hand, it is a relatively easy trait to develop without ever engaging in any sport.

Athletics, except for an infinitesimally small group who become professionals, is, no matter how it is sliced, for fun. If engaging in a sport brings pleasure and happiness to a child or an adult, that's great. If a child acquires self-confidence through a sport, magnificent. If it enables him to meet a compatible group of companions, fine. But it sometimes needs to be remembered by parents that no elegy summing up the worthwhileness and the failures of a person's life would ever bother to mention whether he dropped the ball in a crucial play of a Little League game or whether he did or didn't make a touchdown against Salami High School.

A too common source of frenzied pressures upon, and hurtful criticisms of, a child stems from the parents' enthusiasm that he "enjoy himself at a sport." The hallowed concept of the "all-around" child is appalling. Show me the all-around man, and I'll show you a failure. Among the many things this world needs sorely are more one-sided people. If your child takes naturally to athletics, and really enjoys it, good. If your child doesn't know second base from a starting block, and couldn't care less, but is a proficient student, or an interested artist, hallelujah! Don't be deluded into straining yourself toward making him an "all-around" unhappy misfit.

There is nothing more pathetic, and no one so self-defeating, as the eager father, perhaps himself an ex-athlete, who struggles so hard with his firstborn son to make him love sports that the child inevitably sets his course for any field of endeavor other than athletics. More often than not, it is the father who never himself quite achieved stardom, who is blustering through life with a tremendous lack of self-confidence, and who tries for a second chance to achieve fame in sports through his oldest son. Dad, if you must have a chip off the old block, don't push so hard that you doom yourself to failure. In the first place, don't set yourself up as such a paragon in your son's eyes that he is defeated before he starts, certain that he can never hope to achieve such heights. Admit a couple of your athletic shortcomings to him, so that his first target can be less than the moon. Second, build up his self-confidence in other areas so that he feels sure of himself and will not be afraid to face the possibility of failure in the sport. Third, don't expect him to be well-coordinated muscularly much before he is seven or eight at best.

And at whatever age you start to teach him, don't belittle or deride his efforts. Praise his attempts rather than waiting to praise his successes. Fourth, don't promptly follow each success by the helpful suggestion "But here is how you could have done even better." Fifth, allow him to become skilled enough so that his first exposures to competition are not pure defeat. Sixth, if he hates your chosen sport, show him what good sportsmanship is and let him excel in some other field in which you yourself were admittedly lousy.

Generosity

Teach your child to be generous, to share, to develop a sense of philanthropy. Certainly. But to understand how to teach this lesson, first consider exactly what generosity means.

A young child is honest and direct. She sees something; she wants it; she takes it; she wants to keep it; and she doesn't see any darned sense in letting somebody else have it. What could be more honest?

As she grows older she stumbles upon the fact that if she gives away some *small* thing she likes, she often gets back something *better* in return. This is an amazing discovery. You give away an old toy, and two great-aunts, a mother, and a second cousin jump up and down with exultation, heap praise upon you, talk about it for hours afterward, and sooner or later they present you with a bigger and better toy to take its place. From this point on generosity is established.

As the child grows older, she learns to value and to accept the praise of outsiders for her noble act as more than adequate compensation for the small value of the thing she surrendered.

With still more sophistication comes the ability to be generous, to sacrifice herself by giving away an object of some value, and then to receive the much greater reward of being able to pat herself on the back and to revel in the sure conviction of what a great girl she is.

Generosity and philanthropy, then, are nothing more than an exalted form of old-fashioned Yankee horsetrading. Your child learns step by step from you the benefits of giving things away, first to be rewarded by a material present, then to be rewarded by family praise, then by outside praise, and finally, best of all, by self-praise.

Nothing hard about this. But the first step toward teaching generosity is up to you to initiate. And the evolving stages of philanthropy must be supported by the parents' example.

Compassion and Kindness

These two traits may to some extent be inborn and instinctive. They certainly seem to exist in some forms of animals lower than man. But if they do exist at birth, they are largely either developed or minimized by one's experiences.

Direct teaching and lecturing have but an imperceptible influence upon the development of these traits. They depend almost entirely upon observation of the behavior of one's parents, and imitation thereof, fortified by the praise, first external and later self-bestowed, which results from exhibiting them.

Self-Confidence

Every human being, child or adult, carries with him an appraisal or an image of himself. This self-image consists of his idea of the way he looks and of the way he moves, of his attractiveness and of his desirability, and his own evaluation of how worthwhile or how valueless he is, of what others think of him and why, of his measure of success or failure, of his degree of goodness or badness, of his abilities and achievements, and of his total worth as a human being. It is the person he thinks himself to be.

If he regards himself as a satisfactory person, we say he has self-confidence, or self-esteem, or a good self-image. If he evaluates himself as worthless, we say he has a poor self-image.

Almost instinctively we know that self-confidence is a valuable personality trait. But how terribly valuable it is may escape us unless we think about it for a moment. You could almost use a person's self-confidence as a measure of the success or failure of his whole life. An obituary might say: "He died lacking self-confidence, poor man," or "He died filled with self-confidence, the lucky devil." In a recent seven-year study by the National Institute of Mental Health, it was considered valid to use a child's self-esteem as the sole index of his total psychological well-being.

It is apparent, then, that if self-confidence is so important as to be a yardstick of normalcy, all the efforts made to develop a normal personality in a child will be at the same time aimed ultimately at developing his self-confidence. In a sense, this book is devoted in its entirety to considering how to develop self-esteem in a child.

The more self-confidence the better? Or is there a maximal desirable amount of self-confidence beyond which any more is detrimental? Though we all know persons whom we say are over-confident, there almost surely is no such thing, from the point of view of normalcy of personality, as too much self-confidence, except as a very temporary and transitory state. The sounder the personality, the more self-confidence; the greater the self-confidence, the more we may assume the normalcy of the personality.

How about those overconfident, egotistical, overbearing, people we all know? All such overbearing, overconfident people are merely overacting. They are people with poor self-esteem, so poor that they are frightened and ashamed to allow the real self-image to show through to be ridiculed. If you really possessed the degree of self-confidence these people profess, you would feel no need to demonstrate it to the world.

Temporarily, a child may overestimate himself and his capabilities and briefly hold himself in too high esteem. But this is in no way an abnormal or undesirable trait, because it is so soon self-corrected. He cannot reach for impossible goals without experiencing the deflating influence of failure, which quickly brings his self-confidence into line with reality.

In his first several years of life, a child's self-image is formed entirely of what he understands his parents' evaluation of him to be. As he goes out into the school milieu, to the appraisal of his parents is added what he concludes to be the opinion of class-mates and teachers. Soon he begins to internalize these outside opinions. That is, he begins to be his own critic, to develop a conscience, which is at first nothing more than his concept of his parents' opinion of him but which now becomes an integral part of himself which he cannot avoid. From now on his self-image is composed of his own critical self-analysis, plus what he interprets to be the opinions of his family and his social contacts.

Often when a child is encountering difficulties in his world, a final analysis of the cause of his behavior is that he is "lacking in self-confidence." If you reach this conclusion concerning a child, you review all the factors that have entered into the de-velopment of his personality and you try to improve those which seem to have gone astray. That is, you review the aspects of love and discipline and independence that have been operating all along. If these contributory elements to his personality had all been operating well, only tremendous pressures from the outside world could have sapped his self-confidence.

On the other hand, a child's self-esteem can at any time be nurtured and improved by attention to influences outside the family circle.

Most obviously a capable psychiatrist can favorably influ-ence the child's self-image. In a like, though less predictable, manner, a superior guidance counselor—and there are some—can buttress his self-confidence. Sometimes a sweetheart can par-tially repair an older child's self-image.

Success begets success. With skill, parents may be able to manipulate the child's environment surreptitiously so that he meets with success. Success at first surprises, and then improves the self-image a little. The more the self-image improves, the more confidence the child may muster to strive again for success.

The school environment can occasionally be managed to provide a serving of success. A skilled tutor can sometimes, in a reasonably short period, prepare a child adequately enough in a subject so that he may shine in the classroom. A truly su-perior tutor can often contribute directly to the self-esteem of a child even during the tutoring sessions. A less than good tutor, of course, can make matters worse by deriding the child and by failing to stimulate his interest in the subject and by turning him away from it.

Under ideal circumstances and control, parents can function effectively as tutors, and as morale builders during the tutoring sessions, but they operate from a peculiarly vulnerable base and, unless they are scrupulously careful, they may easily aggravate a sense of failure.

A dedicated classroom teacher, interested in children, and whose confidence is invited by the parents, may be able to contribute measurably to elevating the child's self-confidence. No child suffers damage to his ego from being led to consider himself "teacher's pet" for a time. I know a few spectacularly effective elementary-school teachers who manage to have twenty-odd "teacher's pets" in each class at all times—each child devoutly convinced that he is the favorite. It is easy to see the close similarity between the effective teaching of these gifted classroom teachers and the success of the parent who is equally able to make each of her children feel himself to be in some way her favorite child.

Social and academic clubs at school may, with the cooperation of the directors, be used advantageously to bolster a sagging self-image. It is not the responsibility of the school to initiate such maneuvers. But the polite parent will often find the school more than cooperative. Sometimes parents can assist their child to success through extracurricular or home-assigned class projects.

The field of music offers wide opportunities for providing a child with successful experiences. It may not be possible to become the best piano player or the best saxophonist in the neighborhood, but sometimes it is possible with little skill to become the best five-string banjo player or the best ocarina player in school, if an enlightened music teacher can be found. With a little cooperation from the music department, the best (and only) five-string banjo player in the whole school might be able to enjoy a little favorable publicity, and a measure of success.

Sports sometimes offer avenues of success for the child who

needs more self-confidence. The obvious approach here is to choose a field in which there is no insurmountable competition and in which the child's interest might be aroused. Then to find a good, patient instructor who, in privacy, can give enough lessons to assure that the child's first exposure to competition will result in a tolerable showing rather than humiliation. This, too, is generally an unsafe field for the tutorial hand of the parent, unless the parent is prepared to exercise extraordinary restraint, and patience, and forbearance from any hint of criticism during the learning period. Before you eliminate the field of sports as an operating arena, think carefully of all the minor sports that are now available to children. For a rundown of sports you may scarcely have heard of, consult the nearest large recreation department or the head of the physical-education department at your school.

Don't neglect social skills. Dancing is a valuable asset, particularly if learned in seclusion. An easy familiarity—which may be acquired from a sympathetic and uncritical adviser and by imitation—with the fundamentals of good grooming, flattering dress, dating etiquette, restaurant deportment, opposite-sex small talk, and unembarrassed acceptance of compliments, may all contribute to self-confidence.

An honest effort by the parents to improve their dealings with and attitudes toward the child can contribute greatly to the restoration of self-confidence, particularly if it is done skillfully and with the outside guidance of a professional, either psychologist or pediatrician.

An exceptionally well-run day camp or sleep-away camp may occasionally fortify a child's self-esteem. Usually, however, it requires careful consultation with, and preparation by, the camp leader.

I do not mean to suggest that any one of these devices should be depended upon exclusively. Rather, as many of them as is practical should be employed simultaneously, if there is a significant suspicion that the child's self-confidence is sagging to the point of hindering him.

Responsibility

There is no quibbling with the enthusiasm to develop the characteristic of "responsibility" in our children. What a noble goal, to be able to accept one's responsibilities in life. But how to achieve this personality trait? In fact, what does it mean, to accept responsibility?

Possibly being willing to accept responsibility represents more than a single trait. Perhaps it means first having the ability to be independent, then having the self-confidence to make decisions, and finally having enough thoughtfulness and consideration of others to be willing to do things for their benefit as well as for one's own.

If this is an approximate definition of the characteristic of "accepting responsibility," then at least two parts of it are composed of attaining independence and of developing self-confidence. These components are discussed elsewhere. The remaining ingredient then would be learning to have regard and respect for the rights and privileges of others. How does one best instill this trait into the personality of one's children? I don't know for certain. But it is surely worth our thinking about together.

Many successful parents "teach their children responsibility" by assigning them chores to perform about the home from the time the children are very young. I can't deny this method, and it does teach the children something, but I wonder what lesson is learned. There is no doubt that in some families these chores, whatever they teach the child, become a constant point of friction between the parents and the child, which leads to no end of disharmony. It rather seems to me that if I were assigned chores that had to be performed no matter what, the thing I *might* end up learning, the thing I *would* end up learning, could well be that if you are big enough and strong enough you can make other people do what you want them to do, whether they want to or not, until they themselves are big enough and strong enough to resist. Now if that is the lesson, I wouldn't really have learned much about responsibility. Or I think I might also learn to hate (1) to wash dishes, or (2) to mind my baby sister, or (3) to carry garbage, or whatever. Nor would this lesson have a great deal to offer to further my sense of responsibility.

On the other hand, if I grew up in a family in which, from the time I could toddle, I observed my father frequently offering to help my mother with her tasks, and my mother offering to help my father with his, and if, as I grew up, each of them frequently offered to help me with some tedious or unpleasant undertaking, then I think I just might grow up foolish enough to believe that this was a common state of affairs and a normal way of living in a family.

It seems to me I might even want to have the privilege of offering to help them with their tasks—provided, of course, that they hadn't already convinced me that growing up is such a tough business that I wanted most of all not to grow up. If I learned that it was a privilege to volunteer to help out the people I loved, and even to seek out ways of lightening their burdens, then I think I might really have acquired something of a sense of responsibility.

I am not sure that this is a sound interpretation of the matter, or that it constitutes good advice, but I for one would prefer children to perform chores on a voluntary basis and derive some pleasure out of the volunteering than to see chores assigned, from which arose only arguments.

No one should minimize the importance to the overworked mother and father of receiving help around the home from their children. Indeed, sometimes to preserve the physical and emotional health of the overburdened mother, and therefore to protect the integrity of the family unit, it is imperative that the children be assigned daily chores. My point is that this sometimes imperative assignment of tasks to the children does not simultaneously teach them anything about responsibility. It does teach them the practical lesson of the ability and perhaps the right, of the strong to direct the weak.

The assumption of chores serves the development of responsibility only when the children can be led by emulation and love to volunteer for the chores, and to derive satisfaction from the volunteering.

Do you willingly volunteer to help those who trust you and believe in you? Or do you need to purchase the trust of those who presumably love you by performing chores for them?

9

Sex Education
and the Teaching
of Attitudes

What attitudes should you teach your children? Should you guide them toward tolerance or intolerance? Toward aggressiveness or passiveness? Materialism or idealism? Forgiveness or retribution? If I were foolish enough to try to tell you, you would be justified in not reading any further. Only you can decide what you want your child to believe in. So instead of telling you *what* values, let me discuss *how* to go about teaching whatever attitudes you judge most important.

In order to inculcate values in your children you must first of all be able to communicate with them effectively. But certainly you are aware of the communications gap that exists between our generation and theirs. You have heard it expounded by the pundits. More than likely, you have had personal experience with this gap yourselves. "I just can't seem to reach my son, Doc." "My daughter and her friends speak a different language than I do. We can't seem to communicate."

So our efforts to pass our values along are doomed before we even start. Sheer bunk!

Adults in general, and parents in particular, communicate constantly and very effectively with the younger set. They communicate today; they communicated in the past; and they will communicate in the future. The messages come through loud and clear. And the children hear, they comprehend, and they respond.

The problem is precisely that they *do* get the word—exactly and literally. But the signals we send are not the lessons we would like them to learn. What we call the "communications gap" is nothing but our excuse for the fact that we don't much like what we have managed to teach our kids. We are disconcerted because we have succeeded in passing along to them some of our own ill-conceived values. And they have seen through them most effectively.

We want our children to be respectful, but we teach them disrespect. We want dependability, but we teach undependability. We want initiative; we teach sloth. We want continence; we teach incontinence. Then we bewail the "communications gap."

There are three broad avenues by which we communicate with our children, open channels through which we constantly reveal ourselves, justify our values, and teach attitudes to our offspring.

But remember this. None of these routes avails us much if the child's personality has been skewed by neglect. He single-mindedly puts first things first. If his personality needs repairs, he will direct all his attention toward achieving this end. He cannot at the same time spare the effort to receive ungarbled any communication which is not directly relevant to these repairs. For example, the child in the classroom who is not yet convinced of his acceptance by his family is far too occupied with his defensive role of class clown to concentrate on the spelling lesson.

It is the same with the communication of attitudes. If the child is so busy struggling to interpret his world in a way that he hopes will bolster his self-confidence, he cannot be expected to learn attitudes without distorting them. This is one major cause of the failure of communication between generations. The child with an abnormal personality cannot at the same time be a receptive student.

Misdirected efforts to force values and attitudes on children, which end up as harangues and denunciations of the child, are doomed to failure. Adults who would communicate with children must be as wise as children and put first things first. Be certain that the personality is secure before teaching values, and in the teaching be careful not to mutilate the personality.

When the child is driven to lying in a desperate attempt to protect his unsatisfactory image, it is not the time to lecture him regarding proper values. (In point of fact, aside from further lowering his self-esteem, you would be wrong and he would be right. His sense of values at that moment is much more realistic than yours. He is evaluating the preservation of his personality as more important than telling the truth. From the viewpoint of his future emotional adjustment he is correct. Your values are incorrect.) When your daughter is shoplifting in a vain quest for a clear statement by you of your acceptance of her as a satisfactory individual regardless of her sins, it is not the time to sermonize on trustworthiness.

Keeping in mind that a secure personality is a prerequisite to the teaching of attitudes, let us examine the three channels available for communicating a point of view.

First we have direct verbal confrontation or lecturing. "Sit down, John, I have a few things to tell you." Or "Anytime you want to know something, just come and ask me."

This Channel One is not so great for parent-to-child communication, for parents and children are mostly human. Summoned to a sermon by Mom or Dad, the child reacts even as you or I. "What did I do now? What's the fastest way for me to escape? What's the angle I have to watch out for?"

Equally impractical, the invitation to "come confide in me whenever you have a problem" imposes upon the parent the superhuman restraint of never responding with belittlement or embarrassment. "My child never asks me questions. He never tells me anything," usually means that in the dim past a question or a trust got him in return either an answer that was accompanied by a "helpful" criticism or an embarrassed evasion and changing of the subject. "Yes, Bob, God made children of all colors; but what the hell were you doing in the mud with your new shoes?" Or "Oh, Sally, you mustn't ever talk about letting boys undress you." These spontaneities seal off this line of communication—like forever.

Because of the special vulnerability of the parent-teacher in relating to his child-student, this direct communication is more useful in the classroom than it is in the home.

The second avenue for making contact with the minds of children is the "overheard" technique. Children (and adults) are comfortably receptive to information discussed in front of them but not directed to them. Whether they elect to join in the discussion is immaterial, but, if they do, their contribution must not be scoffed at or demeaned.

This Channel Two is the pipeline most neglected by parents. Particularly appropriate to carrying messages which involve attitudes and the pros and cons of values, it requires some degree of deliberateness to be kept operational. Families that pray together may stay together, but families that discuss values formulate ethics together. Examine subjects aloud within earshot of your children and you will come to understand "spongeability."

This technique is capable of conveying knowledge in both directions. If you are so terribly mature that you can bear to hear, rather than to listen to, what your children say, you might find the square and the circle drawing closer to coinciding with each other.

The third avenue of communication is unfortunately always open, twenty-four hours a day, and it is by far the most efficient way to teach both profitable and harmful lessons. This Channel Three is emulation. Paradoxically, the effectiveness of this channel often leads to behavior that drives a parent into whining, "I can't communicate with this kid." Oh, you're teaching him all right. But, man, what are you "telling" him?

Children are naive enough to want to imitate, especially those they love. And they love their parents through all except the most intolerable abuse. Particularly in matters of attitudes and ethics are they susceptible to influence through emulation. This is so, I remind you, unless they are preoccupied with correcting a personality fault.

The stress of a major personality deficiency may suggest to a child that rebellion and total rejection of his parents are the solution to his problems. He may then act according to the exact opposite of what his parents stand for. Thus the paradox of the "good father" alcoholic with alcoholic offspring and the "bad father" alcoholic with teetotaler children.

One of the frustrations of the pediatrician is the parent who with a straight face complains of a child's behavior—when the child is imitating the parent's faults to a tee. And instead of being flattered, the imitated parent is furious.

Do you teach politeness by jabbing Susie's ribs to get her to say "Thank you" and by twisting Sam's arm to hold the door open for you? Or do you do it by being sure to say "Thanks" yourself, and by unfailingly waiting patiently for your husband to open the door?

Do you teach thoughtfulness by nagging Joan to set the table and Alex to dry the dishes? Or by your husband and yourself frequently volunteering to help each other with the routine tedious chores? And by offering to help the children with their tasks without being asked?

Do you persuade the teenager to keep you informed of his whereabouts by boxing his ears and withholding his allowance when he doesn't? Or by raising him in a family in which the adults customarily let their children know where they can be reached if necessary? And in which a delayed arrival home is faithfully announced by a timely phone call?

As with the teaching of homework, the teaching of attitudes is best accomplished by demonstration.

These, then, are the tools available for establishing attitudes. To illustrate their use, I would like to go over some details of building one particular set of values—attitudes toward sex.

Sex Education

"What about premarital sex if you are mature and are truly in love with someone?"

"Is sex before marriage as bad as adults tell us? Can it have advantages for some people."

"How far is too far in a premarital relationship?"

"What are the limits of sexual relations for teenagers?"

"Is it possible for a girl to set her moral standards too high?"

"What harm is there in going steady?"

"How can we accept sex at the right time when most of our lives we are told it is wrong?"

"Is love possible without sex?"

I have chosen these questions, and all the others cited in this chapter, from questions asked of me by teenagers during my talks on sex education.

In the minds of many educators, professional and parental, sex education means a recitation of biological facts, the time-honored "birds and bees" session between the parent and child when he or she reaches "that age," added to classroom discussions of hygiene and human biology—plus, of course, "information" picked up along the way from peers and from graffiti.

So that you and I won't be talking at cross purposes, please erase this concept from your mind. Meaningful sex education is not a review of menstruation and acne. Nor does it consist of admonitions such as "Don't you ever let me catch you fooling around with boys, you hear?"

Sex education is the building of *attitudes* concerning the whole subject of sexuality.

Does it no longer then involve the teaching of facts? Of course it does. But not just anatomical facts. Sex education is an exposure to *all* the facts of sex, and to an understanding of the reasons behind the facts, and to the formulation of attitudes toward sex based firmly upon these facts.

Values in general, and toward sexual conduct in particular,

are secure against rebuttal and confusion only in proportion to how solidly they are based upon understanding. To have faith is comforting. But to have knowledge that justifies your convictions protects your faith against the blandishments of sophistry and error.

As you know by now, I am convinced that the years of parenthood do not contain enough hours to guide our children toward all the things that would be helpful to them. Therefore we need some sense of priority. Are attitudes toward sex significant enough to the child's future to warrant the time and attention of the parent and the child?

At every P.T.A. meeting devoted to a discussion of sex education, there is the devil's advocate who rises to ask, "Why do we have to teach the kids about sex? Nobody ever taught me and I turned out all right." The softest answer I can think of is: "My friend, you must be kidding. You're either very lucky or very deluded. Who do you suppose produced the statistics of unhappy marriages, divorce, promiscuity, and illegitimacy? Who do you imagine raised and trained the present generation?"

Proponents of sex education are apt to emphasize different points of view. There are those who are upset by the rapidly rising venereal-disease rate, the increasing commonness of promiscuity and premarital intercourse, the swelling numbers of illegitimate births, abortions, teenage marriages, and divorces. They would hope to combat these trends by adequate education.

Others are more impressed with the terrible waste of the wonderful emotions of love and sex. They see so few people whose lives are enriched by the fullest possible enjoyment of love. They are saddened by the abundance of frigid marriages, and of parents who emasculate their sons, defeminize their daughters, and emotionally seduce their own children. They see women who deny their femininity, and men their masculinity; anxious teenagers guilt-ridden over conflicts between their morality and their instincts. They hope that better sexual knowledge might prevent some of these tragedies.

You might say that these opinions stress opposite reasons for sex education. One is concerned with better control of impulses. The other looks toward the greater enjoyment of sexuality. But you would be wrong. These are not contradictory goals. They are indeed one goal, as we shall see. An increased enjoyment of sex involves both better understanding and better control.

I myself believe that both of these concerns are valid and that together they give the teaching of sexual attitudes a high priority. But I would add still another viewpoint, perhaps the most important. An understanding of your own sexual values requires familiarity with human motivation and practical psychology, which knowledge should contribute to the tolerance for, and solution of, many personality, behavioral, and interpersonal problems even beyond the sexual sphere.

There are still those who doubt whether matters of sex should be taught to children at all. Their sincere but confused arguments stem from the belief that sex education may prematurely kindle the youngsters' curiosity and passions. The choice, however, of whether or not to teach just doesn't exist any more.

Children today are constantly exposed to sex. Shall they be left to make their decisions on the basis of a few biased facts? Or have they the right to all the truths before they formulate their values? The only real choice remaining to parents is between *some* information, part of which is false, or *all* information, truthfully expressed.

The distortions of motion pictures, television, books, magazines, and plays, the aberrant behavior of public idols, can hardly, in the spirit of fairness, be permitted to remain the Ph.D.'s of sex education. Who's going to teach this vital subject to your child? Well, in varying degrees, you're starting to get some help from the schools, the churches, and the youth organizations. But you, the parent, have to tackle the job of sex education if you want it done.

In fact, you already have been teaching sexual attitudes for as many years as the age of your oldest child. Most of the things you have done or said in front of your children—or have left undone and unsaid—have had overtones of sexuality, if only because you are a male or a female yourself. Even if you left home now, for good, your very absence would teach your child volumes about sexual behavior.

Just remember that the "new" sex education has little to do with the time-honored dissertation by the embarrassed father upon "the facts of life." The establishment of sound attitudes toward *all* aspects of heterosexual love is the objective, not a recitation of anatomical terms.

How parents may teach this topic is simple to tell. But effectual teaching depends largely upon the pupil and the teacher having a mutual goal. And it is important in sex education for the parent to have considered what this goal might be.

With what purpose might you wish your child to receive an adequate sex education? There are scores of subordinate purposes, but all lead to one ultimate intention. Among your lesser goals might be some or any of these: that your daughter not become illegitimately pregnant; that she not bring embarrassment to the family; that your son not contract a disease; that he be a partner in a successful marriage; that she be content in her role of woman; that he and she be able to enjoy love to the fullest degree and in all its forms; that she make an able mother. Now, all of these—and other—secondary goals are directed to a common end.

The one ultimate goal of sex education is that the individual will arrive at attitudes which, over the years, will bring him the greatest amount of happiness and will subject him to the least amount of hurt. It is only in this context that sexual attitudes make sense and can be held to and defended. Is this not the real purpose for the development of any attitude, sexually oriented or not?

The three routes of communication between parent and child which I have mentioned above are of variable weight. The least susceptible to willful control, and at the same time the most effective, is Channel Three—demonstration, observation, and imitation.

Fortunate children live in the presence of warm, unabashed love between the parents and in a climate of mutual respect, consideration, and self-sacrifice. Their mother is visibly proud of her femaleness. She is aware of, and pleased with, her vital role of guiding, supporting, and maintaining her family. She controls the decisions of the family through gentleness. She regards with pleasure the males in her life. Their father plays his part as the provider, the protector, the aggressor, the decision maker. He seeks the counsel and suasion of his wife. He recognizes and respects her complex contribution to the integrity of the family. Merely growing up in a family with such an orientation toward sexuality would by itself be a superior curriculum of sex education.

On the other hand, the husband who must deride or physically abuse his wife and children, or who must assume a passive, dominated status, detracts from the sexual adjustment of his offspring. The wife who scorns and degrades her husband and children, or who aggressively assumes the prerogatives of the males in her family, distorts her children's sexual attitudes. Unfaithfulness between the parents effectively communicates itself to children of any age. And even accusations of infidelity are not much less harmful.

Exhibitionism, seductive actions, and provocative physical contacts between parents and children, often thoughtless rather than deliberate, are apt to create sexual guilt in the child. Equally, excessive modesty and prudery in the child's presence set the stage for later sexual anxieties. The fad of the parade of the nude parent has passed into deserved oblivion. School-age children of either sex are aroused and resentful when confronted by adult nudity. Equally so, parents surprised in a state of undress who fluster histrionically and flee amidst protestations of shame, create feelings of fright and distorted curiosity in the child.

Affectionate, companionable, physical contacts between parents and children are proper and desirable. Lustful caresses obviously are not. Those who have trouble seeing the difference need help. Today's popular psychologist who says categorically that fathers should never kiss their daughters on the mouth worries me. Experts who cannot distinguish a symbolic salute of touched lips from lovers' kisses are troubled people.

Parents who shrink from affectionate physical contact with each other direct the child away from later mature physical love. On the other hand, the sight or sound of passionate love between adults either terrifies or guiltily arouses children. Children over six months of age should preferably not share the parents' bedroom.

It is plain from the above that the parent *unavoidably* plays a major part in developing sexual attitudes in his sons and daughters. You see, you have already been teaching sex with no embarrassment. And maybe you will believe that you *are* at least a little qualified in the subject.

The second avenue of communication, Channel Two, is under much more deliberate control than is Channel Three. This is the method of teaching by means of overheard discussions. The parent can alter this technique at will, and can avoid it or employ it as he desires. The messages may be incidental casual comments or they may be deliberately planned in order to influence and teach the child.

First, how early should you begin to discuss your opinions, values, and ethics within earshot of your child? At about the time you begin to acquaint him with his own name. Remember, a child's attitudes are jelling long before he reaches his teens. The moral and ethical viewpoints you deem significant are properly overheard by your child even before he can comprehend them clearly.

Here we get into the area where you need help. Most of what you need, though, is self-help. You already have values and attitudes of your own. You have opinions of what is right and what is wrong. But you have seldom discussed your beliefs with anyone, including yourself. So it would be a chore for you even to list them. Even more striking, you probably have not thought much about *why* you believe as you do in sexual matters. Nor have you matched your opinions against the arguments of those who believe differently. Not that you couldn't defend your values. You've just never organized your own convictions.

It's one thing to tell me, or your own child, what your attitudes are. It's quite another thing to convince us enough so that after we have heard the arguments on the other side we still share your values.

It is even likely that you don't know your own spouse's attitudes toward sexual behavior. And still less do you know how she defends her opinions.

Here are some starting points for your role of teacher. Discuss with yourself, with your mate, with your dinner guests what your attitudes are toward ethics, and why. Start when your children haven't the vaguest idea of what you're talking about. By the time they're old enough to comprehend, at least you yourself will be certain how you and your spouse look at things.

Do you believe in premarital intercourse? Ever? Under any circumstances? What value does it have? What price does it exact? Why do perfectly sane people hold to a view opposite from yours? Does your spouse agree with you? If I give you three good reasons why you are wrong, can you still justify your opinion or will you have to modify it?

Which is it better to be, a man or a woman? Which contributes more to the present welfare of the family? Of the country? Which contributes more lastingly to the future welfare of the family?

How much petting will be good for your daughter? How much will be bad? At what age? With whom? Under what circumstances? What will it cost her in future happiness to act differently? What about your son? Does your spouse see it your way? Are her reasons for her opinion more defensible than yours? Under what, if any, circumstances, including engagement and marriage, should your daughter welcome physical contact with a boy? Hand holding? Kissing? Hand on knee? Thigh? Breasts? Genitalia? And why do you think your opinion is correct? I'll bet you two plugged nickels you and your wife (husband) don't come out tie on this one.

It is good for children to know the views of their parents. It is more valuable for them to know why their parents hold these views. Values that are backed up by intellectual conviction are infinitely less vulnerable to challenge during the teens and early adulthood.

Sexual Attitudes and Values— Some Topics for Discussion

Not to direct your discussions, but to encourage your own thoughts concerning what sort of topics might enrich a program of family sex education, I include below a few subjects. Where these seem to have a common-sense justification of which I am aware, I have included it. Your own interpretations of the matters will be better. You might even, in thinking about these subjects, discover something of value to yourself.

"How do I know whether I really am in love with her?"

Well, if your feelings for her are based upon a willingness, even an eagerness, to give up your own satisfactions for the purpose of making her happier, perhaps you are. Are you willing to change your educational plans, if need be, to make her happy? To do without new clothes, to give up old friendships, to forgo your avocational interests, your leisure pastimes, to work harder, to withhold your criticism of her interests, her attitudes, her friends? Then perhaps you love her. Is she eager to have you make these sacrifices for her? Then I'm not so sure she really returns your love, except in a very childish way.

Love is a feeling, an emotion. It is also an instinct, present in all humans from earliest infancy. Like all instincts, it remains for life in some form or another.

The shape of love normally develops at the same time that the mind and body develop. It matures along predictable lines, and its development is influenced by the evolving personality, by knowledge and experience, and finally by hormonal effects. As with the developing body and the developing mind, the orderly growth of love can be partly or wholly stunted by severe environmental conditions, so that it may be prevented from ever attaining its full normal development.

The young infant is entirely self-centered, aware only of his own wants. His love is a primitive emotion which he feels toward those who bring him comforts. He has no way of knowing that the world doesn't exist solely for his pleasure. His love is entirely selfish, because he has not yet learned any relationship more rewarding. We all know a few unfortunate adults who have never passed beyond this infantile stage of love.

Under normal conditions the child eventually learns to experience love without needing to receive any external reward. He loves on the basis of internal rewards—imagination, fantasy, self-praise. At this stage he can love a distant person, even one he has never met. This is the emotion corresponding to "puppy love." More of our friends are stuck at this level.

Continuing to mature, the child begins to feel love in return for love. This preadolescent or early adolescent form of love is unfortunately the tenuous emotion upon which many marriages precariously hang.

Finally, if he is fortunate, the child graduates to the ability to love based upon what he can give to the object of his love, and dependent only upon the return of love. Love normally, then, matures into an emotion *based upon the desire to sacrifice for the beloved,* in return for love. It does not ever normally become a desire to sacrifice in return for rebuff, which is simply masochism, not love.

Along such maturational lines do many of our emotions and personality traits evolve. But they can be arrested at any stage of development, depending upon one's experiences.

As love matures from birth to adulthood, does each successive stage completely supplant the previous one? No, each step forward overshadows the previous stages, which remain active but diluted. The mature person, who has arrived at the summit of self-sacrificing love, still finds his love aroused to a lesser degree by pleasures that he receives, much in the manner of the young child.

How does an awareness of this biological phenomenon help

the parent and the child to establish meaningful sexual attitudes? Consider such questions from children as: *"I know he loves me deeply. What's wrong, then, with letting him have intercourse with me?"*

If he really loves you, perhaps you're right. Does he want you because of the pleasure he can give you? Is he eager to give of himself in order to make you happier? Then perhaps he does love you. Or does he want to have intercourse for the pleasure it will bring *him?* Then he loves you as a very young child loves. Regardless of his calendar age, his emotional development is stunted at age five—he loves to get, not to give.

Does he think he loves you, and willingly risks hurting you emotionally, physically, and socially by allowing you to have intercourse with him? The essence of mature love is the eagerness to bring pleasure, not knowingly to risk harming. He may be guided by stupidity or cupidity, but he is not motivated by love.

Do *you* consider allowing him to risk hurting himself emotionally by having intercourse with you? To feel guilt or embarrassment or fear of fatherhood? How sure then are you that *your* feeling for *him* is really mature love? Are you loving on the basis of giving or getting?

Is it possible that his desire for intercourse represents a need to prove his independence and his masculinity to you, to his friends, to his parents, to himself? Then his "love" for you is a personality abnormality, an inadequate ego, latent homosexuality, an unresolved Oedipus complex, momism, or what have you— but it certainly isn't love. And do you, knowing his reasons, consider having intercourse with him "to help him"? Then your feeling for him is sympathy, sorrow, maternalism, or masochism, but it doesn't resemble love.

"What's so wrong with unmarried college kids living together if they like it and if no one gets hurt?"

Well, nothing really, if you have oriented your life toward settling for mediocrity and second best. The trouble is, you get no better than you bargain for.

If you learn to be content with ham hocks and turnip tops, it's hard to adjust to caviar and artichokes. If you are satisfied to be half educated, it's difficult to go back to finish your schooling. If you adjust to the shallowness of playing house and to irresponsible fornication, it's not easy to replay the scene with sacrifice, respect, and fulfillment. If you will trade "The Arrangement" for the wonderful magical world of the newlyweds—and will suffer the one you "love" also to make this cheap swap—go to it.

Intercourse with love is an experience, an adventure, a fulfillment, an ultimate *gift to the beloved.* Intercourse with fear is a thrill, a cheapness, an amusement-park ride. Intercourse without mature love is simply a metabolic function.

When intercourse is part of a total commitment of mature love, it can be an emotional experience of such magnitude and depth that it is worth planning for and worth waiting for. If you are not willing to accept a lesser gratification, it is important to avoid accustoming yourself to shoddy substitutes.

Pearl Buck's writings on sex education raise the thoughtful comparison between the emotional experience of intercourse with a prostitute and the exhilaration of intercourse in the married bedroom. Which is cousin to teenage experiments? What is the reward—or the fee? And who pays it?

BOY: "I love you deeply. I want to devote my life to you. I promise to marry you, to be loyal to you, to love our children. Now will you have intercourse with me?"

GIRL: "Of course, under those circumstances."

BOY: "O.K., will you have intercourse with me for two dollars?"

GIRL: "Hey! What do you think I am?"

BOY: "We've already established what you are. Now we're dickering about your price."

"I love her. She makes me feel wonderful when she is near. When she touches me or kisses me I feel like a giant. I think of her constantly when we are apart. I love her, though I don't like the friends she goes with, the way she feels about school,

*her habit of fibbing, the way she squanders money, her atti-
tude toward religion, and I don't trust her judgment."
"I love him. I trust him and believe in him. We feel the
same way about a family, a home, education, the irrelevancy of
money, the sacredness of loyalty. We have the same interests,
goals, friends, and values. I love him though he can't bear to
sit close to me, to have me hold his hand, to put his arm around
me."*

These are good relationships for an affair or for friendship.
They are malformed, doomed to failure, incomplete qualifications
for mature heterosexual love. They are employment for the
divorce lawyer, certain anguish for the child they spawn.

This third aspect of love that you might want to contemplate
is the fact that *normal* mature heterosexual love is composed of
two elements, physical and non-physical. Each is itself a powerful force; but neither can long survive without the other.

We have no common word for the non-physical part of heterosexual love. It is part companionship, part joy in simply being
together—together in fact, together in mind. It includes respect
for the thoughts and moods and ideals of each other. It involves
an acceptance of responsibility toward each other. It includes the
sharing of values and goals. Insofar as time is a measure of love,
it is the larger part of mature male-female love, for it occupies
many more hours than does physical love. It is most often the
lacking element in unsuccessful marriages, for without this kind
of love, physical love cannot be sustained.

Physical love too is a powerful constructive force which, used
in a normal way, is both desirable and essential. Physical love is
natural, God-approved, and to be anticipated and wholly enjoyed
under appropriate circumstances. It too is divisible into two
elements, romantic love and venereal love. The latter consists of
both intercourse and precoital physical contact. "Intercourse"
means "communication between," and sexual intercourse can,
and should, be the ultimate communication between two partners
in love. Romantic love consists of all the lesser physical contacts
and fascination between persons of opposite sex.

The sum of the above, which most pay lip service to but few think about, is that mature love is a composite of physical and non-physical attractions and that the two can only be coexistent. The one without the other is incomplete, immature, unstable, barren, and doomed to dissolution.

"What's so wrong with finding out before you get married whether you and a girl are suited to each other by having intercourse a few times?"

The price of the knowledge may be paid for the rest of your life, for memories are hard to erase.

"What's wrong with it if we have already announced our wedding date?"

Not much, but weddings do get canceled. People do change their minds between announcements and weddings. And occasionally they change their minds because of disappointment in the discoveries they make regarding the ideals of the loved one.

For some, a personal code of sexual conduct, impervious to arguments and blandishments, can best be based upon understanding the reasons behind human behavior. How a man will react in a given situation always depends upon just two things: (1) the environment he confronts—the extrinsic factor, and (2) the intrinsic factors of the man himself—that is, his emotional makeup and his knowledge.

In a sexual reaction between two persons, each becomes in effect the environment of the other. So the resulting behavior is determined completely by the *personality* and the *knowledge* of both individuals. I remind you, in addition, that personality itself is determined in the main by the three factors with which we have been concerned—love, discipline, and independence. Furthermore, personality is composed largely of one's past experiences. Today's knowledge is tomorrow's personality.

The infant, born with certain potentials, is nevertheless barren of facts. As he learns about the type and quantity of love felt for him, about the quality and amount of discipline focused upon him, and about the way his future independence will be dealt with, these facts, added to his potential, become his personality. What is at one moment his conscious knowledge becomes at the next his subconscious self. Thus it is clear that today's experiences are not simply gone and forgotten tomorrow, but rather have become part of tomorrow's personality—as much a part of you as your nose or your arm.

To summarize this, as it will be applicable to sex education, we may say that when two persons participate in a sexual relationship the behavior of each will depend upon the personality and knowledge of both. Therefore an aberrant personality structure or false knowledge on the part of either participant will tend to result in abnormal behavior on the part of both. And, further, that it is not possible to have a sexual experience in the present which will not affect you in the future—affect you more or less, affect you beneficially or adversely, but nonetheless affect you.

The applications of these simple facts of human behavior to sex education, and to the establishment of codes of personal conduct, through understanding of your own motives as well as the motives of others, are almost unlimited in number.

It has been wisely noted that a girl should not wait till Saturday night to make up her mind what she is going to be willing to do in the back seat of a car that Saturday night.

Whether she will permit hand holding, genital caresses, or intercourse is more rationally decided in advance. An important consideration in this decision must be the knowledge that what she experiences Saturday will remain a part of her personality for all the Saturdays of her life.

A sexual relationship that might inadvertently result in dissatisfaction, disgust, embarrassment, unpleasantness, humiliation, inadequacy, failure of fulfillment, anxiety, or other unforeseen distresses cannot be wiped away and readily forgotten. Attempts in the future to achieve the pleasures of licit intercourse may be handicapped by unsummoned recollections of the past.

Also, if despite the disadvantages of discomfort, inexperience, fear of discovery, and haste, an emotionally and physically satisfactory sexual experience *is* achieved, the later guilt that just might assail the partners could also mar the attainment of ideal physical surrender to a spouse or lover. Emotionally one reaps tomorrow the harvest of the good or harmful seeds that one sows this Saturday night.

Having some understanding of the reasons for human behavior helps in discussing the pros and cons of such other queries as "Why shouldn't I: (1) engage in premarital intercourse, (2) go on unescorted dates, (3) encourage boys to caress me, (4) wear excessive makeup, (5) drink as much as I like, (6) wear sexually enticing clothes, particularly since (a) all my friends do, (b) you and your friends do, (c) they do on TV, in movies, in books, in ads, and in the papers?"

The logic is impeccable, if . . . If you assume that your peers, your parents and their friends, and the celebrities behave as they do because it is in their best interest and because it brings them the greatest happiness, both now and in the future. But first, before so assuming, you must examine the possible causes that actually lie behind the behavior you observe.

We know that behavior is largely dictated by personality structure—by partly uncontrollable and unconscious emotions. Personality is in turn determined mainly by satisfactory experiences with love, discipline, and independence, mostly with regard to one's own parents and family. Unsatisfied love needs, neglected discipline needs, unfulfilled independence needs, are irrepressible. They are more important to their owner than any other consideration in his mind. They compel him to action in an effort to correct them—compel him more forcefully than any other desire for happiness he may have—compel him to action which to an outsider may be incomprehensible since it often leads to his self-hurt, even to the extreme of self-destruction.

What might be the reason that some of your peers welcome premarital intercourse, smoke pot, and shop-lift? Do some of them, do all of them, come from families where they never gained acceptance, where discipline was withheld or misapplied, where independence was systematically squashed?

Is their behavior based upon what will bring them the most happiness? Or are they striving in desperation for what they lack, trying to forget, hoping to convince themselves, attempting to hide behind a pretense, anxious to pay back their parents?

Do the hippies whose biographies make the newspapers come from families where discipline has been nil, where acceptance and love have been so minimal that the parents scarcely know what their children are doing, where independence has been supplanted by neglect? It is no surprise that often the families are affluent; material gifts are just not a requirement of personality development.

Do you think alcoholics drink because they believe it contributes to their happiness? Ask one. They know fiercely and intellectually what misery it causes them. But they drink from the compulsion to escape the knowledge of their personality deprivations.

Perhaps you will say, "I have thought about it, and these are not the reasons why *my* friends are sexually permissive. Besides, too many people act this way for them *all* to have personality problems." Before you feel sure, talk to your friends about their families, and know that there are hundreds of thousands of teenagers and adults with despairingly serious personality problems.

Maybe you yourself have a personality aberration. So perhaps it is necessary for you to be promiscuous or to try drugs. But sometimes by understanding why humans behave as they do—including your own parents—you can see through their behavior to what they really feel and how they would like to behave. And understanding sometimes helps to see things in a different light. It sometimes helps you to react a little differently to them.

In understanding parents it pays to try to remember certain little-thought-of facts. First, none of them has had any training in being parents. Bright as they may be in many things, their training in how to act as a parent is zero. In fact, any pointers they may have picked up from friends or from books are as apt to be wrong as right.

Second, it is highly likely that, all evidence to the contrary, they love their children, including you.

Third, they are all tied up with their own personality quirks, so that often what they intellectually *want* to say and do bears no resemblance to how they actually manage to speak and behave. The father who constantly berates and belittles his child may well be driven by his own sense of worthlessness to fear that he has failed the child as a father, both in endowment and in helpfulness. He is often the same father who proudly tells all his friends what he truly believes—how wonderful his child is.

The mother who constantly nags or refuses to trust the child she adores may be driven in her behavior by a rejecting long-forgotten association with her own mother. And so it goes. It helps, sometimes, to understand—not to forgive, but to understand—what causes people, parents and lovers included, to act as they do.

"My parents think that I'm a failure. Johnnie's parents are divorced. Why shouldn't we have sex together if it makes us both feel better?"

After you both have improved your self-confidence, and after you emotionally and financially can afford to marry, perhaps you should. But until then, you would be using each other, not loving each other. You would be hurting him further by agreeing with him that he is not capable of better things than promiscuousness. And he would be telling you the same thing. You can't bring yourself happiness by hurting someone else. You bring yourself guilt and self-deprecation.

Toward understanding sexual behavior, it is valuable to recall that the elementary motivating force of human behavior is the maintenance or the creation of a satisfactory self-image.

The adolescent with a normal personality will have a reasonably good self-image, so that he will be motivated to defend it only when it is under severe attack. But the more askew the personality, the more unsatisfactory will be the adolescent's self-image. And the more desperately will his actions be forced by the need to bulwark his self-image by whatever behavior he imagines may be successful.

His sense of values may be so heavily weighted by the urgency of bolstering his malformed ego that his choice of activities may seem incomprehensible to a neutral observer, who falsely assumes the individual to have the same sense of values as his own.

How much of your friends' behavior, in whatever field, including sex, is dictated not by intelligent appraisal, not by altruism or materialism, not by emotions of love or sympathy or avarice, but by the compulsion of ego defense?

How much of your own morality is based upon, or sacrificed to, this urge? And in your own instance, is it truly necessary? Or successful?

"Cathy and I hate the world of our parents and their fouled-up society. We resent their dedication to money and status. We reject their false standards that tolerate war and poverty. We can't debase our love for each other by living apart until we might be able to marry. What's wrong with that?"

Parents and older children alike need some understanding of rebelliousness if they are to achieve a meaningful understanding of sexual behavior. The development of independence is a prerequisite to normal maturity; and rebellion is an integral part of attaining independence. A totally submissive teenager is clearly in need of professional help. Rebellion is a natural consequence of normal personality evolution and maturation.

But there are different kinds of rebellion. There is beneficial rebellion, which is helpful to the individual, to the family, and directly or indirectly to society. And there is harmful rebellion, which is ultimately destructive to the individual, to the family, and to society. Rebellion is to be neither categorically condemned nor embraced, but rather it should be understood, so that it may be judged to be probably successful or probably unsuccessful.

Successful rebellion is needed to complete the child's self-image by demonstrating to his own satisfaction his ability to assume independence of thought and action. To achieve this goal, the rebellion clearly must not conflict seriously with his own values, or permanently with society's, for either of these situations would create conditions that would ultimately weaken his self-image. The more adequately the personality has already been formed, the more easily will successful rebellion be accomplished.

Unsuccessful rebellion is that which leads to serious conflict with the child's already established sense of right and wrong, and thus arouses guilt. Or it leads to long-term rejection by society and the inevitable consequence, deterioration of the individual's self-image.

The less complete the personality, the more drastic and desperate will be the rebellion, for the more compelling are the child's needs for convincing proof of his adequacy. In the case of a seriously disturbed personality, virtually no proof can be convincing enough, and the rebellion will be both futile and self-destructive.

The questing teenager who lets his hair grow to his shoulders in order to express to himself and to his world his competence to make his own decisions in his maturity, is a far cry from the distraught teenager with no belief in his ability to cope with society's demands, who must therefore rebel totally, in an effort to survive emotionally, and who adopts a rebellious hair style as a result of his nonconformity.

The long hair, the lying, the stealing, the rejection of education, the indifference and sloth of a teenager who is not yet seriously disturbed are often an older child's more sophisticated restatement of the five-year-old's plaintive "You don't love me." It is often a test question aimed at the parent. The hoped-for answer is: "Yes, I do love you. I love you very much. I don't like what you are doing. But I love you and believe in you enough to love you just as much despite what you are doing. My love for you is solid and unshakable, and not contingent upon your actions." If the answer that is actually forthcoming from the parent is not satisfactory to the child's self-image needs, the next rephrasing of the question may be still more reckless and urgent.

Do you believe in and trust someone you love because you love him? Or does someone you love first have to prove himself worthy of your trust and belief? Differing answers to these two questions are often responsible for the gulf between teenagers and their parents—the gulf that leads to more and more rebellion in a quest for the "right" answer from the parent.

The relevancy to sex education of an awareness of these motivations for teenage behavior is that abnormal or unsuccessful rebellion often takes the form of sexual activity, to the detriment of the young person's partner who misinterprets his advances as a manifestation of sincere love.

Children who are having a hard time convincing their parents, and a hard time convincing themselves, that they are ready for, and capable of, independence may well turn to sexual activities to establish their competence. Sex is, after all, only for adults, and one incontrovertible way to prove you are adequately adult is to father or mother a child.

"Dad, is it O.K. for me to put my arm around my date and kiss her?" Sure, it's great, if she'll let you. And if you do it because you like each other. But if you do it on Main Street my guess would be that affection had nothing to do with it. I would guess that you don't think much of yourself, and need to show passing strangers, as well as your date, how successfully you have grown up—you hope, but don't really believe.

"No, Dad, it's not because I don't have any self-confidence that I neck on Main Street. It's because I've got so much self-confidence that I don't care what others think of me." This reasoning is obviously false, because if such actions were really a measure of self-confidence, then the boy would feel equally at ease urinating or undressing on Main Street. But in what way is the logic misleading? Simply in that emotional stability (normal personality) does *not* imply that one is able to ignore the opinions of others. This, indeed, is rather close to the definition of a psychosis. Self-confidence rather means, among other things, that one does not have any compulsion to call the attention of others to oneself.

"Mom, you're so old-fashioned. I just have to go steady with one boy, because that's what everyone else does nowadays." If this came from a self-confident, emotionally mature daughter, regardless of her calendar age, I might indeed agree with her. Childhood sweethearts can make sound marriages.

But if it came from an inexperienced and immature daughter, my own translation of her words would be: "I don't think I've got much to offer, and if some boy shows any interest in me I'd better count my blessings." My reaction would be to wonder why I hadn't discussed such a situation within her hearing years before. To wonder why her self-image was so poor. And to discuss with my spouse how best to give the child confidence at this late date.

Adolescents have the right and the need to know and to understand this motivation in their peers. The time-honored mother-daughter warning that boys may deliberately get them into "trouble" needs equally to be contemplated by boys. Girls may deliberately get them into "trouble," in a bid to escape their own intolerable situation. There are more helpful ways out of this dilemma than procreation. It is perfectly reasonable, and sometimes helpful, for both parents and teenagers to be aware of these influences upon the sexual behavior of themselves and of their companions. From understanding and discussions may sometimes come resolution or avoidance of problems.

"Isn't it true that it hurts a boy and girl emotionally if she refuses to 'go all the way' with him after they have been necking?"

"Modern" thinking concerning sexual activities is sometimes beclouded by technical jargon and misinterpretation of psychiatric concepts. A classic self-deceptive argument is the unqualified plaint: "But inhibition is bad for you." No psychiatrist, rational or irrational, ever defended such a notion. In this loose use of the word, "inhibition" seems to mean "the denial of instant gratification of a desire." However, the delay of an impulse for the sake of a future pleasure is not only not "bad for you" but is rather a beneficial form of ego building.

The ability to postpone immediate gratification in favor of a future reward is properly called self-control. It is neither "inhibition" nor "frustration." Self-control is proof to your self-image that you have successfully passed from the infantile need for immediate gratification to the mature ability to forgo an immediate pleasure for the sake of a greater future pleasure.

Arm yourself and your children with this defense against the sophistry that falsely proclaims, under the banner of "psychiatric wisdom," "Do it now. Don't risk the harm of frustrating yourself." The only harmful form of frustration is the inability to acknowledge and examine an impulse and to dispose of it advantageously by an appropriate choice of (1) gratifying it, (2) postponing it, or (3) redirecting it.

Inhibitions arise only from refusing to recognize an impulse, from denying its existence, and from forcing it, unexamined and unresolved, from the consciousness. Constructive self-control is a far cry from frustration in sexual relationships.

A more sophisticated misinterpretation of psychiatric facts, which deceives even some of our professional counselors and sex educators, comes from the following "reasoning": Psychological anxieties do arise from conflicts between a child's values and his or her behavior. A boy or girl who feels that promiscuity may be wrong but who nevertheless engages in premarital intercourse, creates just such an anxiety within himself and thus suffers emotionally. But the problem can be neatly solved, and the conflict resolved, by convincing the child that his original values were wrong!

Thus, presumably, a young girl engaging in sexual activities which conflict with her conscience, and experiencing as a result emotional depression or ulcerative colitis, can be cured by leading her not to change her actions but to reconsider her values. In this way her conscience no longer questions promiscuity, and she can engage in premarital intercourse without paying any emotional price.

There is only one glaring fault with this logic. It just ain't so! The fallacy lies in the assumption that the new, permissive values which condone the behavior will be able to be maintained in the future against the lessons of experience and of widening exposures to the opinions of society. The "solution" actually serves only for the moment. As knowledge challenges the substitute values, the old conflict rises from the ashes.

Consider the future of the "college arrangement" in terms of the above.

This same analysis of human behavior confounds even the

gifted members of the learned "Committee on the College Student of the Group for the Advancement of Psychiatry." Their misleading advice to educators and to young persons is to the effect that the enlightened college student rightly has a free choice to decide between premarital intercourse and postponement. Such a presentation demonstrates rather sadly the occasional inability of the intellectually gifted to think.

Let me suggest an analogy. "A college student with acute appendicitis has a free choice to decide for himself whether or not to consent to an appendectomy." True or false? Actually he has no freedom of choice at all, *unless* he is first made aware of all the relevant facts. Unaware that he has appendicitis, and of the consequences of appendicitis, and ignorant of the favorable risks of appendectomy, the student could have no meaningful freedom to choose.

It is the same with sexual decisions. The student has free choice only *if* he has first been acquainted with all the facts upon which to base a decision. Against the many risks of premarital intercourse, there are no known medical facts to indicate that promiscuity is in any way physically or emotionally beneficial. So, in the final analysis, neither the knowledgeable nor the ignorant student has any real freedom of choice in this behavior except the choice of whether to hurt himself and his partner or not.

"What's wrong with petting?"
"In dating, how do you know how far to go?"
"Should a girl let a boy kiss her on their first date?"
"Why are some girls so much more popular than others?"

No serious answers to questions about dating and petting can be formulated without some attention to the subject of popularity. Many adolescent decisions concerning heterosexual relationships stem from the perfectly natural desire for popularity.

Man is instinctively a social animal. Furthermore, approval and acceptance by his peers reinforce his self-image. By and large, the greater the teenager's self-confidence and the more secure his personality, the less will be his need for popularity, and the smaller will be the price he is willing to pay for peer acceptance. Theoretically, the completely self-confident human would have little need for popular appeal.

The more severely stunted personality will correspondingly be willing to pay a higher price in seeking the popularity which it more urgently needs. This accounts for some of the more flagrant behavior that bids for popularity at whatever cost.

The most severely deprived self-images will pay the highest price of all—capitulation. Terrified to risk self-anticipated deroga- tion, they will dare to seek popularity only with animals (com- monly horses) or with confessed rejects (currently "hippies"), or they will withdraw completely to seclusion.

The parents' own personal need for approval seems often, too, to play a dominant role in how strongly the child will be urged to pursue popularity. The seriously insecure parent may force his child to try for popularity at the cost of the child's happiness or at the price of denying the child's own ethics.

If the achievement of popularity is a normal goal of virtually all adolescents, how does a parent counsel a child to go about attaining it? The subject is of course far too complex, too sub- jective, and too individualistic to fit into the scope of this book. (A book I would recommend to boys and girls, mothers and fathers, for its compassion and wisdom on this subject, is the 64-page *Becoming a Woman*, a Dell Purse Book.) Here I would merely like to emphasize just two basic facts concerning popu- larity.

1. *Popularity is not successfully gained at the price of sacri- ficing your own ideals and values.*

The teenager can be helped to see that those of his colleagues who appear to be enjoying temporary popularity at the high price of conferring favors which represent a sacrifice of self- esteem and of future pleasure, are those for whom he can prop- erly feel sympathy but not envy. They represent the unfortunate toll exacted by inadequate family life—inadequate in love, disci- pline, and independence.

Popularity with members of their own sex often appears to teenagers to depend upon being accepted by the "in" set of the community. This may require behavior for which they are not old enough or which conflicts with their own standards and values. When acceptance is purchased at this price, the result is anxiety, self-doubt, and psychosomatic symptoms.

To avoid such entanglement, the adolescent needs to have been made aware (1) that the "popularity" of many "sophisticated" groups is more infamy than it is prestige, (2) that such false popularity is short-lived, and exceedingly over-priced, and (3) that his parent not only will not push his child toward such a relationship but will forbid it if necessary.

Popularity with the opposite sex is similarly not a purchasable commodity. Decisions concerning dating and petting which are made with the thought of gaining popularity are self-defeating.

Kissing and petting, when they are truly signs of admiration and respect, are delightful. When they are the offered price for popularity, they purchase only a loss of respect and a prominent part in the seller's tales of conquest.

2. *Popularity of a permanent sort accrues to the person who makes himself sensitive to the needs of his colleagues.*

The youngster who thinks about making his associates feel that *they* are popular, admired, accepted, and worthwhile, who concerns himself with making others feel at ease and self-confident, is the one who himself generally becomes popular.

"What do I have to do to become popular with this or that group?" No one ever becomes popular with a group; you become popular with individuals. If several persons to whom you are attractive happen to go together, then you are "popular with the group."

"O.K., then how do I get a boy or girl to like me?" Forget about what you can do to attract his attention. Concentrate on making him feel interesting and popular. Smile. When he says something—anything—ask him to say more. Don't match his statement with one of your own. "I hate homework." "Really? Why? What else do you hate?" Not "Me, too; especially French—it just bugs *me* because . . ." And not "Gosh, *I* don't; *I* think . . ."

If you want to get anyone to like you, you must look for his good points and overlook his bad points and weaknesses. If you *must* let him know his faults—forget it; go look for someone else whom you can persuade to like you.

Don't tell him how much better you are at something than he is.

It is clear that there are at least two common pitfalls that parents seek out and fall into with regularity in dealing with issues of popularity involving their children.

Motivated either by their own sense of insecurity or by an overeagerness to see their children attain "happiness," and apparently without any thought of it as sex education, many parents enthusiastically push their young adolescents into the social pool long before they are ready.

Often I hear: "When do I have to start dating girls?" and "At what age am I supposed to try to be popular with the boys?" The only true answer I know is: "Never, unless you feel like it."

Many utterly normal, and potentially happy, boys and girls, even through their high-school years, are not anxious or ready to embark on the boy-meets-girl route. Too often parents and society create an unnecessary and provocative social relationship between adolescents who are not themselves all that eager.

There are days in a pediatrician's life when he concludes that he has only two kinds of children in his entire practice— those who eat too much and those who eat too little. On other depressing days his charges seem to divide into those who are too fat and those who are too thin. The worst days are those when all children, according to their parents, seem to be either too active in their socio-sexual pursuits or not active enough.

One of my favorite people is the mother who worries herself —and her pediatrican—gray because her teenage daughter has no boy friends. Jennie eventually appeals to a boy, who then spends all his time mooning on her doorstep and monopolizing her time. Mother is soon back at the doctor's worrying about her daughter's going steady. The doctor is now a wiser man. "How fortunate you are, Mrs. Brown. Only two weeks ago I had to counsel a mother who was concerned about her daughter's lack of sex appeal."

The other popularity pitfall involves the unwillingness of

parents to support their teenagers by saying "No!" When morality must take second place to popularity we might as well all call off the game and go home.

It is still psychiatrically proper in this day and age for parents to say "No" to a teenager's announcement that he or she is going to spend the night with an unchaperoned date. Or going to a party at the home of a friend whose parents will be "tolerantly" absent. Or on a drinking spree. Or for a drive in an unsafe car.

The plea "Everyone else's parents lets them" is a euphemism for "The other parents don't care; or they are too uncertain of their child's popularity to risk endangering it; or they are being bamboozled in the same way you are."

The argument "You're too old-fashioned" deserves the answer "Yes, that's what gives me the right to assume the responsibilities of parenthood."

More often than you may believe, despite the face-saving arguments and rantings that may ensue, your willingness to forbid an unacceptable escapade gives the child the welcome "out" that he needs. His "face" is saved with his peers—it's not that *he's* "chicken," but his dad is "square." He avoids a situation that could involve him in guilt and anxiety. And he learns that his family thinks well enough of him to believe that he can be socially accepted without needing to buy his popularity.

These, then, are a few of the concepts and topics which bear directly upon sex education for the child in the home. You may well think of others, some more relevant to your family's orientation. These relatively complex philosophies concerning human values and behavior do not lend themselves readily to communication by silent observation and imitation. They certainly do, however, need to be backed up by adult example that the child can observe.

Nor do they fit easily into a direct lecture approach from parent to child. They are best taught to the child by being made subjects of conversation and discussion between the parents, or with other adults, in the presence of the child. The child is not particularly expected to join actively in the conversation, but if and when he does, he should be neither excluded nor belittled.

I am hoping to suggest that any one or several of these topics, or other, better ones of your own choosing, would provide years of brief discussions at mealtimes, during TV commercials, during automobile trips, while waiting for the rain to stop during ball games, and so forth. None would make much sense, or hold a listener's attention, if approached as a three-hour do-or-die harangue.

For testing your own knowledge and giving you some practice, they also make pretty good topics for exceptionally dull dinner or cocktail parties.

Religious orientation toward sexual morality I have omitted, not from lack of importance, but from lack of broad enough knowledge on my part. I am confident, though, that nothing of what I have said is contrary to any of my readers' religious beliefs.

Physical and Physiological Aspects of Sex Education

There are many details of anatomy, development, and physiology which constitute the lesser part of sex education but which parents find difficult to discuss. These simple facts are communicable by direct presentation, the Channel One of communication, though a few might easily be items of family discussion. Schools are doing a better and better job in this field, and there are many comprehensible books on the subject for parent and for child. Among the better ones is the series of booklets prepared by the Joint Committee on Health Problems in Education of the National Education Association and the American Medical Association.

This series is called the "Sex Education Series," and includes:

1. *A Story about You*—for children in grades 4, 5, and 6
2. *Finding Yourself*—junior-high age

3. *Approaching Adulthood*—senior-high age
4. *Parents' Responsibility*—for parents of preschool and early-school-age children
5. *Facts Aren't Enough*—for all adults dealing with children

They may be obtained, for thirty cents each, from:

> National Educational Association
> 1201 Sixteenth Street, N.W.
> Washington, D.C. 20036

or:

> American Medical Association
> 535 North Dearborn Street
> Chicago, Illinois 60610

Among the topics of anatomy and physiology considered reasonable for pre-teenagers and adolescents to learn on the subject of sex are these:

Anatomy and terminology of male and female genital organs
Conception—roles of mother and father
    Development of embryo and fetus
    Genetics
    Determination of sex
    Twinning
    Contraception
    Prematurity
    Abortion
Birth
Physical development
    Puberty—in boy, in girl
    Physical changes
    Emotional changes
    Masturbation, homosexuality
    Rate of sexual excitation, male versus female
Physiological changes
    Menstruation

Seminal emissions
Erections
Acne
Venereal diseases

These are the topics that come first to mind when sex education is mentioned. Yet clearly they are the less important part of the subject.

The questions, relevant to this aspect of human biology, which go unanswered in the mind of the child are varied almost beyond belief.

"Is it true that men cannot impregnate women in the daytime?"

"In the way girls have menstruation, what happens to boys?"

"Can you get V. D. by manual contact with genital areas?"

"Is the time a woman is menstruating the time she is fertile?"

"How many hours before intercourse must I take the pill sold at school for a dollar to be sure of being safe?"

Teaching the Anatomy and Physiology of Sex. Since no comprehensive coverage of sex education is intended here, I don't pretend to deal thoroughly with these aspects of anatomy and physiology. But I would like to stress a few points of special significance.

The teaching of attitudes, of behavioral motivation, of the origins and purposes of ethics is far more important than the learning of biological facts such as proper terminology, fetal development, and menstruation. No boy becomes a better lover, no girl a better wife, by mastering terminology.

Most parents, including professionals, are uneasy with the terminology of sexual anatomy, and uncomfortable with a presentation to their own child that concerns sexual intercourse. Such qualms and embarrassment are utterly normal and need not be seriously struggled against in an effort to impart sexual knowledge to children. While it may be necessary for a grade in biology to identify the clitoris, the penis, the hymen, and the testes by their proper names, it does not materially contribute to a child's sexual adjustment to be so able. If the words come easily to you, use them; if they stick in your throat, don't avoid the subject just to avoid the words. I would settle for "a thing," "a place," "a hole," or even "a whatsis."

Nor is it necessary to discuss intercourse in a manner that either causes you to show embarrassment or forces you to try to choke back your reticence. It is, of course, unfair to convey to the child that physical love is sinful or ugly or bad or immoral or forbidden. It is *not* improper to let the child know that some aspects of love are intimate, private, personal, and indeed sacred to the point that you have difficulty discussing them in a detailed manner or even in discussing them at all. To be sexually sophisticated and free from crippling inhibitions does not require that you should be able to discourse coldly on intimate matters.

In fact, I am not sold on the idea of presenting sexual information in such a thoroughly detached manner (if this were possible) that the teacher and the student would feel as little personal involvement as they might in discussing the weather. I am not convinced that sexual fulfillment needs to include the ability to discuss in the locker room the experiences one has had with one's wife during the previous week.

Premarital Intercourse. Arguments for premarital continence which depend upon threats include such negative warnings as premarital pregnancies, hasty teenage marriages, venereal disease, and abortions. How much such warnings have influenced promiscuity in the past—or whether they have influenced it at all—is unknown. Their impact on the morality of tomorrow's youth will certainly be minimal. How much they have detracted from legitimate sexual participation and pleasure, to the detriment of the family and the individual, is more easily imagined.

It is at least probable that positive arguments for continence which are based upon the ultimate pleasure of the individual and upon consideration for the rights of others are easier to defend against the counterarguments of one's teenage peers. Nonetheless, reasons based on fear seem to be the birthright of every child, and whatever their value they should be accurate and factual.

Contraceptives. There are some who see "the pill" as a prime cause of the allegedly increasing promiscuity. However, there have always been methods of contraception readily available, and there has never been, nor is there yet, a completely safe contraceptive method.

The rhythm method is effective, under ideal circumstances, say 90 per cent of the time. It cannot ever be completely effective, because conception has been known to occur on each day of a woman's menstrual cycle.

Mechanical and chemical contraceptives have been successful upward of 95 per cent of the time.

Anti-fertility pills, taken properly and under the direction of a physician, have achieved a success rate of 98 per cent or better. Thus, under ideal conditions, which seldom exist in premarital intercourse, "the pill" has a failure rate of "only 2 per cent."

Now if it *is* going to make some difference in influencing the moral behavior of an individual for him to know his odds with the wheel of roulette, he should know that science has improved his odds from one out of ten to one out of fifty. I would want all youngsters to know that a failure to protect, whatever the odds, amounts in the long run to a 100 per cent failure to the people involved. Then there is little comfort in having been 98 per cent safe.

I cannot help but note, however, that most early premarital experimentation with intercourse is done without *any* contraceptive efforts of any sort.

Abortion. The truths of abortion need to be understood too, if they are to be mentioned at all. "Safe" abortions can be obtained by an American girl for between $1000 and $2000—cash. She generally has about forty days in which to raise the money in time.

"Unsafe" abortions can be had for somewhat less. A "safe" abortion involves a mortality rate of under 1 per cent; good odds except for the few who make up the 1 per cent, who are themselves 100 per cent dead. The percentage of those who live but are thereafter sterile is not much higher. The greatest price of abortion, however, above that of money, life, or sterility, is the unpredictable, sometimes shattering, effect it may have upon the future emotional and sexual lives of both the male and the female participants.

Venereal Disease. The threat of venereal disease is surely the most ignoble reason for practicing morality. Is it ever effective? I don't believe it. I do think, though, that youth has a right to know the facts, to make whatever use it can of them.

Unadorned, the facts are these. Venereal diseases are rapidly increasing in this country again. They are often not easily diagnosed until they have produced irreversible damage. They are becoming more difficult to treat as the causative germs are becoming more drug-resistant.

They cause all sorts of problems for the physician to solve, including sterility, deforming arthritis, idiocy, paralysis, disintegration of the nose, and deformed offspring. They are contracted by—and, worse, they are transmitted by—pretty girls and ugly girls, educated boys and uneducated boys, sweet girls and sophisticated girls, gentle boys and tough boys, white and black and yellow, wealthy and poor, squares and swingers, clean and unbathed, urban and rural, old and young, professional and amateur.

Both syphilis and gonorrhea are most often transmitted by sexual intercourse, but they can also be caught through genital foreplay and homosexual practices. They are rapidly disseminated, because a boy or a girl who is willing to have sexual intercourse with *you* is almost always willing to have had in the past, and willing to have in the future, intercourse with others, sometimes lots of others. Unless, of course, you are really the most devastatingly irresistible lover in the world.

Physical Changes at Puberty. Physical and emotional changes that accompany adolescence, and their normal variations, can confuse and temporarily sadden and hurt children who are not prepared for them. They are much more likely to hurt children seriously and permanently whose *parents* are confused by these changes and therefore treat them in a misconceived manner. It is of some importance for adults to be aware of the wide range of normalcy in these matters in order better to comprehend and support the adolescent.

Girls mature *on average* younger than boys. Appearing about two years prior to the first menstrual period, the first physical signs of puberty are usually nipple changes and early breast development. Anywhere from eight to fourteen years of age is common for these first signs.

Boys start physical adolescence with an enlargement of the penis, testicles, and scrotum, sometime between the ages of ten and sixteen. Thus the *average* age for the onset of puberty is earlier for girls, but obviously some girls mature at a later age than many boys.

Adolescence being a period of rapid bodily growth, and the age of onset being so variable, children of the same calendar age as their friends suddenly find themselves misfits—too tall, too short, too curvy, too childish.

Girls who mature young need to have their newly prominent curves and height greeted with dignity and delight in the family lest their posture and self-image suffer along with their self-confidence.

Boys and girls who must endure the indignity of maturing late need parents who are themselves convinced of the normalcy of the lateness, and who can support their sometimes distraught offspring with confidence in the future. Since the genitalia do not change appreciably in size from birth to puberty, boys may discover with anguish that their visible claim to masculinity has become dwarfed in proportion to their bodies by comparison with the burgeoning displays of peers who have entered puberty ahead of them. Few boys have the temerity to approach their fathers for an explanation of this belittling phenomenon. The wise father is aware of his prerogative to reassure without being bidden.

Emotional and Social Maturation at Puberty. More meaningful even than the vast differences in physical maturation are the equally great variations in emotional and social maturation. While these correlate vaguely with physical growth, the emphasis must be upon "vaguely." Some children are socially mature as soon as they are physiologically grown up. Others, equally normal, are not ready for, nor interested in, mixed parties and dating until years after puberty.

An eagerness for heterosexual social activities, much like independence, develops naturally in boys and girls, provided that it has not been seriously thwarted by the parents. But it cannot be successfully forced. The validity of this observation is painfully evident on all sides. Yet countless parents continue to urge their sons and daughters into socio-sexual activities before they are ready.

I know the extreme futility of such a warning. Who is expected to heed? Not those parents who themselves measure their own happiness in terms of social activity. Nor those so insecure that they must get their kicks vicariously through their children. Nor those who passively coerce their adolescents by exposing them to a socially precocious environment. Nor apparently even those who ingenuously protest, "But I only urge him to for his own happiness" and "I don't want her to be hurt by being left out because of her shyness."

How fortunate are those children whose parents can afford to let them wait to grow up sexually at their own rate.

Do you have any questions about your role as parental sex educator as I close this chapter? Are there details and subjects you feel are uncovered or improperly presented? I sincerely hope so. This has been the briefest introduction to the subject; hopefully a prod to your curiosity to encourage a reappraisal of your own thoughts on the matter. And perhaps to urge you to consider supporting your school and your church to get on with their contributions to this important phase of child education.

Now if you are still unconvinced of your ability to give your child the advantages of good sex education without embarrassing yourself, would you mind leaving this chapter bookmarked for your teenager to read?

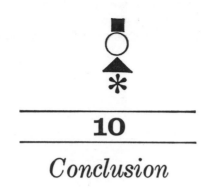

10

Conclusion

Now I face a most unpleasant assignment—closing this book while there are yet so many things unsaid. My third-grade English teacher would want me to end with a résumé of important topics. But before I begin my summary I want to describe one other topic, a special environment recommended for "brain-damaged" children and referred to as the structured environment. These special surroundings contain so many of the factors which contribute to the normal personality of all children that the subject may adequately remind you of some of the suggestions offered to you throughout this book.

The Structured Environment

In a previous chapter I discussed the subject of the "brain-damaged" child. This abhorrent term refers to children who have the personality syndrome which includes labile emotional responses, short attention span, poor muscle coordination, and physical hyperactivity. It does not have any direct reference to intelligence, and the IQ's of these children vary from as low to as high as those of any other group of children. Part of the prescribed handling and teaching of children with these personality traits is that they be provided with a "structured environment."

What exactly is a "structured environment"? "Structured" means that the child's environment should be planned, simple, direct, understandable, meaningful, non-confusing, directive, and supportive. These children learn best, and learn well, if the following conditions are adhered to: The person doing the teaching should be authoritative, direct, and convincing. He should issue straightforward orders, not complicated or obscured by unnecessary explanations, and he should not offer the child choices. He should be careful to say only those things he himself believes in, knows to be true, and which he can back up if the student shows any inclination to doubt him. The directions should not be obfuscated by a bribe; there should be no condition attached such that "if you want this, do that." Rewards, especially praise, should be direct, immediate, and short. If the instructor erroneously issues an order which cannot be backed up, and if the child chooses to disregard the order and to disobey, the instructor should drop the subject and turn to another rather than further demonstrate to the child the instructor's fallibility. Thus the child develops confidence in the teacher and is able to learn from him and to have faith in him.

The instructor should correct the child when he commits an error, but should take care to see that it is the answer that is criticized and not the child himself. He should teach as few subjects as necessary, and as patiently and as long as necessary, until each is mastered by the student, before passing on to other lessons.

He should deliberately allow the child to succeed frequently, even if he, the instructor, has almost to manufacture the success. Thus he encourages, through self-confidence, the child's desire to try again and harder.

He should be consistent in his teaching, always presenting the same fact again and again until the student comprehends, and should avoid giving conflicting information or instructions from moment to moment. He should allow the child voluntarily to develop his own independence and should be careful not to push the child, by direct statement or by implication, into attempting something that the child is not himself convinced he is ready for. Further, when the child does venture to make an independent decision, the instructor must be careful to praise the effort, and not to criticize unduly or to ridicule the erroneous result. The instructor should be lavish in his admiration of the child himself, beyond the praise that may be bestowed for effort and for achievement.

The instructor must not tolerate destructive or harmfully aggressive behavior, but while controlling it he must be conscious of criticizing the action and not the actor. Once an incorrect answer is corrected, it is forgotten, and not referred to in the future. There must be no belittling or derogatory attacks by the instructor upon the person of the child in the eagerness of the teacher to get across a lesson.

This, in essence, is what constitutes the "structured environment" within which these children are capable of learning well.

You are not likely ever to have the need for dealing with a "brain-damaged" child. Nevertheless, it seems important to me to point out the environment in which it is agreed these special children who have difficulties in learning are best able to achieve their full potential. It is strangely and remarkably identical with the environment in which *any* child can best develop his personality to its fullest capacity. These special conditions of learning are just as applicable to the "normal" child as to the "brain-damaged" child. Simple lessons without confusion and without derision, heavily laced with love.

Summary

The total health of the individual can be thought of as divisible into two aspects, physical soundness and emotional well-being. In the case of the child, the physical aspect of health has been the beneficiary of impressive progress during the past five decades.

Advances in his emotional health have been considerably less conspicuous. It is this emotional constituent of health in the developing child which has been the subject of this book.

A reasonably normal personality is an *absolute* requirement for the child; it demands precedence over *all* other goals. Its importance is approached only by the need for tolerable physical health. There can be no assurance of successful learning, of appropriate motivation, of happiness, of the establishment of rational values, morality, or attitudes, or of the improvement of society unless and until the child's personality needs are met first.

The healthy personality stands squarely upon three, and only three, legs. A large number of factors *influence* the emotional soundness of the child. But they are all of secondary importance to the sole unconditional requisites—love, discipline, and independence. These three factors alone will not automatically result in perfectly fulfilled children and adults, but without them there can be no surety of healthy maturation toward an emotionally stable adulthood.

The demand for love, discipline, and independence will be satisfied (or unsatisfied) by the family, by the community, and by the school. A great deal of correction or a great deal of distortion can result from the influence of the neighborhood and of the educational system. However, the major source of help or hurt to the developing personality lies within the family.

No matter how involuntary their participation, and despite how often it may be restated that "it is unfair to blame the parents for the child's shortcomings," it is nonetheless the mother and father who have the greatest opportunity to provide the child with the three essential ingredients. The parents cannot resign from this responsibility since (1) they come to bat first in this league, constituting almost the entirety of the child's environment until he attains school age, and (2) they occupy a singular status in the child's mind because he recognizes his dependence and reliance upon them.

Both the community and the school will participate in the offering or withholding of love, discipline, and independence. And they will also influence the child indirectly, through the mother and father, as the parents' relationship to the child is altered by the degree of parental satisfaction with the child's performance outside the home. Neither the school nor the community, however, has the opportunity under our social structure to work from the start, as do the parents, upon an unmarked slate.

The love that is required for healthy emotional development is that based upon unstinting acceptance. It is love given simply because the child is alive and here. Other forms of love are pleasant for the child; but they are not essential, and they may even be harmful if they detract from, supplant, or precede the love which is unearned by the child but deserved purely because of his being—because of being living flesh and blood created by Mom and Dad, hopefully in a moment of mature passion.

This non-demanding love must not only be present; it must be effectively communicated. It is not shared impartially with siblings or peers. It is uniquely the child's own. It is not dependent upon performance.

Love, or praise, or acceptance which the child purchases by some attainment is satisfying. But it can be exceedingly dangerous to the preservation of emotional health. Deserved love must never come earlier than blind love. And it must never loom large in proportion to this blind, undemanding love. Further, it must occasionally be earned without much effort and, once it is earned, the child should be given time to enjoy it before he is faced with the next demand. Defeat is a great teacher. But it is purely destructive unless it is preceded by (1) adequate unearned acceptance and (2) a satisfactory draught of success.

Discipline is the second essential factor in emotional health. Discipline is teaching. It is teaching engaged in because you love. It is not punishment.

Punishment is not teaching. Punishment is a price exacted for failure. It is not a requirement for a normal personality. It is sought by the child only when his emotional health is poor. Punishment is not guidance; it is retribution. You punish your neighbor's child; you discipline your own. Punishment is good for the deliverer; it serves to release fury and to calm the punisher. Since normal human parents need release from frustration, punish your child if it is desirable for your own personality equilibrium. But don't think that you can pay your debt of discipline needs in the currency of punishment.

If the cycle of family formation is to be continued, independence, in preparation for the assumption of adult responsibility, is a third necessity for the child. Independence is rebellion. By its nature, it cannot be urged on the child; it must be fostered indirectly. It cannot for long be both successful and self-destructive; the two are mutually contradictory. Parental trust, which must underlie normal independence, is given; it is not earned. But it cannot be given apart from the protection of discipline and the support of love.

So important in the value scale of children of all ages is the fulfillment of this triad of requirements, and the resultant attainment of emotional health, that these needs will be esteemed, until obtained, in excess of any other prize. Therefore, no mature approach to life's challenges—no successful "formal" education, no acceptance of attitudes, no facing of responsibility—can command the child's attention until his personality needs are first satisfied.

Attempts to pass on a standard of values to a child, to nurture the proper attitudes and ethics, and to instill desirable character traits are doomed from the start if the child does not first have a personality that he is himself satisfied with. Further, trying to teach these elusive and complex subjects by methods which themselves weaken and belittle the personality is equally ineffectual.

On the other hand, given the student with a well-adjusted personality and a secure self-image, the need aggressively to teach these subjects disappears. Simple emulation suffices, under this happy circumstance, to impart the most complex lessons of ethics, behavior, and character structure.

Give away your love to your children, and you will receive back more love than you can encompass. Guide your children to reality, and in the doing you will enrich your own understanding. Welcome their evolving independence, and you will be supported by the strength that you have helped them attain. Then you will truly realize that no other task in life is so worth the effort, so demanding of skill and knowledge, so challenging of the imagination as the job of the earnest mother and father.

Index